PENGUIN BUSINESS
WHO BLUNDERS AND HOW?

Robin Banerjee is the chairman of Nucleon Research Pvt. Ltd, a global clinical research organization. He served as the managing director of Caprihans India Ltd between 2012 and 2022, and has held senior management positions at Hindustan Unilever, ArcelorMittal Germany, Thomas Cook, Essar Steel and Suzlon Energy.

Robin is a chartered accountant (FCA), cost and management accountant (FCMA), company secretary (FCS) and master of commerce (MCom). He is the recipient of two lifetime achievement awards from *CFO India* (Feb 2023) and Manufacturing Today (Oct 2023).

Robin holds board positions at several companies, chambers of commerce and business schools. He is a much-sought-after keynote speaker, a popular columnist, a business coach, a philanthropist and a gym enthusiast.

PRAISE FOR THE BOOK

What the Corporate Leaders Say . . .

'It's human to make mistakes and the corporate world is no different. Despite the fancy management degrees of the top echelons in most of the fancied corporations in the world, there has been many an instance of glaring blunders which the world has seen. Robin comes out with his second book, post the very successful one earlier on "corporate frauds". Given his vast experience in the corporate world, Robin has gathered a wealth of knowledge on the intricacies of the corporate world. This book deals with "corporate mistakes" which have shaken the world and taught humanity some invaluable lessons. I am sure readers would enjoy reading it as much as I did.'

—**Sunil Agarwal**, *MD, InCred; Former MD, Deutsche Bank*

'At a time when a major part of the public narrative is dominated by the Insolvency & Bankruptcy Code, Robin's latest book is both timely and topical. It is nobody's case that mistakes are a sin and, hence, unpardonable. The fine tag line "The Dumb Side of the Corporate World" subtly endorses this. When mistakes are "made" rather than "happen", the author has an issue. And this is precisely what he has chosen to describe, illustrate and draw experiences from. As always, Robin's style is conversational, anecdotal and provocative. This will be a useful book for many audiences, those who have made mistakes and want to introspect and learn from them, and those who haven't but want to learn from those who have, but without passing judgement. Over to you readers for an enjoyable drink and an educative read.'

—**Ashok Barat**, *Chairman, Path-Finder Consultants; former-MD, Forbes & Co.; Vice President 2019–20, Council of EU Chambers of Commerce; Former President, Bombay Chamber of Commerce and Industries*

'A classic treatise by Robin. It is a very engaging, informative and easy-to-read book! It will make you reflect and introspect! I thoroughly enjoyed reading it!'

—**S. Bhaskar**, *President, Institute of Internal Auditors-India (2018–2019); Chief Internal Auditor, Tata Capital Ltd*

'Success stories have many narrators and many fathers. But stories of failure are often swept under the carpet or are simply justified or externalized. This book brings stories of failure into the limelight. The author tells story after story—of how lack of professionalism spells demise of family businesses, how macho M&As falter on implementation, how poor corporate governance destroys mighty business empires, how inability to innovate derails erstwhile market leaders, and how overstretching with debt kills companies— several recipes of failure, indeed! These stories should act as red flags to the readers, and if they take necessary steps in the nick of time, the author's purpose, I believe, will be served.'

—**Debnarayan Bhattacharya**, *Vice Chairman, Hindalco Industries; Vice Chairman, Novelis Inc.*

'Even while driving on a straight road, we keep an eye on the rear-view mirrors while looking ahead through the windscreen—in business life, this holds true too. Business cycles are getting shorter and technology is disrupting industries. This book from Robin helps us look at possible areas of failure as we navigate the VUCA world.'

—**Partho Dasgupta**, *CEO, Broadcast Audience Research Council; Chairman, Meterology Data Pvt. Ltd*

'Good decisions come from experience. But experience come from bad decisions. However, most books and case studies in management are about successful companies. Drawing on details from diverse industries, Robin identifies the reasons for failures and how managers can learn from mistakes to build enduring organizations. This book is a must-read for every management professional.'

—**Ramesh Ganesan**, *MD, HDB Financial Services Ltd, Member, Board of Governors, IIM, Tiruchirappalli*

'[The] first 50 years of the 21st century will be remembered for innovations, start-ups, M&As and business blunders. Robin has showcased plenty of real-life instances of business mistakes so that readers do not fall prey to them. I am confident that this book will become a precious treasure to all connected with businesses—small or big.'

—**Ajit Gupte**, *Chairman and President, NMIMS Business School Alumni Association Board*

'The book is a back-to-basics reminder of the fundamentals of leadership. It serves as a pedagogical guide to those who love to learn from mistakes. The refreshing real-world examples make it an easy-read for a practical approach to building businesses.'

—**Abhyuday Jindal**, *MD, Jindal Stainless*

'The book is well researched and beautifully written, engages the reader and has innumerable examples with succinct analysis. A complex subject well explained in a lucid and interesting way! It is a must-read for all!'

—**Sushama Kanetkar**, *Authorized Representative for India, Commonwealth of Pennsylvania, USA*

'Robin takes you through the graveyard of once-great companies and narrates a compelling story of how they got there—how blunders in quality, innovation, debt, M&A and greed took them there. It is a must-read if you want to successfully navigate in this unforgiving world of modern business, where if you don't change fast, you will succumb faster.'

—**Sunil Khanna**, *MD, Vertiv Energy Pvt. Ltd; Former Chairman, CII Maharashtra State Council*

'Hidden under wraps behind many corporations which otherwise appear successful are unacceptable stories of poor governance, poor management, failing boards and oodles of unacceptable management practices. The entire journey of value creation seems to be travelling on a road full of potholes for values! This is a well-investigated book of such corporate tales. Read on, and get a first-hand feel of corporate thrills from the eyes of Robin, the corporate James Bond!'

—**Adil Malia**, *CEO, The FiRM; Former President HR, Essar Group;*
Former Director, Coca-Cola

'Robin's well-researched book provides insights into how many of the issues facing corporates today are a result of leaders having made wrong choices. The impact of their decisions can often be devastating and far-reaching both for them individually and, more importantly, for their organization. Robin has analysed some of these instances, drawn conclusions from them and attempted to provide alternatives on how such situations could be addressed in future. It is a "must-read" for all leaders who want to make a difference.'

—**Sunil Mathur**, *MD, Siemens Ltd, India; Deputy Chairman,*
CII Western Region 2019–2020; President, Bombay Chamber of
Commerce and Industries

'In today's complex corporate world, Robin's ability to identify the central issue (among many), dissect it further and explain it in lucid fashion comes to the fore. Great read!'

—**Saurabh Nanavati**, *CEO, Invesco Asset Management Co.;*
Former CIO, HDFC Standard Life Insurance

'The book on "corporate blunders" is very timely and useful, especially for the small and medium enterprises, who are always trying to do their best during difficult times. Learning from numerous easily worded examples in the book, it should go a long way in helping the business community run their businesses better, especially new entrepreneurs. I suggest that every entrepreneur reads this book and grow.'

—**Chandrakant Salunkhe**, *President, SME Chamber of India*

'It is a fascinating and well-researched presentation, covering all major business predicaments right from minor follies, quality compromises, disputes and conflicts, poor governance and un-befitting capital structure, that may eventually culminate into business failures. This brilliant work makes compelling reading for business professionals to design a guiding framework in their corporate philosophies and culture, to avoid walking over the ubiquitous fault lines.'

—**Dr (Ms) Renu Shome**, *Director,*
The Council of EU Chambers of Commerce in India

'This book is a bold and transparent narrative on the disastrous consequences of compromising on ethics and quality in trying to make a business more profitable. It is an absolute must-read for every CXO/promoter/entrepreneur—who wants their businesses to stay relevant in a rapidly changing environment. The lessons learnt from blunders by industry leaders should resonate very strongly with leadership teams focused on creating and growing a sustainable business respected by customers and regulators.'

—**Santanu Syam**, *Director and Chief*
Operating Officer, Angel Broking Ltd

'There are several books that extol business successes, but very few on business failures. This book teaches the reader that businesses are indeed not failure-proof, but there are certain mistakes that can be cautiously avoided to put your brand on the track to success. In this well-researched book, the author explains logically how the lack of relevant innovation, consumer transparency, good governance and professionalism, among others, may cause companies to fail. Blunders such as brand fatigue, mismanagement of finances, lack of good leadership and not keeping pace with new technology are explored in detail with innumerable case studies and examples. This title is a must-read for budding as well as seasoned entrepreneurs and working professionals to understand what not to do when running a business, in turn helping their brand reach greater heights.'

—**B. Thiagarajan**, *MD, Blue Star Limited;*
Former Chairman, CII Maharashtra State Council

'Robin has done it again. Like his previous books, this one is also interesting, informative and easy to read, and can be appreciated by a wide spectrum of people. I hope you enjoy reading it as much as I have. Happy reading.'

—**Firdose Vandrevala**, *Chairman, The FiRM;*
Former Chairman, Motorola; Chairman,
CII Western and Eastern Regions; President, AIMA

'This book is a sensor that will help corporates sense early on if they are on their way towards a fall. It is a potential fall detector. The book will be a great addition to corporate and management school libraries.'

—**Pramod Panda**, *Sr Programme Director, Centre for Advanced*
Financial Research and Learning (CAFRAL); Member, Board of
Studies, SVKM's Mithibai College, Mumbai

'The book is very cognizant of how critical decisions, inflexible traditionalism and momentous mismanagement have resulted in big industry blunders and lost billions. I liked Mr Banerjee's unique insight into all the realistic cases discussed in this book. I strongly recommend it to all entrepreneurs.'

—**Satish Wagh**, *Chairman and MD, Supriya*
Lifescience Ltd; Chairman, CHEMEXCIL

'Thanks to Robin for this unique book! While success stories inspire us to "do more", we draw our caution from stories of failures to "do it right". Too much noise around "Thunders of Success", while "Blunders of Failures" remained hidden so far!'

—**Vikesh Wallia**, *Regional Director,*
Western Region, Institute of Directors;
Former Board Member, Times Group

What the Educationists Say . . .

'Robin's book is a great read and re-read for executives, managers, leaders and students. I have read a number of books which explain success stories, but hardly any book that makes you learn from mistakes. It is said that there are no failures, only feedback. However, the book explains that if feedback is ignored, these blunders result in disasters. It is interesting to know "who blundered" and "what we can learn" from "how they blundered!"'

—**Group Captain D. P. Apte (Retd)**, *Director, MIT School of Business; NLP Trainer; Author of* Reboot Your Mind

'Replete with a wealth of stories, Robin's book is another reminder that the many-spangled blinkers of (mis)governance and self-aggrandizement often misguide corporate leadership to drive even the best of pre-eminent organizations towards a path of insignificance and ultimate demise.'

—**Dr Bibek Banerjee**, *Senior Dean, Strategic Initiatives and Planning, Ahmedabad University; Professor, Amrut Mody School of Management*

'This extensive research work of Robin has idiosyncratically brought out obvious impacts of ill-crafted strategies in the corporate world. Leaders of the present Industry 4.0 era will get plenty of application-oriented learning points which he has brought out through extensive causative analyses of many leader-made disasters. I am sure the millennials, aspiring to be tomorrow's leaders through generation transfer of family businesses, will also be immensely benefitted from his words of wisdom. The book is a must-read for all corporate leaders, business strategists and consultants.'

—**Dr Prof. Paritosh Basu**, *Chairperson, MBA (Law), NMIMS School of Business Management, Mumbai*

'Well-researched, lucidly written and documented, this is a fascinating compilation of the most famous business follies, blunders and failures of various economies around the globe—from outright fraud, quality compromises, lack of vision and failure of management to innovate and adapt to new market realities. As a seasoned CEO, Robin has brilliantly arranged and integrated management theories, cases and actual business practices in this sequel which make it a compelling read.'

—**Dr Achintan Bhattacharya**, *Director, Bandhan School of Development Management; Former Director, National Institute of Bank Management* and *National Insurance Academy*

'Robin's book is a nuanced observation of the ever-changing and precarious world of business where sometimes even a trivial negligence might make you stumble, which will ultimately lead to an abominable collapse of a glorious empire. This riveting and engrossing work not only exposes the deep secrets of the business world but also provides remarkable insights about how to avoid possible hurdles on the slippery road to splendid profits. This book creates a niche space for itself because it takes us deep into that very abyss of doom which lies just next to the zenith of triumph. A lucid account of the lessons to be learnt from these falls and failures has made the reading not only enlightening but also intriguing and engaging.'

—**Dr (Ms) Lily Bhushan**, *Principal, B.K. Shroff College of Arts & M.H. Shroff College of Commerce*

'Robin, the financial wizard, has woven his magic again! A compelling and gripping read, this book is simply unputdown-able! It deals with a topic which has not been explored before, that is, corporate mistakes. It is a fascinating account of the follies and blunders committed by huge names in the business world. Read it to understand how even big businesses run by astute minds flounder. This book is probably the only one of its kind!'

—**Dr (Ms) Sunanda Kar**, *Educational Director, Rajasthani Sammelan; Former Principal, Ghyanshyamdas Saraf College of Arts & Commerce*

'The book is a delightful guide, full of important information about the modus operandi of business houses for those of us who want to learn or enjoy every aspect of the business world. Robin takes the readers on a dark, twisted and hilarious journey into the floundering working pattern of corporate houses in a very simple and lucid style.'

—**Dr Sangita Laha**, *Dean of Faculty, National University of Study and Research in Law*

'The book is worth reading. The objective of the book is to create awareness about several common mistakes which businesses have committed over time. The author has very categorically pointed out how many business houses focus on the marketplace of today but fail to anticipate the future and, in turn, encounter unenviable stumbles. The book has rightly pointed out how the greed of a few people, for both family-owned and public companies, has put their shareholders in the dock.'

—**Dr Suresh Chandra Padhy**, *Vice-Chancellor, Poornima University*

'In a simple, articulative and efficient manner, Robin has presented us with failure stories, stumbling blocks for businesses and what not to do. It is a one-of-its-kind book that will make us wiser about corporate pitfalls. A fantastic read!'

—**Dr Professor Ms Swati Padoshi**, *Director, Dr. G.D. Pol Foundation, YMT College of Management; Founder and Facilitator, moveurcheese.com*

'In an uncertain, volatile world, leading a business is often like steering a ship in a stormy sea. There is no guarantee of safe arrival, yet that is what all captains will go for. Knowing what not to do is often a better strategy in such cases. Robin makes an excellent analysis of corporate blunders made by industry stalwarts and shows how such moves can be avoided in the business world. If you want your business to survive and succeed in the long term, not keeping this book in your personal library may be the biggest blunder you would make.'

—**Dr Professor Subhasis Ray**, *Xavier Institute of Management Bhubaneswar (XIMB), Xavier University*

'It is an excellent read for corporates, entrepreneurs, management students and future managers. The meticulous examples make one understand how to take sensible decisions and "what not to do" in business!'

—**Dharmendra Sharma**, *Management Trainer and Visiting Faculty, NMIMS, Welingkar, SIMSR, XIMR, ICAI*

'The book is an excellent read. The author takes his readers on a journey into the common mistakes which businesses have committed only to perish. The root cause of all the mistakes is management greed. The lesson is that the corporate leaders, who desire to enhance profits, bypassing "good governance" principles, ultimately lead businesses into oblivion.'

—**Dr Professor Vinod Sople**, *Dean (Research), ITM Group of Institutions, Mumbai*

'Every business empire is built after many failed attempts!! Business is a harsh teacher; for some it is patience; for others it is connections or status by birth. Robin, in *Who Blunders and How?* has explained it all, brilliantly and lucidly in a matter-of-fact manner, where events unfold like a story. The author's attempt is an invitation to read and understand how the "blunders" in business win acceptance in the world of corporates driven by stock market indices. The book is an excellent effort to make comprehensible for the common reader a difficult problem dealt through stories of modern-day corporates!'

—**Dr M. Sreedharan**, *Director, Indira Institute of Business Management*

'Reading this book, you'll learn from the success and failures of many leading organizations and be able to identify fatal mistakes in your own entity that may lead to failures. It is a captivating book on business traps, predicaments and reasons for abrupt burnouts.'

—**Dr Professor Bigyan P. Verma**, *Director, SIES College of Management Studies; Former Director, GNIMS*

What the Authors Say . . .

'Just as compromising quality to save cost is non-negotiable, so is reading a book by Robin. There are facts that freeze as you go on. In a country running rife with small and big businesses, one expects failures as well as triumphs. Between these pages is the magic of the shoulda-woulda-coulda world that relates how things are often not deliberated but happen invariably!'

—**Maya Bathija**, *Author of* Paiso: How Sindhis Do Business

'Robin's perspective and analysis of corporate blunders is very insightful, coming very close to his other book on corporate fraud. Some blunders are deliberate and some happen when wrong circumstances collide with good intent. Knowing which is what, is very important for managing companies to know. I strongly recommend that all senior managers and leaders read this book and build their body of knowledge.'

—**Dr Sumit Chowdhury**, *CEO, Gaia Smart Cities;
Technology Adviser, BARC India; Visiting Faculty,
Carnegie Mellon University; Author of* Rules of the Game

'Judging the book by its cover may not always be right but some covers excite the readers' imagination, as the intrigue they behold becomes a precursor to what they seek to uncover. Enticing in theme, exhilarating in choice, enduring simplicity in narration igniting curiosity, Robin's book is an exquisite choice, not just for a reading aficionado but also for every person who feels the need to know the hows and whys as to how the big guns in the corporate world despite infallible success fall prey to the ignominy of an unprecedented fall. A compelling read with incisive analysis, this book is an asset to all those in the business of leading and managing to get an insight into how focus on creating fame and fortune distracts companies from choosing sustainable value-based options.'

—**Professor (Col) N. Ram Gopal**, *Professor,
IBS Business School; Former Associate Director,
MIT School of Business; Author of* Defying Destiny

'The book is immensely useful for anyone who wishes to survive and lead in the corporate world. With examples from around the world, Robin takes his readers through a corporate tale of terrors while providing a happy ending in the form of a message. The gamut of issues covered in the book serves almost every learning need for managers and entrepreneurs.'

—**Damodar Mall**, *CEO, Reliance Retail;*
Board Member, IIM Bodh Gaya; Author of
Supermarketwala: Secrets to Winning Consumer India

'Companies often blame extraneous factors for their debacles. Robin proves it otherwise by narrating a series of bountiful blunders and less-talked-about business bloopers committed by key insiders that led to the downfall of companies—big and small—in recent times. The author's incisive analysis and suggestions will definitely provide valuable insights to all corporate leaders who want their companies to soar higher.'

—**Dr Sibichen K. Mathew**, *Income Tax Commissioner*
and Certified Fraud Examiner; Author of
When the Boss Is Wrong *and* Making People Pay

'This is an excellent and well-researched business book. Deriving deep lessons in how to run a business from a plethora of real-world case studies on corporate blunders, coupled with Robin's leadership experience, it provides the reader with an unmatched resource for business management and strategy.'

—**Ashutosh Mishra**, *Head Sales, ANZ Australia; Former Executive*
Director, Goldman Sachs; Author of Happiness Is All We Want

'This book is worth reading. The objective in this book has been to create awareness about several common mistakes which businesses over time have committed. The book provides numerous examples why businesses fail and the reasons behind it. Failure can be rooted in bad management, misguided leadership, strategic failings, market changes or just bad luck or often a combination of all these. The book provides insight for the readers to understand the numerous reasons for businesses to fail, how to prevent it or be aware of it before it is too late.'

—**Dr Suresh Chandra Padhy,**
Vice Chancellor, Poornima University, Jaipur

'What an apt topic to write [about] and who better than a seasoned professional like Robin as the author—a deadly combo! Real stories from the corporate world about glaring mistakes made by hugely successful corporations at a point in time, who have withered due to these, are staring into our face. This book shares them in a tell-all manner for professionals to learn the much-needed lessons so that we emerge wiser! It will help you make sound business decisions and choices as you internalize the essence through each of the examples. Read this book to know it from a practitioner's perspective.'

—**Dr (Ms) Aparna Sharma**, *HR Consultant; Former Country HR Head, Lafarge India; Author of* Between U & Me *and* Reality Bytes: The Role of HR in Today's World

What the Journalists Say . . .

'It is a practical and easy-to-read handbook for managers to understand why a business fails or what traps it should avoid. Examples of how companies deal with challenges from disputes, conflicts or innovation have made the book interesting. Robin calls a spade a spade. He deglamourizes M&As, just as he argues that innovation can yield better and quicker results if it is made relevant. His advice to family-run businesses is to let some professionals take charge of the operations, while he rues the fact that too many companies have a public relations network that is not fully aware of what is going on in the company and why. His final punchline is reassuring: Make no mistake—perfection is a myth.'

—**Ashok K. Bhattacharya**, *Editorial Director,* Business Standard

'Yet another thoroughly researched and engaging book on corporate malfeasance. The author shines a bright light on the cover-ups that big companies try to get away with.'

—**Antoine Lewis**, *94.3 Radio One host; Literary Festival host; Former Editor of* Savvy Cookbook

'An essential read for every manager who would like to learn important and lasting lessons for their organization, through someone else's mistakes and at someone else's cost!'

—**Anuradha Das Mathur**, *MD, CFO Collective; Founding Dean, The Vedica Scholars Programme for Women; Founder and Director, 9.9 Media*

'Over the years, thousands of books have been written on what makes a company successful. This, despite the fact that most companies fail. Hence, Robin's latest effort is a rare book, which deals with the lessons one can learn from the failures of others.'

—**Vivek Kaul**, *Editor, Vivek Kaul Publishing; Author of* Easy Money *trilogy; Contributor, LiveMint*

'When businesses and brands stumble, fail or succumb to unexpected market upheavals, it could sometimes be because of unexpected reasons that are beyond the ken of those who manage them. But often it is because of inherent fault lines such as ownership patterns, quality of management and simply the failure to perceive the larger long-term trends. With contemporary examples from around the world (as well as a focus on Indian enterprises), the book is a thorough attempt to bring insights into why companies commit blunders, and it is an essential read for anyone seeking to understand the 'whys' and 'hows' of averting corporate mistakes.'

—**Sanjoy Narayan**, *Former Editor,* Hindustan Times

WHO BLUNDERS AND HOW

The Dumb Side of the Corporate World

ROBIN BANERJEE

PENGUIN
BUSINESS

An imprint of Penguin Random House

PENGUIN BUSINESS

Penguin Business is an imprint of the Penguin Random House group of companies whose addresses can be found at global.penguinrandomhouse.com

Published by Penguin Random House India Pvt. Ltd
4th Floor, Capital Tower 1, MG Road,
Gurugram 122 002, Haryana, India

First published by Sage Publications India Pvt. Ltd 2019
Published in Penguin Business by Penguin Random House India 2024

10 9 8 7 6 5 4 3 2 1

The views and opinions expressed in this book are the author's own and the facts are as reported by him which have been verified to the extent possible, and the publishers are not in any way liable for the same.

ISBN 9780143464594

Typeset in 9.5/13.5 pt ITC Stone Serif by Fidus Design Pvt. Ltd, Chandigarh
Printed at Replika Press Pvt. Ltd, India

www.penguin.co.in

This book is dedicated to the five most beautiful women in my life:

The very reason of my existence—my mother; my significantly better half—Ananya; the reason of my life—daughter Roshnai; and the two most wonderful creations of God—Arahana and Aheli.

CONTENTS

ACKNOWLEDGEMENTS

To err is human, to forgive is divine and to acknowledge is celestial! Whether writing this book has been an error or not, only time will tell. But there is no doubt that while penning down my thoughts on who blunders and how, I learnt a lot, gained many experiences and met several noble souls willing to aid with their views and expertise.

My several places of employment have also been my temples of learning from the mistakes I have made and seen others committing. Hindustan Unilever, my alma mater in professional life, taught almost daily what not to do. 'Do not come to office unshaven,' said my financial controller (who became the chairman), Keki Dadiseth, when I was just a young management trainee. I learnt that there is no substitute for good grooming. 'Don't make the mistake of bribing government officials for quick permissions,' said my then general manager boss—the late Shunu Sen—a marketing legend of his time. Ethical practice stands in good stead in the long run. I kept learning from the many hiccups.

After almost two decades, I moved to Germany to join Ispat International (now ArcelorMittal), the largest steel company in the world. When I was the managing director of its German operations, Lakshmi Mittal told me 'not to make the mistake of assuming even the audited financial numbers as correct especially when prepared by the government-owned companies'. This sane advice was very worthy while I negotiated with the Government of Romania to acquire their largest steel plant. Malay Mukherjee, the ex-chief operating officer of ArcelorMittal, gave me the sermon—'Do not make the mistake of stocking up by buying iron ore and coal, thinking the price is low. In the long run, you can never buy low and sell high,' he said, 'hence purchase to produce and sell.' What a learning! I have seen many companies going under while trying to speculate on inventory.

After returning to India, I joined Thomas Cook, a global travel and forex company. I learnt from the mistakes of making too many acquisitions quickly. It's important that mergers and acquisitions (M&As) should be phased out; each acquisition needs to be treated as a newborn baby to be taught how to walk first and then to run. The process cannot be hurried.

Joining Essar Steel as its executive director and then Suzlon Energy as its Group chief financial officer (CFO) and member of its global boards, I learnt a lot from the mistake of drowning oneself with borrowings. Debt is like a double-edged sword: on the one side, it helps to fund dreams, on the other, if not handled with care, it can make enterprises bleed.

Ruben, my brother, editor-in-chief *Outlook* magazine group, has always been encouraging in whatever I do. No wonder that he corrected several faux pas in the initial manuscript.

How could I ever achieve anything if my better half, Ananya, would not have been patient with me, encouraging in my endeavours and, of course, correcting continually all the goof-ups I kept committing.

Dr Roshnai, our darling daughter and a medical professional, keeps her keen eyes on me whether she is in India or abroad, correcting my mis-steps and trying to make my journey of life more seamless and worth living. Abhishek, my son, took immense trouble to correct several oversights and omissions in my initial draft.

My mom, who keeps wondering why I still burn the midnight oil and keep poring over books, papers and the laptop; her implicit inspiration is worth in platinum.

I am obligated to my childhood guru, Debnarayan Bhattacharya, vice chairman of Hindalco. So many mistakes he has pointed out as I rode the train of my life. He went through this book carefully and, as usual, pointed out several bloopers.

Two of the managing partners of the FiRM, Firdose Vandrevala and Adil Malia—a consultancy firm advising businesses how to avoid mistakes and operate seamlessly—have been my friends, philosophers and guides in my endeavours. Both gave great guidance to avoid the snags that crept into the manuscript.

A book of this magnitude could not be completed if my family and friends would not have pointed out the numerous lapses I committed while dealing with them. They encouraged me in all my ventures, without which nothing would have been remotely accomplished. My unpretentious obeisance to Ashok Chatto-padhyay, Abhyuday Jindal, Ashok Bhattacharya, Ashok Barat, Achintan Bhattacharya, Adil Malia, Ashutosh Mishra, Anupam Dasgupta, Antoine Lewis, Ajit Gupte, Dr Aparna Sharma, B. Thiagarajan, Dr Bibek Banerjee, Dr Bigyan Verma, Chandrakant Salunkhe, Dharmendra Sharma, Gr Capt D. P. Apte, Damodar Mall, Debabrata Mukherjee, Firdose Vandrevala, Gopal Sehjpal, Harsh Chopra, Dr Jagdish Pol, Dr Lily Bhushan, Prof N. Ram Gopal, Partho Dasgupta, Dr Paritosh Basu, Maya Batheja, Dr M. Shreedharan, Prakash Iyer, Pramod Panda, Pramod Banerjee, R. Mukundan, Ramesh Ganesan, Dr Renu Shome, Rimjhim Banerjee, Sanjoy Narayan, Sanjay Kapoor, Sangeeta Pendurkar, Saurabh Nanavati, Satish Wagh, Santanu Syam, Dr Sangita Laha, S. Bhaskar, Sushama Kanetkar, Sunil Khanna, Dr Swati Padoshi, Dr Sibichen Mathew, Dr Sumit Chowdhury, Sudipto Panda, Soumitro Panda, Dr Suresh Padhy, Sunil Mathur, Sharmila Karve, Sanjay Tolia, Dr Sunanda Kar, Sunil Agarwal, Dr Subhasis Ray, Sunil Pathare, Kashmira Mewawala, Kapil Pathare, Uday Khanna, Vivek Kaul, Dr Vinod Sople and Vikesh Valia.

Manisha Mathews, my commissioning editor at SAGE, has been simply outstanding. She handled the manuscript with great professionalism, guiding me through the several lapses as I went along finalizing it. Her predecessor, Sachin Sharma, has been equally good, to make sure that the book contains the 'who' and 'how' of every blunder illustrated. Vandana Gupta, my editor, has been superb in her endeavours in rectifying numerous manu-lapses, so did her predecessor Guneet Kaur. Anupama Krishnan has been great in designing an attractive cover design. This book may not have reached so many of you—my wonderful readers—without the lovely work done by the admirable marketing brain,

Shafina Segon. I sincerely thank Vivek Mehra, Aarti David and the whole of SAGE's splendid team, who straddled through the several snags as we went along the path to highlight the business mistakes, which all of us need to avoid, to make our lives more glitch-free.

I apologize for my inadvertence for not acknowledging so many, who have helped me as I went along with this project of writing on business blunders. I am sure of bungling in not acknowledging every one of you who added value to this effort and to my life. My humble gratitude to each one of you—my gurus, guides, folks, buddies and confidants. Thank you all for being with me through the thick and thin of this ever-challenging life, which has been peppered with aberrations, delusions and slip-ups.

My deference and salutation to all of you!

INTRODUCTION

Kingfisher and IndiGo airlines started their operations in India around the same time in 2005–2006. Indian flyers are aware that while Kingfisher folded up in 2012 due to huge accumulated losses and a severe fund crunch, IndiGo sprinted ahead with great gusto to make and raise tonnes of money. Kingfisher, sharing its name with a popular lager, headed by the liquor baron Vijay Mallya, never made any profits.

Why is this contrasting performance, given the same market to serve? It is no rocket science to conclude that IndiGo airlines would have managed its affairs well, while Kingfisher could have utterly goofed up! On-time performance was the focus for IndiGo; but Kingfisher continued to repeat its wrongs—premium pricing with delayed and mismanaged flights.

With the same business environment, Kingfisher Airlines focused on the glamour quotient and IndiGo concentrated on a low-cost business model. Kingfisher foolishly concentrated on making its air hostesses wear designer outfits a few sizes smaller and signing up expensive models for its commercials. The splashy airlines kept digging its own grave through some lousy strategies based on an awful understanding of the aviation business and piling up debts.

To make matters worse, the booze-scion Vijay Mallya did everything else other than focusing on the airlines business, which was on the downhill for long. He has been a regular at Formula One's global travelling circus—co-owning a team, working closely to launch swimwear calendars every year, owning a cricket team and taking keen interest in its player selections. These extracurricular activities left very little time for Mallya to do anything meaningful. To top it all, his fatal mistake was the acquisition of the loss-making low-cost aviation company—Air Deccan—to start and run a five-star airlines.

Instances of errors and bungles proliferate the world of business. Big names have eaten humble pie, some have tripped and tumbled on their way, and many have bitten the dust. Understanding how so many of them ended up at the wrong side of business prosperity and knowing who they were will help you avoid some quicksand of business life.

Most of you will recollect the dream camera of yesteryears, Kodak—the compact gadget for amateurs to capture the perfect 'Kodak moment' for posterity. Kodak was synonymous to photography as Xerox was to photocopying. However, if today you are looking to buying a photographic equipment, Kodak will be farthest from your mind.

How did Kodak fail to continue its hold on the camera market? Kodak made the inexcusable mistake of not recognizing opportunities emerging in the digital photography space, a technology incidentally invented by Kodak itself way back in 1975. This was in spite of a market research study Kodak undertook in 1981, which deduced that the company has about a decade to prepare itself from a digital onslaught. Sadly, during this ten-year window, Kodak management did very little to prepare itself for the technological disruption. More so, the business team followed a silo approach by ignoring the developments within their own research team.

Why did Kodak do this? Kodak feared that developing and promoting digital photography will kill its ongoing lucrative 'film-based' business model. And what was the result? Kodak continued to decline as the disruptive 'film-less' technology replaced the 'film-based' method of clicking pictures.

A classic mistake many corporates do is not carry out meaningful innovation while good times prevail. Nokia and BlackBerry also fell into this trap of overconfidence and lack of managerial foresight. It is a blatant error to commence innovating only when a crisis strikes or the business collapses—in fact, it becomes too late to do much.[1]

A glaring instance of businesses not recognizing what the market wants and refusing to adapt to change took place in the auto market in India. When I was a kid, I remember my father would revel in the occasional indulgence of going to my uncle's place in an Ambassador taxi, the then India's only domestically produced passenger vehicle since 1958. The distinct rounded silhouetted cars with spacious bench-like seats became India's symbol of high social standing and nation's hope of self-reliance. But as time passed, things went haywire. The lovable 'Amby' manufacturer Hindustan Motors failed to fire the desires of the new generation of drivers exposed to new car models available since the 1980s. Even when the company saw smarter and sleeker cars on the roads, they stuck to the age-old plump look, failing to meet customer expectations. Ultimately, it had to stop making my lovable Amby in 2014, as no one would buy such elephantine-looking fuel guzzlers anymore.

Many big companies, names and brands—loved and revered—have succumbed to their own follies. It is an unforgiving world of modern business—adapt or perish; transform or die; progress or capitulate. Change fast or succumb faster. Some mis-steps, few miscalculations, and the intolerant market may punish for long.

Blunders and mistakes essentially are value destroyers—years of toil can be annulled; assets created can get demolished or diminished; and entrepreneurial dreams can get wrecked.

Every business is tested for endurance and accomplishments. But only a few extract strength and wisdom from their trying experiences. These are the ones who are known as success stories. Instances of who blundered and how will tell you the stories of things going awry and lessons that can be learnt—to alter adversities into ascendancies.

Good–Great–Gone

There are loads of business books extolling the virtues of successful companies. In fact, one of the passkeys to writing a popular book is not to dwell on failures for too long.

Built to Last and *Good to Great* by Jim Collins are two of the best-known business books, eulogizing greatness. These books discuss factors of whether a new company would survive long term and characteristics which have made companies leap from being good companies to great companies.

The author had to, however, eat his words and correct his theory of greatness through *How the Mighty Fall*. Even his so-called great companies with a sunny outlook made mistakes and many stumbled. Some successful companies just fell into mediocrity or collapsed. **Circuit City, Motorola, Bear Stearns, Lehman Brothers** and **Zenith,** once great organizations and acclaimed in success-books, fell from positions of power and triumph.

Jim Collins describes a five-stage process of how corporates rise and fall:

- To begin with, hubris born of success (businesses attributing triumph to their own superior qualities and failing to question their significance when conditions change)

- Next stage, undisciplined pursuit of more (businesses over-do, moving into areas where the factors behind their original success no longer apply)

- The third stage is denial of risk and peril (warning signs soar, but bosses convince themselves that all is fine; this may arise at the stage of greatest apparent success)

- Followed by the fourth stage of grasping for salvation (search for new solutions or a saviour boss or a new acquisition)

- Ultimately to the fifth stage: capitulation to irrelevance or death

Collins says that firms with a never-give-up approach, at times after reaching the fourth stage, have bounced back, including IBM, Nucor and Nordstrom.

Something similar happened when the bestselling book *In Search of Excellence* was published. The authors faced embarrassment when many of the companies they profiled in the book, such as **Atari**, **Xerox**, **Wang Laboratories** and **NCR**, proved to be anything but excellent.

Worse was the celebration of **Enron** in *Leading the Revolution* by Gary Hamel. While the books were arriving in the stores in 2002, the energy-trading company was blowing up.

There are many other famous books applauding the virtues of great companies only to find later on that many exalted entities have committed grave errors to face humiliation and downfall.

'What goes up must come down' goes the famous phrase. Reasons for slipping might not only be mistakes committed but could also be a change in environment, government policies, economic catastrophes or lack of finance.

Every institution, no matter how great it is, will be vulnerable to decline. You could yourself recollect how numerous iconic brands or businesses, lauded for their successes, have disappeared into obscurity. There is no law of nature that the powerful will remain at the top.

There are many instances of celebrated brands collapsing. During the 1960s and 1970s, **Pan Am** was the go-to airline for the glamorous in America. But it made the mistake of mismanaging its financial affairs. When the Gulf War-related fuel price hike took place, unable to bear the shock, the airlines collapsed in 1991. Another instance of slip-up pertains to the famed **Borders** bookstores. Founded in 1971, this global outfit folded by 2011 as it failed to keep pace with the e-commerce mode of selling. In another stark example, even after producing 35 million cars for over a century, **Oldsmobile**, the once-popular auto brand, faltered in the 1990s as the company made the grave error in not developing sleeker and more fuel-efficient cars, and had to close down in 2004.

We have all witnessed the regular demise of many brand icons. Anyone can fall, and many eventually do. However, some do recover and may come back stronger.

The bottom line is: No business is infallible and gets accentuated by committing blunders.

Why Success Vanishes?

I often wonder why some companies and brands, without which it was difficult to carry on our daily lives, often throw in the towel. Look at the instances cited in the previous sections and how they have crumpled over time. Seemingly successful companies have often tripped very badly on their journey pathways.

There are, however, companies which continue their successful expeditions unabatedly. When I was a kid, I used to brush my teeth with Colgate toothpaste, and I do it even today. I had Lipton tea since the days I commenced drinking the energizing beverage. I still enjoy it. Horlicks was the health drink which my mom made sure I had every morning. It is as popular even today among mothers—and to top it all, I still love it.

Why such dichotomies? What makes some companies trip? What makes the others tick?

There is no single reason for businesses treading the path to obscurity. There are usually multiple bungles and causes which lead many a business to hit the door of hopelessness. In fact, many a time, reasons for failures are not even known to the outside world.

Reasons for tripping in the business world could be many. Many glaring and famous ones have been covered in this book.

Let me cite a few instances of business gaffes here.

Sometimes consumers get tired of using the same product—some sort of brand fatigue hits them with the brand owner failing to spot it. When I was in school, no movie was complete without the customary screening of the fever-and-pain brand medicine—**Saridon**—advertisement. Such was its impact that as soon as the advertisement would get screened, many, including me, would get an instant headache! Bored with the ad and fed up with the staid positioning, consumers moved on to other analgesics.

Some businesses make cardinal errors of not keeping pace with competition—technology, quality, packaging, positioning, advertisement, delivery and service.

If you ever visited Mumbai in the 1980s and 1990s, or you belong to the megacity, the only cabs which you would have noticed were the endearing Premier Padmini, made in India by the **Premier Automobiles** for over four decades. When the more fuel-efficient and reliable Maruti 800 cc cars hit the market in the mid-1980s, immediately one could smell the possibility of the impending business disaster for the iconic Pad or Fiat (the car was originally licensed from Fiat, Italy). Hindi cinema immortalized *kaali–peeli* (black–yellow) Premier taxis—eventually folded in 2000, unable to stand up to competition.

Managing businesses through inefficient and inexperienced management has been a bane for many.

Indian drivers loved their **Dunlop** tyres. Headquartered in a posh building in Kolkata, the company used to rule the roost in the 1960s and 1970s. So was **Jessop & Co.**, making railway wagons in India. Both failed miserably in practising proficient management.

Consumers change the way they buy or consume. New ways of shopping have killed many old giants.

See how retailers go in and out of fashion. **Sears** and **JCPenney**, two of America's biggest department stores, are in danger of flunking—victim of poor mall traffic, popularity of online shopping and mistake in not adopting to changes in consumers' buying habits. Two exemplary Indian department stores leave me with fond memories—**Haralalka** in Kolkata and **Akbarallys** in Mumbai. Both stood for decades as their city symbols. But now they are pale shadows of the past, unable to change quickly their product-dispensing habits. Customers needed to 'ask' for products displayed 'behind' the counters, while their nimbler competitors had commenced changing their method of storing merchandise right in 'front', to make consumers touch and feel them. By the time the iconic stores changed, it was too late for them to catch up with the rest. Skipping adaption of simple changes made these great brands miss the bus of continuity and growth.

Blunders of short-term actions and making money on the sly have led numerous businesses to either shut shops or continue with ignominy.

Satyam, once India's information technology (IT) major, and **Enron**, the darling of America's energy sector, both had painful exits owing to grave errors committed by doctoring financial numbers. Accounting scandals to prop up business performance falsely have led the Japanese conglomerate **Toshiba** and the largest British retailer **Tesco**[2] into a tailspin, and their vaunted brands have been smudged. Management greed has destroyed many and spoilt reputations of thousands of corporations built over time.

Most mistakes are sheer errors and unintended, but some are caused with an intent to defraud or make a fast buck. Eventually, the result is similar—blunders and slip-ups do leave dark marks on a corporate's history. Goof-ups often create flutters, generate abhorrent distrust, alienate customers and demotivate employees. Eventually, it may lead to bankruptcy and the end of an enterprise built over time. However, if business bloopers are handled with care and caution, mistaken indiscretions become mortal mis-steps, to be forgiven and forgotten!

Endurance and Ethos

Not a single company that was listed in the first Dow Jones index (DJI) in 1896 is listed today (General Electric was the last company to lose the DJI listing status in June 2018). Some of the first listers still exist as part of other conglomerates, but most have faded.

Why do some companies last for centuries, but most do not? While many do not read newspapers anymore, how does *Bennett Coleman and Co.* publish one of the most successful newspapers, *The Times of India*, since 1838? When hundreds of hotels go belly up every year, why is Mumbai's Taj Mahal Palace of Tatas still functioning with glory since 1903?

It has been observed that companies in the business for everyday needs such as food, drinks and accommodation have longer lifespan. Family-owned businesses seem to last longer and perform better. There are other human institutions such as temples, churches, mosques and educational institutions with longer longevity, with more than the average lifespan of 40–50 years.

What makes some businesses last longer than others? The answers to durability mainly lie within us. Just think why many of us live longer than others do. The good news is that what works for humans also works for business enterprises.

Sensible eating, regular exercises, maintaining height–weight balance, moderate drinking and no smoking are known to be the elixir of life. None of these are unknown. Yet many of us do not follow the basics. Poor work–life balance, engaging in frequent fun-time binges, long hours of sedate lifestyle and consuming liberal doses of sugar–salt–oil in food are rather common indiscretions that limit our longevity.

Business durability works on similar principles. Not adapting to changing customer habits, inefficient management, debt overload, unresolved conflicts, unethical behaviour, lethargy, overconfidence and a myriad of other reasons of business blunders lead to curtailing of an organization's life cycle. No reason is unfamiliar, yet business basics are often not adhered to, leading to organizations tripping sooner than later.

Health, whether it is personal or business, is fundamentally the product of multiple decisions and choices made by us, by recognizing what truly motivates us. We do not always make decisions—even important ones about physical or financial well-being—based on careful calculations of risk and reward. Rather, our conduct is strongly determined by our feelings, character, surroundings and available options.

We may be able to nudge one another towards wiser decision-making and healthier lives. Similarly, community pressure and societal acceptance play a wide role in improving an enterprise's endurance, building positive business ethos and a healthy financial performance. Not recognizing this principle of societal pressure would be a miscue.

(Mis)takes (Mis)understood, (Re)defined

Unlike success, mistakes are difficult to define. The definition is nebulous, contentious and often misunderstood. In trying to redefine, it is customary to consult a dictionary to find out what it is: 'a thing which is not correct; an error of judgement'. It could involve decisions based on information gap, deliberate act, careless move or pure bad luck.

Slip-ups could range from being as minor as typing an incorrect spelling to significant ones of misconstructing a contract clause to convey an opposite meaning. Mistakes can be termed 'macro' and 'micro'. When a doctor misjudges a serious ailment, or an engineer misreads the impact of smoke bellowing from an overheated machine, catastrophic consequences of macro implication could emanate. 'Micro' mistakes are usually correctable, like recruiting an inefficient employee. While errors could be trivial, these could also be calamitous.

Mistakes could be 'overt' or 'covert'. A rail company can incur a huge damages if its driver, through sheer error, overshoots a signal—this is an overt error. A covert blunder could be involved if the railway carriage fails to stop when brakes are applied. The consequences of both are similar—probable loss to lives and properties, but the reasons could be attributed to controllable (driver negligence) and non-controllable (malfunctioning brakes) causes. A serious look, however, would convince you that both the mistaken instances could teach you lessons—drivers to be trained and brakes to be checked properly.

Negligence, sloppiness or 'lapse' could cause mistakes. The sloppy act of pressing the accelerator instead of the brakes while driving could result in a serious consequence. Negligence leading to an error in 1999 caused a Mars orbiter that **Lockheed Martin** designed for NASA to be lost in space, as the engineers at Lockheed used English measurements while the NASA team used metric measures.

There could also be 'deliberate' acts of hara-kiri, like doctoring the financial results to raise share price or structuring a Ponzi scheme to dupe unsuspecting investors. Not-so-deliberate acts leading to 'inadvertent' outcomes may include taking a position on a commodity only to find the price judgement going wrong.

While mistakes and blunders usually result in 'negative' outcomes, there is something 'good' about these. Tracking why they were made and what led to them could teach us many a lesson to avoid them in the future. Albert Einstein aptly said, 'Any-one who has never made a mistake has never tried anything new.' Slip-ups often help us to slip less.

Mistakes Are Inevitable but Learning Lessons Is Optional

'Oh, that was a big faux pas', 'Wish we would have done it differently' and 'It would have been great not to do it' are some repenting remarks many of us would have uttered. These are ways to express disgust and contrite when we realize the fault.

Everyone commits errors, whether of omission or commission. No mortal or business can ever say it has not blundered. The problem, however, is that no one talks about their failures and seldom admits them. No bragging sessions take place on muddles made and losses suffered. But the truth is that all have grown up taking mis-steps including our first baby steps.

The terms blunders, mistakes, errors and failures are often used interchangeably. A mistake or blunder is a wrong action, and failure is the outcome of incorrect deeds. By committing errors in examinations, the outcome could be poor results. In business, the misstep of taking too much debt could result in the failure to repay borrowing commitments on time.

Mistakes are great educators: These help us learn from other people's howlers and teach how not to repeat them. To err is human,

Introduction

but the astute learn from them. Just think of athletes—numerous trials and errors, serious hard work, and plentiful mistakes and failures lead them to perfection. The business world is no different.

Mistakes have a strange behavioural side. While we hate to make and admit faults, most of us love to point out when others commit them. We would do a world of good if we can acknowledge the dictum—errors are inevitable and are normal for of all us to commit. This is because most business managers look at slip-ups the wrong way. Starting a blame game takes away the thunder of learning from failures.

Not all mistakes can be classified in the same way—some could be commendable involving exploratory or hypothesis testing, while others could be blameable, arising out of violating set procedures or lack of ability. Leaders need to inculcate a culture of learning from goof-ups, avoid blame games and make the team comfortable when things flop. Do not pontificate on 'who did it', but involve the team in reporting catastrophes, analyse mistakes and identify key acquirements. Dissecting 'trustworthy' failures and discouraging 'blameworthy' aberrations would go a long way to building an organization where success builds on blunders, bloopers and bungles.

Why This Book?

This book will make an honest attempt to lay down the possible major faux pas in running businesses. I hope that this knowledge will help you to evade some traps of the trade and teach you some tricks.

Take any business magazine or business non-fiction book. Stories are mainly on triumphs—successful start-ups, effective M&As, great marketing strategies, innovative products and so on—that provide an adrenaline rush. On the contrary, the literature on struggles, failures and blunders is very hard to come by.

It is no secret that success is often built on a bed of fiascos and flops. Unless you fall, you do not learn; unless you try, you cannot fail; and unless you fail, you cannot grasp.

Blunders and bloopers are subsets of failures. See a mistake as just a mistake—not as mine or yours. It being mine brings guilt, and yours brings annoyance. Only realization brings improvement. Learn from mistakes—the best way to move ahead. This book is all about looking ahead for more blunder-free days.

Good decisions come from experience, but experience comes from bad decisions. This is a truism. Inexperience is our greatest experience.

No mistake—whether good or bad, intentional or involuntary, catastrophic or trivial—is deliberated or diagnosed often. It is not in human genes to bring our muck out from the closet and use the open air to cleanse. We would usually allow the grime to settle on its own or hope it evaporates someday, even at the peril of the stink sullying the business air around. This book, however, brings into the open many mistaken steps in the business world— and most of them will teach us a lesson or two. I hope we will all be wiser by analysing some famous, frequent and common mistakes big businesses have committed over time.

The stories told will help you to answer several queries and should enable businesses to be run with fewer hiccups. The chapters will provide you with numerous real-life instances of 'who' encountered the business quagmires and 'how' they fell into the occupational snags and snares, more importantly, 'what' the possible lessons are to be learnt to fix the blunder booby traps.

References

1. Financial Times. Business leaders are blinded by industry boundaries. Financial Times [Internet]. 2019 Apr 22. Available from: https://www.ft.com/content/731ce4b4-62a7-11e9-9300-0becfc937c37

2. BBC. Tesco: Where it went wrong. BBC News [Internet]. 2015 Jan 19. Available from: https://www.bbc.com/news/business-30886632

QUALITY QUIVERS AND QUANDARY

When you visit your favourite restaurant, you expect to gain a similar experience as you had the last time; when you pick up your toothpaste every morning, you expect the same brush-feel you had the previous day; when you want to savour a chocolate piece to pep your mood up, you anticipate the same taste you had the previous occasion. The expectation of repeating a previous positive experience is unending when using a product or service.

It all boils down to the provider of the goods and services to make available quality in a consistent manner.

If you get a jolt by a sudden drop in service or get shocked by an unexpected fall in the quality, your confidence as a consumer will take a nosedive when you procure it the next time.

Can you imagine that you get into the world-famous **Toyota** car only to find out that the brakes may not work at high speed! Quite a few Toyota cars sped out of control due to either accelerator pedals getting trapped in ill-fitting mats or faulty pedals stuck in half-depressed positions. The company recalled a whopping 10 million cars in 2009 and 2010 for problems relating to unintended acceleration. Toyota was fined $1.2 billion in March 2014 in the United States, and it admitted that it misled consumers, leading to incidents where vehicles sped out of drivers' control.[1]

Where was the problem with Toyota, a company long considered gold standard for reliability? It committed the cardinal error by showing a lack of concern for quality and hiding information about defects in its cars—an appalling behaviour by one of the highest-selling car companies. What was the result? Toyota lost its top car manufacturer position soon thereafter.

It may sound weird for a company of Toyota's image to fiddle with safety practices and give a go-by to good-quality practices. When its cars faced safety-related problems, the company said that it had recalled all vehicles fitted with faulty floor mats—though, in reality, it had not—essentially, it lied![2] Horrifying mistakes by the company which prides itself for providing quality products at reasonable prices!

President Akio Toyoda repeatedly admitted Toyota's quality and safety problems to its rapid growth, which outstripped its ill-trained workforce. He nailed the problem on human resources saying that the company could not train enough personnel to keep pace with its speedy growth. He acknowledged that the warped and misguided approach incorrectly focuses on product and sales volume first, with safety and quality becoming a secondary priority. Toyota's inverted strategy during the rapidly expanding period, which commenced a decade back, was the undoing of its long and carefully cultivated brand goodwill, which it is still struggling to get back.

Quality is sometimes sacrificed at the altar of cost. That could be a grave blunder. When the manufacturer finds that the cost needs to be reduced to fight competition, many a time businesses cut corners on quality. Needless to mention, quality does not come free. It has a price. The moot point is: It should not be under-specified but should be adequate in accordance with the seller's commitment. It also need not be over-specified. When a customer buys a Ford Fiesta, surely it is not expected to provide the quality of an Audi car. But the Ford car needs to be safe, functional and deliver on its promises. Quality is often a trade-off corporates commit, and to compromise on it is hara-kiri.

General Motors (GM), makers of Saturn ION and Pontiac G5, tried covering up safety lapses with its ignition switches. Airbags are one of the most important safety features in a car—opening up as soon as there is any crash. But if it does not open, what do you make of it? This is what happened in 2005 Chevrolet Cobalt, where airbags failed to open up. The ignition switch was prone to be turning off, leading to cutting the engine and disabling systems such as the power steering and the airbags.

More surprisingly, from a widely quoted e-mail of 2005, it is understood that GM engineers rejected the idea of adopting a new design for the ignition switch, as it would cost 90 cents (yes, less than one dollar!) per vehicle.[3] Utter incompetence and callousness were prevalent in this very famous company. During the last decade, 124 deaths were related to the auto safety system failures, recalling 2.6 million vehicles, and GM was fined $900 million in September 2015.[4]

Embarrassments to such huge brands as Toyota and GM are one issue, but the utter failure of the quality systems of companies of international repute, resulting in loss of human lives, is of very serious concern.

Airbags not inflating automatically to protect passengers during accidents is a disastrous snag. Japanese maker **Takata's** airbag reflected propensity to explode in humid conditions. It has been linked to at least 14 deaths, more than 100 injuries and recall of tens of millions of vehicles worldwide.

The reasons for Takata's hara-kiri are several. One, the company struggled to keep up with a demand surge for its airbags through the early and mid-2000s as it bagged new customers like GM. This could have resulted in shipping goods without performing adequate checks on quality. Second, airbag modules would get wet during transit, arriving wet at the automakers' assembly plants on leaky trucks, resulting in their frequent malfunctioning. The company's overt focus on timely delivery meant it was ignoring logistical disasters and manufacturing issues. Although way back in 2004, Takata conducted secret tests on 50 airbags where steel inflators in two of the airbags cracked during the tests, a condition it observed could lead to rupture. But instead of alerting about the possible danger, Takata's executives discounted the results and ordered lab technicians to delete the testing data from their computers and dispose of airbag inflators in the garbage.

These grievous errors led to estimated liabilities totalling a whopping $10 billion, and 19 automakers recalling over 45 million inflators worldwide because of rupture risks. These awful quality snags ultimately pushed the largest Japanese company into bankruptcy in June 2017. This brought to an end the 84-year-old Takata group that developed Japan's first driver-side airbag system in the 1980s with Honda. (In April 2018, Takata was taken over by the Chinese-owned Key Safety Systems for $1.6 billion, forcing Shigehisa Takada, its chief executive and grandson of the company's founder, to resign. The company has been rebranded as Joyson Safety Systems.)[5]

Quality snags have led to massive car recalls for long, and most brands of cars have fallen victim to poor-quality management. The situation has only grown worse over the years. Over a lengthy period, the auto industry looks to have lagged focus on basic safety practices, though there are reasons to believe that the auto sector is becoming more sensitive to this issue of late.

Honda was facing massive recalls due to airbags and other causes. Honda's chief executive officer (CEO), Takahiro Hachigo said in February 2016 that the company expanded too rapidly and risked losing the freewheeling spirit of creativity that has been Honda's hallmark. He lamented the fact that the company rolled out products at a speed and scale that exceeded its means.[6] It chased sales targets, rather than creating and delivering quality products it was known for—a colossal error of growth ambitions overtaking quality consciousness.

Quality defects could be observed everywhere—after all it's generally the man–machine intervention which creates a quality product.

But should there be anything wrong, the quality quandary can be minimized hugely if manufacturers recall their merchandise—preferably on their own. This, however, has not always been done by the makers as they try to hide under the garb of some shady reason. Product recalls are embarrassing but significantly better when the manufacturers own up their mistakes. It helps to regain much lost ground in the company's goodwill.

Products have fallen short of quality standards time and again. Some manufactures recalled their products. Many did not do so with consumers suffering the abject apathy of the makers.

In June 2018, US packaged food giant **Kellogg's** recalled its Honey Smacks cereal due to potential salmonella (a bacteria causing serious illness) contamination, which apparently has been linked to 130 instances of sickness and 34 hospitalizations. The reason seems to be its manufacturing being done at a third-party factory where quality parameters could have gone rather lax.[7]

Similarly, Besnier-family-owned **Lactalis,** one of the largest dairy producers in the world, was forced to recall 12 million tins of baby milk from its home market in France and abroad, made in its factory in Craon, north-western France, after salmonella bacteria were discovered in them in late 2017. Dozens of children fell ill after consuming the baby formula. Several French retailers came under severe fire after they admitted selling Lactalis products affected by the quality scare, when they should have been removed from shelves. The company said that its French baby-food factory might have been exposed to salmonella since 2005, and if this were true, it was a significant quality faux pas. The dairy group's CEO apologized and said in June 2018 that it was an accident and halted production at the Craon plant.[8,9]

Quality bloopers, when acknowledged by the marketers, are forgivable. But when the makers refuse to acknowledge the problem, it is any company's catastrophic calamity.

Children's car seats with defective buckles could severely endanger the child and make it difficult to free a child in an emergency. **Graco Children's Products,** an American baby products company, failed to recall promptly about six million child car seats with defective buckles.

When parents complained, Graco refused to consider that the buckles were defective. Some guardians accused that they had to cut straps to free a child. Graco insisted that the problems with the buckles stemmed from contamination with 'foreign material such as food or dried liquids'. But investigators dismissed that explanation, saying that buckles getting dirty with food and drink was 'completely foreseeable', and not an excuse. The American National Highway Traffic Safety Administration forced Graco in

January 2014 to recall the products. The company initially refused, but only to relent a month later.[10]

The manufacturer refused to acknowledge quality issues, while parents and the safety regulators insisted that there was a problem. What a dreadful corporate behaviour, especially when it is linked to safety—be it children or otherwise!

Quality has never mattered more than it is now. Today, you can compare an endless array of products from around the world just with the click of a mouse. Shoppers are smarter and have more information available than ever before. They can view user-generated reviews on subjects as wide as holidays to houses, and compare the value–price hypothesis. Quality feedback is easily available, with social media instantaneously broadcasting any quality annoyance. It is now an unforgiving world—manufacturers and marketers better beware!

Garbage in Garbage out

The famous computing world adage implies that poor-quality input will result in poor quality of output or service. It is true, everywhere and always.

Trust in input quality certified by established producers is often assumed sacrosanct. The plastic-film-making company which I manage assumes that the quality certificates from manufacturers of plastic granules used as an input can be taken for granted and need not to be quality tested every time before usage.

But when this trust is wrecked by vendors, it results in calamitous consequences. Manufacturers and marketers sometime commit the cardinal error of taking this confidence for granted by compromising on its quality promise.

Currently, a concern in input quality compromise is India's over $20 billion pharmaceutical industry, a global supplier of value-for-money generic medicines. Health regulators in the United States, Europe and the United Kingdom had barred several Indian manufacturing units from producing medicines, including bulk drugs, for their markets because of deficient standards and lack of reliable data from medicine trials. Worse, drug companies have been warned several times about concerns relating to lab workers testing samples repeatedly until they obtain desired results and discarding of unfavourable test results. This is a blunder by Indian drug companies, making them face a serious global credibility test. It may be mentioned here that in addition to Indian exporter-manufacturers, such cautionary steps have also taken place in several other exporting countries from time to time.

There are several instances of pharmaceutical misdemeanours pertaining to product quality. Quality-related transgressions have serious long-term adverse implications on the company involved. To say the least, these mistakes need to be avoided at any cost.

When US Food and Drug Administration (FDA) inspectors visited, in 2013, the Chikalthana plant of **Wockhardt**, which produces a generic version of the heart tablet *Toprol XL*, they found urine spilling over open drains, soiled uniforms and mould growing in a raw material storage area.[11] These serious transgressions could affect not only input items going into the manufacture of medicines but also the finished product, tarnishing the manufacturer's image globally. Not to unlearn, Wockhardt's plant in Gujarat, which makes sterile injectable drugs, was found in 2016 by the FDA to have failed to follow procedures to prevent microbiological contamination of drugs claiming to be antiseptic.[12]

Wockhardt's or any other firm's lack of good manufacturing process adherence is a matter of perspective, discipline and sense of purpose. If customer requirements (especially for drugs and food items) are not taken care of seriously, the outcome could only be catastrophic—and cost-reduction mentality is mostly the prime culprit.

Quality concern erodes the edifice of trust. It equally applies to sourced items, which may either be used for further manufacturing or sold as such, like traded commodities. Sometimes it is possible to contain the damage if the businesses and authorities move swiftly to put in place stringent quality assurance standards. But a lackadaisical approach is a business killer.

Tailpiece

Quality is not definable. It is to be perceived, sensed and experienced. Peter Drucker, the famous management author, said, 'Quality in a product or service is not what the supplier puts in. It is what the customer gets out and is willing to pay for. Customers pay only for what is of use to them and gives them value. Nothing else constitutes quality.' If quality is to be treated as a gospel for an organization, every input item needs to match the quality expectation of the product or service it goes into.

Quality Sacrifice at Profit's Altar

Quality is uncompromisable. Customers assume that quality is given. The good news is that most suppliers are attempting it. The bad news is that some businesses feel that cost is the king, sacrificing quality to enhance profits.

Customer satisfaction is all about customer loyalty—an ability to make the customer buy your product or service repeatedly. In simple terms, quality helps customers to return, but not to return products or services sold. It is of paramount importance to focus on customer needs to precede company's priorities.

Organizations need to have a culture of trusting customers. If customers complain, the organization should believe that the concern needs to be fixed without quarrels. The sales team and company's employees should have adequate authority to satisfy customer needs. There should not be any quagmire of bureaucratic steeplechase to resolve customer complaints or arguments on cost to be incurred to set things right.

A significant instance of corporate quality deceit was by **Ranbaxy Laboratories**, which is now owned by Sun Pharmaceutical Industries. Once the second-largest Indian drug maker, it has been a poster child for manufacturing problems. In 2015, Ranbaxy paid a $500 million penalty to US authorities as part of a settlement that included pleading guilty to two charges of violating drug safety and data manipulation.

What did Ranbaxy do? Between June and August 2007, the company knew that certain batches of *gabapentin* (also known as *Neurontin*), a drug used for treating patients with epilepsy, had tested positive for 'unknown impurities' and had unreliable shelf life. But Ranbaxy kept mum over the adverse findings.

How did the fraud come to light? Dinesh Thakur, an American-educated chemical engineer, was hired as a research executive by Ranbaxy, way back in 2003. Since the day of joining, Thakur was looking at whether the drugs produced, in fact, work.

While working for Ranbaxy, Thakur's three-year-old son developed an ear infection. The standard treatment is *amoxicillin clavulanate*, a strong antibiotic drug made by GlaxoSmithKline (GSK). Ranbaxy makes a generic version of this drug. Thakur applied it on his son based on his paediatrician's advice. Unfortunately, the drug did not work, and his fever persisted. As is normally the case, he went back to his paediatrician. She changed the manufacturer to GSK, and his fever came down within a day. Thakur's suspicion for Ranbaxy's drug quality grew stronger.

Thakur found that Ranbaxy's drugs' 'bioequivalence' (generic drugs having the same effect as the branded drug) data were either made up or did not exist. Thakur asked, 'Does the drug work as intended?' Thakur had his doubts. He reported to the FDA in 2005. The agency's investigation found that Ranbaxy had a 'persistent pattern' of submitting 'untrue statements'. On at least 15 new generic drug applications, auditors found more than 1,600 data errors. This meant that their drugs were 'potentially unsafe and illegal to sell'. Ranbaxy was falsifying data to receive approval of its generic drugs.

'In essence, Ranbaxy used the fraud as a competitive advantage to build and grow the business in the U.S.,' quipped Ranbaxy's former vice president Vince Fabiano.

Another glaring instance of pharma sector deception took place in India's second-largest generic drug manufacturer, **Dr Reddy's Laboratories.** The company apparently ran an 'uncontrolled custom quality control laboratory' to test its drugs into compliance. They would destroy records of drugs failing tests, retaining only those that showed passing the tests. This is not unique and, unfortunately, Ranbaxy's earlier behaviour was somewhat similar.

The US drug regulator inspected three manufacturing sites between November 2014 and March 2015. Taking cognizance of the findings, the agency warned Dr Reddy's in a letter of November 2015 about the existence of an unknown lab where drugs were tested, routine retesting of samples until they logged acceptable results and not recording the failed tests and improper data management—all serious charges of hoodwinking.

Data falsification is a major malady. Many companies have been involved in this unseemly behaviour. The so-called quality-conscious Japanese manufacturers of **Kobe Steel**, **Takata**, **Mitsubishi Motors** and **Toyo Rubbers** have all involved themselves in data deception. Similarly, **Tata Steel** UK is under investigation by The United Kingdom's Serious Fraud Office owing to possible inappropriate testing and certification procedures.

A global organization which has suffered over time from quality miscarriages is **Johnson & Johnson (J&J)**. A string of manufacturing snags has threatened its image as one of the world's most trustworthy brands. In recent years, the company has recalled Tylenol pain-reliever capsules, contact lenses, artificial hips, injectable antipsychotic drugs and liquid Motrin for infants.

William Weldon, a life-timer with J&J, who was the CEO between 2002 and 2012, had been criticized for focusing too much on cost-cutting and too little on quality. No wonder the quality parameters took a back seat over a long period in J&J. When the CEO focuses on cost and profit, and not on quality, the outcome could be tragic.[13]

Even a food-product giant like **ConAgra Foods**, in business for 100 years and a Fortune 500 company, slipped in basic hygiene. Problems emerged in Southwest Georgia's peanut country when a whistle-blower squeaked that ConAgra had found salmonella in peanut butter at its plant in Sylvester, Georgia, United States. But when plant officials were confronted, they refused to acknowledge and cooperate with the FDA. The government finally demanded the records three years later and verified the whistle-blower's claims, after hundreds of persons fell sick due to salmonella-tainted peanut butter produced at the plant in 2007. It was found that ConAgra knew peanut butter made in Georgia had twice tested positive for salmonella in 2004. The problems were not fixed by the time of the outbreak.

ConAgra ultimately admitted to a misdemeanour count of shipping adulterated food, pleading guilty in 2016, agreeing to pay $11.2 million. This was the largest criminal fine ever imposed for a food-borne illness in the United States, to resolve a decade-long criminal investigation into a nationwide salmonella outbreak caused by contaminated peanut butter.[14]

The matter was clearly a case of factory conditions being suboptimal. Following the outbreak, the company upgraded its Sylvester plant to address issues that contributed to salmonella contamination. The company also instituted new and enhanced safety protocols and procedures for manufacturing, testing and sanitation.

The issue is: Why didn't it do it earlier? Why should a company of ConAgra's stature wait to make thousands sick? It all boils down to one strategic intent: Is it profit over quality or the other way round—organizations need to always sort this basic conundrum. The sooner they recognize that quality precedes profits, the better off they would be.

Profit is not bad—in fact, it is the reward for good entrepreneurship. But abating quality to bloat earnings would be an enormous error any industry can ever commit.

Tailpiece

We, as consumers, take for granted the safety of food and medicines we consume. We always count on the firms that prepare and package the things we consume to be just as anxious about the quality of their product as they are with the profit they pocket. There is nothing wrong for businesses to optimize cost, enhance turnover and improve profit. But if it is done at our cost and peril, that is doomsday in the making. It is well known that squeezing a lemon too much and too quickly will only bring out its bitterness faster!

Quality: A Cult

Quality is a culture, a philosophy, a faith that needs to be practised over and over again. It is not a one-night stand which gets over sooner than later. It is a love affair which an organization needs to promote, pamper and practise over its lifetime.

Developing quality products and services to ensure a satisfying experience by customers is the trait every successful business will depict. Any slackness in this tactic will be an inerasable mistake.

Companies have failed miserably on various occasions to follow this simple principle of following a culture of quality. Great names have fallen on their face when near-term goals made short shrift for long-term value creation.

The lack of a quality culture can lead to disastrous consequences.

In an instance, the most horrifying day, perhaps, in the history of any industrial nation was 3 December 1984. Victims recall seeing their neighbours foaming at the mouth and dying around them; the infamous **Union Carbide** pesticide plant, spewing a deadly cocktail of methyl isocyanate and other gases, killed over 2,000 people—some say 20,000—who lived in the adjoining slums, with tens of thousands of others afflicted for life. The world's worst industrial disaster made Bhopal an international byword for a chemical catastrophe.

Revelations from employees and company technical documents, as well as reports from the government's chief scientist, exposed basic operating errors, design flaws, maintenance failures, training deficiencies and cost-saving measures—all led to endangering safety at the plant.

To cite just an instance of complete quality apathy, interviews by the *New York Times* with company employees reflected the following episode: When employees discovered the initial leak of methyl isocyanate at 11:30 PM on 2 December, a supervisor—assuming it was a water leak—decided to deal with it only after the next tea break. In the next hour, the reaction taking place in a storage tank went out of control. 'Internal leaks never bothered us,' said an employee. Workers said that the reasons for leaks were rarely investigated. The problems were either fixed without further examination or ignored, they said.[15]

Such accidents usually happen because of a series of wrong decisions involving both distant managers and on-the-spot engineers. A lack of quality concern for the manufacturing plant has left behind ghastly human and physical scars, which are visible in this Indian town even today.

Fast forward several decades to the present, a lack of quality culture prevails even today among certain enterprises.

Samsung, a famous consumer goods company, had its flagship phone—Samsung Galaxy Note 7—exploding spontaneously. The company had to kill the product in October 2016. Initially, the South Korean giant announced that the defect was caused by faulty batteries from one of the suppliers. But repeated internal tests failed to confirm this.

While over $17 billion of Samsung's market value was knocked off the day it announced the stoppage of Note 7 production, the customer trust it lost was invaluable. Quality problems do irreparable harm and may take ages to recover the trust once bestowed.

What led to the Samsung fiasco? While the truth may not ever be known, what seems to have transpired is the company's hunger to fight its smartphone rival, Apple. Samsung planned to cram increasingly sophisticated features into its devices. It was possible that Samsung's supply chain failed to deliver increased require-ments of components within the desired time targets. This could have led to technical problems or to cutting corners.

The *New York Times* stated that Samsung's corporate culture may have compounded the issue. The paper reported that based on two former Samsung employees, who asked not to be named for fear of retribution from the company, described the work-place as militaristic. A top-down approach was followed with orders coming from people high above who did not necessarily understand how product technologies actually worked—a sure recipe for quality disasters.[16]

The market was not surprised with the fiasco, which was not the first one. Just before this smartphone mess-up, 34 different models involving 2.8 million washing machines were recalled in 2016, when over 9 machines reportedly exploded during 2011 and 2016. The machines apparently had a defect where their tops were not properly secured. Too much machine pressure while in operation caused the top to blow off, potentially resulting in injuries. This was a clear case of poor attention to safety in quality. (Samsung seems to have learnt its quality-optimizing lessons since this fiasco, with a stream of new launches having gone through without any quality hiccups.)

Tailpiece

Organizations need to create a culture in which employees live quality in all their actions—being passionate about excellence as value system instead of just obeying orders from the top. Quality cult involves creating an environment where employees not only follow quality guidelines but also 'see' others taking quality-focused actions, 'hear' others conversing on quality and 'feel' quality in their blood. Not looking at quality as an ethos within an organization will be a mistake.

In Closing

Businesses nowadays have little choice but to shape up and remain relevant—and total-quality adaption would be fundamental. After discussions on who tripped on quality's alter and how, let us shift our attention to what should be done to fix quality. Build four core value beliefs of an organization to build a 'culture of quality':

- Leadership emphasis is the key. Do not make 'quality' a hog-wash. Make the top team believe that quality is imperative.

- Make quality a brand statement. Is it producing defect-free goods and ensuring customer satisfaction? Focus on both—which need refreshment from time to time.

- Create peer pressure and collective pride among employees as opposed to top-down dictates; hone quality culture throughout.

- Instil quality consciousness at grass-roots level. Employees should be allowed to learn from mistakes and be free to apply prudence to non-conforming situations.

When the culture of quality ensues, the customers' tolerance for lack of quality will dwindle. Confuse not—this is the true test.

References

1. Jensen C, Tabuchi H. Toyota to recall 6.4 million vehicles. The New York Times [Internet]. 2014 Apr 9. Available from: https://www.nytimes.com/2014/04/10/business/international/toyota-to-recall-vehicles.html

2. Ross B, Rhee J, Hill AM, Chuchmach M, Katersky A. Toyota to pay $1.2B for hiding deadly 'unintended acceleration'. ABC News [Internet]. 2014 Mar 19. Available from: https://abcnews.go.com/Blotter/toyota-pay-12b-hiding-deadly-unintendedacceleration/story?id=22972214

3. Mackey R. Highlights from house hearing on G.M. defects. The New York Times [Internet]. 2014 Apr 1. Available from: https://thelede.blogs.nytimes.com/2014/04/01/live-updates-from-house-hearing-on-g-m-defects/

4. Shepardson D. GM ignition switch criminal case is dismissed. Reuters [Internet]. 2018 Sep 20. Available from: https://www.autoblog.com/2018/09/20/gm-ignition-switch-criminal-case-dismissed/

5. Financial Times. Key Safety Systems completes $1.6bn Takata acquisition. Financial Times [Internet]. 2018 Apr 12. Available from: https://www.ft.com/content/a697e0de-3dfd-11e8-b7e0-52972418fec4

6. Financial Times. How upstarts drive progress at Honda. Financial Times [Internet]. 2018 Apr 1. Available from: https://www.ft.com/content/47e06526-30f5-11e8-ac48-10c6fdc22f03

7. Lardieri A. Kellogg's Honey Smacks cereal linked to 30 more cases of salmonella. US News [Internet]. 2018 Sep 5. Available from: https://www.usnews.com/news/health-care-news/articles/2018-09-05/kelloggs-honey-smacks-cereal-linked-to-30-more-cases-of-salmonella

8. Financial Times. Lactalis to pay damages over salmonella conta-mination. Financial Times [Internet]. 2018 Jan 14. Available from: https://www.ft.com/content/22f8569e-f91c-11e7-9b32-d7d59aace167

9. Willsher K. Lactalis to withdraw 12m boxes of baby milk in salmonella scandal. The Guardian [Internet]. 2018 Jan 14. Available from: https://www.theguardian.com/world/2018/jan/14/lactalis-baby-milk-salmonella-scandal-affects-83-countries-ceo-says

10. Jensen C. Car seat maker Graco under investigation for delayed reporting of defect. The New York Times [Internet]. 2014 Dec 1. Available from: https://www.nytimes.com/2014/12/02/business/car-seat-maker-graco-under-investigation-for-delayed-reporting-of-defect.html

11. Business Standard. Urine spills staining image of Wockhardt's generic drugs. Business Standard [Internet]. 2013 Sep 28. Available from: https://www.business-standard.com/article/companies/urine-spills-staining-image-of-wockhardt-s-generic-drugs-113092800025_1.html

12. USFDA. Warning Letter. USFDA [Internet]. 2016 Dec 23. Available from: https://www.fda.gov/iceci/enforcementactions/warningletters/2016/ucm534983.htm

13. The New York Times. J.&J. chief to resign one role. The New York Times [Internet]. 2012 Feb 21. Available from: https://www.nytimes.com/2012/02/22/business/j-j-chief-to-resign-one-role.html

14. The New York Times. ConAgra agrees to pay $11.2 million in salmonella outbreak. The New York Times [Internet]. 2016 Dec 13. Available from: https://www.nytimes.com/2016/12/13/business/conagra-agrees-to-pay-11-2-million-in-salmonella-outbreak.html

15. Diamond S. Union Carbide's inquiry indicates errors led to India plant disaster. The New York Times [Internet]. 1985 Mar 21. Available from:https://www.nytimes.com/1985/03/21/business/union-carbide-s-inquiry-indicates-errors-led-to-india-plant-disaster.html

16. Mozur P. Galaxy Note 7 fires caused by battery and design flaws, Samsung says. The New York Times [Internet]. 2017 Jan 22. Available from:https://www.nytimes.com/2017/01/22/business/samsung-galaxy-note-7-battery-fires-report.html

FAMILY BUSINESS FALLACY

The biggest incubator of entrepreneurship is a family business. However, the flip side is that family businesses do not last through generations, falling by the wayside, usually by the second or third generation. While the ones which last over generations make enormous contributions, over time the family shareholding usually falls below one-fourth—implying marginalizing many a family holding that had built many an empire. The issue is: What ails them?

Just look at several global household family business names that have caved in over time. The financial services firm **Lehman Brothers** and the pharmaceutical giant **Warner-Lambert** are some names which have either lost their independence or simply disappeared into the oblivion.

Similar stories exist on the Indian side. The big names ruling the Indian business horizon in the 1950s either have fallen like ninepins, crashing into obscurity or are still stuggling to somehow exist.

Some of you may still recollect the hallowed groups and names such as **Martin Burn** (which built Kolkata's iconic Victoria Memorial), **Lala Shri Ram** (who had once made DCM a household Indian name), **Walchand Hirachand** (maker of the first Indian ship SS Loyalty), **Karam Chand Thapar** (promoter of JCTs and Ballarpurs), **Kasturbhai Lalbhai** (who made Arvind textile brands well known) and the **Khataus** (my mom loved their sarees).

Recent instances of families toiling to keep their heads above water involve the steel to shipping conglomerate owner, the **Ruias**; the *Videocon* brand owner, the **Dhoots**; and the infamous *Bhushan Steel* people, the **Singhals**.

Families are supposed to be the harbinger of togetherness and oneness of culture, but family businesses are not bereft of their share of problems—greed, ego, incompetence, prejudice, partisan and intolerance. There are numerous stories of dynastic declines—some steady but many abrupt. Competition, mismanagement, deregulation, technological change or simply family-related issues have led several family corporates to doom. While many families ruined their businesses, numerous others have succeeded enormously.

Think of *Walmart, Ford, Dior, Mars, BMW, Henkel, Foxconn, Lukoil, Suzuki, Samsung, Mahindra* and *Bajaj*—all are family-run global giants. About one-third of the S&P 500 index consists of family-run businesses; and about one-fifth of the companies in the Fortune Global 500 (world's largest businesses by sales) belong to this genre. Emerging groups like the Jains (of the Times Group), Mittals (of Airtel fame) and Wipro (reinvented by Azim Premji) will resonate with every Indian. In spite of many mistakes in family businesses, the 'lucky sperms clubs', as Warren Buffet calls a family enterprise, are still going strong.

A family enterprise, for many of us, conjures the images of the neighbourhood grocery stores selling from bread to batteries. Over four-fifths of businesses are family owned, generating over two-thirds of global GDP, with mom-and-pop shops forming the bulk. These businesses are as old as the business world of today—the first form of business ever developed.

Strange as it may seem, many family businesses just fight for survival. They are happy with their continuity and do not aim for greater success or adding value to their shareholding. Surprisingly, subsistence is the mantra for these businesses and not advancement. It is obvious that business outcomes would falter due to wavering desire for bigger attainment.

Family businesses continue to be an enigma. These businesses are often seen as stable, but conservative. Their behaviour may often seem secretive and many times irrational.

This dichotomy is the problem for family businesses. Some are stable, forward-looking and reliable employers caring for their employees, while others display a closed structure and secrecy, arbitrary management style, doubtful professionalism and lack of understanding to changing business needs. Some rest on the laurels of their past glory, depict conservatism and behave in an old-fashioned manner—modernity and progressiveness elude many a business family.

Passing the Baton

Family businesses run the world. It is but natural for any family to realize that the patriarch will neither live forever nor will his or her health permit them to carry on indefinitely. Yet families find it difficult to hand over their mantle to ensure business continuity. The handover of the business baton to the next generation has never been easy and often gets involved in murky family feuds. The bad news is that the average longevity of most family firms does not exceed three generations. Squabbles over succession kill generational entrepreneurship.

Many would have heard these statistics about the longevity of family businesses. Only 30 per cent of all family businesses make it to the second generation. Just 10 per cent remain active, for the third generation to lead,[1] and only 3 per cent last for more than four generations or beyond.[2] Statistically, only about 1 per cent of family businesses will advance from the fourth to fifth generations. This is very bad news!

Sir Adrian Cadbury, the author of a British report on corporate governance and chairman of the confectionery firm founded by his grandfather, mentioned that when the patriarch hands over to the second generation, at that point, the failure rate is highest.[3] This is the 'crunch time'. It will be a mistake if business families do not heed this profound observation.

Potentially, the most toxic issue in a family business is the transition from one generation of a family to the next. The big mistake families do is not to think about continuity early enough.

The main problem—succession—is not a regular issue. Hence, families are generally not good at handling it in their businesses. Not much experience vests within the family as succession mostly takes place once in a few decades.

Then, there is the interplay of love, emotion and attachment. More often than not, parents become incapable of making a rational assessment of their kids' leadership abilities. It becomes more challenging when the children are not capable enough. Family feuds, misunderstandings and wrangles emerge.

There is another psychological reason—the senior generation often assumes that they are indispensable and believes that they add value by dint of their accumulated experience, wisdom and age. It is a myth.

Family businesses can suffer from the distinct possibility that children or grandchildren of the founders may not match their brains, personality or character. It becomes more challenging where weaker members of the household do not start learning or neglect to master the tricks of the trade from the stronger members.

Most parents are unaware that while their offspring might be sharing half of their genes, they may not match their disposition or intellect. The problem commences when they assume that their children are 'just like them'. When parents try to script the lives of their children with those of their own or their unfulfilled dreams, the situation becomes complex.

The amazing success of some of the best family firms perhaps reminds millions of business owners that they can prosper and thrive and yet not surrender their family ownership control; but little do they realize that no family can continue in perpetuation without a successful succession.

Every family business is different when it comes to passing the baton, and each one will need its own unique solution. *Hershey* confectionery, founded in 1894, did it on time, every time. So did the *Tatas*, a diversified Indian conglomerate founded in 1868. The legendary brands remain as fabled.

Failing to name their successor or to plan for an eventuality is practised by many, including the rich and famous. The veteran Italian octogenarian designer **Giorgio Armani** has not announced who would replace him at the helm of the company. He, however, decided to transfer part of his fashion empire to a foundation created in 2016 in a bid to prevent any takeovers or a break-up of the group with his heirs holding the remaining stakes. His indecisiveness on his successor became manifested when he said: 'Believe me, it is horrendous to decide what to leave to whom, if it is right or not right.'[4,5]

A similar story goes for the other fashion designer known the world over—**Roberto Cavalli.** He, too, has so far failed to find someone to take over the company that bears his name.[6]

These two instances of Italian fashion gurus not deciding on their successors could be recipes for an impending disaster when it comes to maintaining the legacy of the hard work done to build the internationally known high-end style brands.

Statistically speaking, globally one in two families will need to pass their baton to their next generation in the next five to seven years. A survey by Edelman, a public relations (PR) firm, reported in the *Economist* that the public's confidence in family enterprises falls once the baton is passed from the founder to the next generation. It is disturbing to know through a PWC survey in 2016 of over 2,800 family business senior-executive interviews in 50 countries that 43 per cent of family businesses did not have any succession plan in place[7]—a blunder which family head honchos can ill afford to make.

This headache is pronounced in the Gulf region than anywhere else, says the *Economist*. Here, 80 per cent of the enterprises producing more than 90 per cent of its non-oil wealth are family controlled. The number of relatives hankering for jobs in these firms is exploding. This is because the population is young and the governments are desperate to shift workers from the public to the private sector primarily due to unstable energy prices. The matter of succession is so serious in the Middle East that it is estimated that over two-thirds of Saudi families have at least one succession dispute tied up in courts.

In Japan, however, succession takes place in a somewhat strange manner. Men in their 20s and 30s are adopted by families to rescue biologically ill-fated families and thereby ensure a business inheritor. Thousands of people are adopted every year and, amazingly, the overwhelming majority are adults. The sliding birth rate in Japan and the prerequisite to have a male as the business face to the world has necessitated the concoction of family business continuity.

Two key reasons have caused the family business succession bungle: poor leadership and hostility. Though, normally, the eldest son of the family is anointed with the prized possession of the succession baton, historical evidence shows that he rarely is the most competent. There could also be other claimants, such as brothers, sisters, their spouses, cousins, and the list could be endless, and one of them could even be more talented. Incompetent heirs and family brawls are the worst enemies of family business endurance.

Tailpiece

What should be done? Do as good chefs do for complicated recipes—break it up into stages and cook! To avoid internecine tussles and to display professionalism, business reigns could be handed over in stages. First, hand over the management control and then the ownership. The founder-entrepreneur could pass on the management to his siblings retaining the shareholding with himself. This is a good way to handle generational transition. But not taking even these baby steps would be a grave disservice to the business continuity.

Family Handicaps

While families are harbingers of togetherness, strangely often the family system becomes a stumbling block.

A family enterprise is usually formed from a single founder–owner or founder couple. Most of the times, it is formed by employing relatives who usually join the business in their quest to find a job. The *Economist* reported in a 1997 study 'Generation to Generation', carried out by four family business pundits, that about three-quarters of family firms in America adopted this form. A further 20 per cent are sibling partnerships, and 5 per cent are 'cousin consortia'. This business formation structure may not be too different in other parts of the world.

Contrary to popular belief, the family patriarch could be prejudicial in the long term. The founder brings in two great values to an enterprise: one, his goodwill with the financiers and, two, possible close relationship with the political class. As the business grows, difficulties to obtain the right talent from within the family with the proper attitude multiply. Children and relatives may not be bequeathed with the prowess of the entrepreneur. The family starts missing the 'patriarch advantage'. Either the right expertise will need to be found from within the family tree or outside talent will need to be tapped. Or else, the business could fall into a ditch.

To find a talent from within the family could be a big challenge. Many of the members may be useless. Some may be disinterested. A few may be more of a baggage than an asset. Anand Mahindra, the Mahindra Group chief, an Indian conglomerate that has been run by the **Mahindra family** for three generations, once quipped in disgust: family companies are mostly stuffed with family members '99% of whom should not be there'.

The biggest long-term risk for Indian family firms, wrote the *Economist*, is not competition probes, shaky finances or lacklustre profits. It is that the kids may not be up to the mark. It would be an error not to recognize these usual family traits.

Unless these businesses reach out to professionals on time, new challenges could constantly keep cropping up. These internal challenges get compounded due to increased competition, war for talent and uncertain financial performance. If not handled quickly, these would hinder the future business considerably.

The presence of too many family members creates another problem. If the family multiplies swiftly, ownership becomes more and more diluted. In addition, the business often cannot grow fast enough to accommodate everyone. Suppose the owner has two children; then they, in turn, have two each; the family has already grown to 6, excluding the patriarch. And these children have another two each: the numbers would become simply too big for one business to take them all, with ownership for each family member getting diluted with the generational flow.

The existence of relatives and a surfeit of them is usually a big handicap. In some families, it is expected that all who wish to join the family firm will find a place. This can have shattering effects, particularly if the jobs given are plum and cushy. Intra-family friction can emerge. An internecine warfare does immense harm to an organization. Decisions could be stunted. Innovations could be by-passed. Moreover, professionals in the organization would either sit on the sidelines till the slugfest gets sorted out or find another employer to work for. At the end, the company suffers due to the mistakes of the shareholders, albeit the members of the family owning it.

The **Mulliez family** of France, who owns one of the largest retail empires in the world (owner of Auchan supermarkets and Decathlon sports shops), has over 700 family members. Wendel, one of Europe's largest listed investment firms, supported by the **Wendel family** for over three centuries, has more than 1,100 family members.[8] Just imagine the struggle they face to cut the cake and share the booty!

The American-Jewish **Pritzker** empire, which included the Hyatt hotel chain and the Royal Caribbean Cruise Line, had to be broken up when Jay Pritzker (co-founder of Hyatt) died in 1999. The empire was divided among the 11 cousins, who all wanted very different things from their inheritance. The well-structured business empire was torn into pieces by 2011 due to the patriarch's lack of foresight and planning.[9]

Such large ownerships create their own problems, apart from the high dilution of ownership. Who is the real owner? Who will be calling the shots? Family members who are mere shareholders are likely to press for higher dividends, whereas those who are managing the businesses may desire reinvestment seeking growth; the bigger the family, the greater the skirmish.

Some business families have just the opposite problem—too few children. For example, the dwindling community of Parsis in India, the diligent-enterprising lot involved in various businesses, is running out of family members. With just over 60,000 Parsis still remaining and diminishing, succession in their businesses is a big problem. The 150-year-old **Tata** Group's fifth-generation patriarch Ratan Tata has run out of family members—handing over the reins of this steel-to-power conglomerate to a non-Parsi professional, Natarajan Chandrasekaran. Similar issues will also arise to the other notable Parsi enterprises like the families of Pallonji Mistry, Nusli Wadia and Adi Godrej. Professionalization at the highest level of the organization of these outfits would only help—and not recognizing this eventuality would be a grave error on their part.

An unexpected death or ill health can throw a family business off-balance. The *Economist* reported that researchers who studied more than 5,000 family companies worldwide to see how vulnerable they were to health shocks among family members found that the unexpected death of a CEO could decrease performance by up to 30 per cent and the death of a spouse or child by 10 per cent. Even the hospitalization of a family owner had an adverse effect. Clearly, not planning for an eventuality in any family is a mistake which a business can ill afford.

As if the impediments are not enough, poor ethos sometimes can also be a family handicap. Many family-controlled businesses often treat business money as their own, even if there is public shareholding or it is listed in the stock exchange. Examples of such companies are aplenty—look around and you will find companies with such poor governance. They would also perhaps employ their relatives without concern for their qualifications, experience or proper vetting. These are weighty blunders, making the proper functioning of family businesses more unsettling in the long term.

Family Business Fallacy

Tailpiece

A business within the family is a potential wealth creator. But there are too many imponderables that need to be navigated to keep the family business-ship sailing on course. Not maintaining sharp eyes on the undercurrents and the unknowns could damage or sink the enterprise.

Family Infighting

The biggest risk a family business can have is its probable squabbles among its relatives. Who gains and who loses in the battle for transmission of wealth and power to future generations is the harbinger of family hostilities. Family tiffs often destroy painfully created enterprises.

The heart of family infighting stems from identity—who is more powerful or who is being threatened. Self-esteem and personal identity are two poisonous thoughts that can play mayhem in a family's internal relationships.

Frictions from rivalries between parents and children, brothers, sisters or other family members who hold positions in the business or derive income from it are business killers. It is very important to acknowledge the feelings of hostility among the players. Non-recognition of the problem itself is a big mistake that can kill any business.

A significant cause for conflicts is the lack of communication, more so, miscommunication. It would be a mistake not to encourage transparent communication and openness within the family and across groups. When family members do not engage in healthy discussions, disputes tend to become personal rather than issue based, complicating matters. Proper communication goes a long way to heal wounds of misunderstandings and misgivings.

Just because business entrepreneurs are brothers, sisters and cousins, it does not mean much. They need to establish and practise strong structured business relationships. Not doing so will be a blunder. The person who has started and nurtured a business will, in all probability, have blind love towards the enterprise. And that may be the precursor of the problem. Instances when decisions are influenced by feelings towards relatives in the business, when prejudice exerts a negative influence, when decisions are taken just because it worked in the past without considering the changing circumstances and when a company is run more to honour family traditions than business needs, are all a catastrophe in the making.

Family squabbles can destroy years of hard work. **Karmann**, the coach-building company which created the classic Volkswagen Karmann Ghia and other cars, became bankrupt in 2009 after over a century of growing with the fledgling automobile sector. It produced bodies and body components for the high and mighty, including the Mercedes-Benz, BMW, Renault, Porsche and Volkswagen Group. Wilhelm Karmann Jr, a second-generation entrepreneur, breathed his last in 1999.[10] It took just another 10 years for the third generation to make the company defunct. The Karmann family could not see eye to eye among each other.

Even a company like Karmann established as early as 1901 could not overcome internal bickering, though it would have met many serious business challenges over its long history. Simmering jealousies, feelings of unfairness and inequalities took a dreadful toll.[11]

While enterprises can survive hundreds of years, founders do not. Unless the family booty is fairly distributed and succession delineated, matters can only come to a head.

Family bickering can ruin the business edifice built over blood and sweat. The tale of the **Kwok family**, one of the richest Asian families, is worth looking at. Kwok Tak-seng founded the company, **Sun Hung Kai Properties**, to become the second-largest business group in Hong Kong and then left it to his wife and three sons, Walter, Raymond and Thomas. This quartet got on well until Walter Kwok was kidnapped by local gangsters and held in a wooden crate for several days until a ransom was paid, rumoured to be HK$600 million ($80 million). The after-shocks of the kidnapping divided the household. Walter accused his brothers of fighting over the size of the ransom, the rest of the group tried to oust him from his role as the chairman of the family trust, and the fight went on for years, bringing ill-reputation to Hong Kong's largest property developers. Walter Kwok, aged 68, died in 2018.[12]

Almost all families have conflicts and misunderstandings. However, most manage to keep the family feuds private. A public slugfest obviously makes the troubles more difficult to resolve. It is a blunder to wash the dirty linen in public.

How do families behave and create conflicts while running a business?

Nearly half of the family firms interviewed in a PWC study said that they have argued about the future direction of the family business. Nearly two-fifths said that they have bickered about the performance of family members employed in the business. Over a quarter of the family businesses fought about the setting of remuneration levels for family members actively involved in the business. And, worse, over 70 per cent of the family businesses surveyed did not have any procedure for dealing with disputes between family members.

While these observations are from a study conducted among the Middle East business families, interpretations may not be too remote for the families from any other geographies. Many business families thus keep making the blunder of not planning for the rainy days in their relationships.

Tailpiece

What is the raison d'être for faltering family firms? Infighting and succession are the primary reasons. A PWC report stated that strife in family businesses is rarely caused by poor business performance; most conflicts arise because the family owners feel that their needs are not being met. Rivalries also surface when situations are unclear or not properly understood. For the survival and continuity of the family and the business, not recognizing these conflicts and not managing them would be a grave oversight.

Floundering Father

Bizarre it may sound, but the problems of a family entrepreneurship usually begin with the founder. Weirdly, the senior generation may feel threatened by rivalry from his own progeny or from a relative or even from a smart professional manager whom he would have employed. Contrary to common sense, father–child antagonism is commonplace. And it is very damaging and affects business continuity significantly.

As the entrepreneur feels that the business is his baby or mistress, he may often refuse to 'let go'. The kid could be well equipped to take on and could be waiting in the wings for years to take over the mantle, but dad could be preventing the natural succession in business to take place. While mentally the father would love to have his offspring to help him in his business, but to hand over the reins may impinge upon his pride or masculinity.

The resentment created by these behaviours is very unsettling for the child. It could lead to feuds, disagreements and a lack of harmony in running the business. Such one-upmanship is a value destroyer in any organization which has been built over the years by the family patriarch. This is a grave behavioural mistake which the family head needs to avoid at all costs.

I know of a live instance in Mumbai. A fairly well-known office-furniture-manufacturing company was started by an engineer. As the company grew, his son, who was trained in finance, joined the business. While the father was a stickler for designs and a perfectionist with regard to furniture models, his son wanted to reduce cost and enhance profits. Introduction of new designs meant more cost. His son was dead against the idea, saying they had enough models to play with, and there was no necessity to keep experimenting with newer designs. Conflict commenced. The father thought his son wanted to usurp his position and ruin the company. The relationship came to such a head that the son had to leave the business. The father is now holding the business reigns, and God alone knows what will happen when he breathes his last.

Take another instance where a high-profile father–son's open slugfest had affected the carefully crafted corporate brand image built over decades.

Thomas J. **Watson** Sr could build the fabulous International Business Machines (IBM) but could not manage to provide his son Tom Jr with a smooth handover. Tom Jr was an ordinary student, and that is where the first signs of father–son disconnect started. Joining IBM as a salesperson, Tom Jr's performance did not meet the standards of his father. Tom Sr often humiliated his son. The Second World War triggered an opportunity for Tom Jr to join the US Air Force—and there his performance was exemplary. His outside experience gave him more confidence. However, the father–son feud never ended. And it took place even in front of their employees. Eventually, in 1951, Tom Sr anointed his son as IBM president. But till his death in 1956, Tom Sr did not allow his son to operate with full authority and responsibility.[13]

The love–hate battle of father and son did not auger well for the organization. Had Tom Sr let go his ego and sense of insecurity, IBM could have perhaps shone more during the time than what it has already done.

Tailpiece

Many business leaders think that they are either indispensable or can rule from their grave. The thought of immortality makes them blind. Not doing what a family patriarch should do—not leaving a will, not anointing a successor or ignoring internal feuds—is an avoidable gaffe.

Sibling Strife

The tales of Cain and Abel, the first two sons of Adam and Eve, are well known. When brothers fight for the single birthright, the success of one means doomsday for the other. The seeds of fraternal rivalry are sown due to circumstances.

Brotherly conflict is as old as the hills. A story in *Psychology Today* reported in the *Guardian* suggests that more than a third of us have challenging relationships with our brothers or sisters even as adults due to some childhood rivalry that never dissipated. Any hopes of an ultimate long-term ceasefire tend to arrive only in our old age—when all our abilities to fight desert us. In any case, it becomes too late to make any useful impact of any truce.

While brothers can work together naturally due to genetic reasons and there are numerous instances of successful coexistence, the challenge comes when they are locked in a given space sharing resources to attain their goal—there is space enough for only one top dog! Disputes emerge.

Family feuds can last decades and erode millions of dollars of firm value. In the annals of family grudges, the quarrel of the Kansas-based family **Koch** (pronounced coke) is one of the biggest, nastiest and longest running. The whole slugfest is essentially about whether a set of two brothers have cheated the other two out of $2 billion. The four Koch brothers were split into two warring camps. On one side were Charles and David, who almost entirely owned Koch Industries, America's second-largest privately held company after Cargill, the grain conglomerate. On the other side were William (he was David's fraternal twin) and Frederick. William and Frederick contend that they were tricked when they were given nearly $1 billion in 1983 to give up their stake in Koch Industries and are now owed billions more. For nearly two decades, the two Koch factions had not spoken a word to each other and not even at their mother's funeral in 1991. They communicated only through their lawyers.[14]

The brothers finally reconciled in 2001, at least on paper, but not before spending millions of dollars on lawyers' fees and unable to concentrate enough to build their businesses—a completely avoidable faux pas committed by a family. The two families could have easily gone their separate ways accepting their differences, without spending loads of money on disputes which led to nothing and adversely affected business performance.

Sibling antagonism created the rise and fall of the **Mondavi family**, which brought wine to the nation of coke and cocktails. The well-known family waded through times of sheer brilliance and sibling rivalries, egged by one-upmanship between parent against child and brother against brother.

Cesare and Rosa Mondavi arrived penniless in the United States from Italy in the first decade of the 20th century. Settling first in Minnesota and then in California, the family achieved an almost unthinkable prosperity within 20 years as Cesare entered the wine business. He educated well his two male children, Robert and Peter, with an idea to bring them into his business. Robert's character was established early on. He was such a taskmaster that even on his honeymoon he spent time conducting business.

In 1943, Robert and Peter persuaded their father to buy a Napa Valley–abandoned vineyard and winery. Their father's condition was that the two brothers must work together—but it ended in a bitter battle.

The two brothers, Robert and Peter, bickered over how to run the business; the quarrel culminated in 1965 when the brothers famously came to blows. Out of that battle, their mother, Rosa, stood behind the less ambitious Peter, and threw out Robert, then in his early 50s, from the business.

On his own, the discarded son, Robert, with his children, Michael, Marcia and Timothy, created the Robert Mondavi Winery— perhaps the single most important event in the history of the California wine industry.

Robert, not learning from his own ill experience with his brother, foolishly placed his two sons Michael and Timothy Mondavi in competing roles to judge who would be the best fit to take charge of the company.

Sibling wrangles emerged. Michael wanted to concentrate on mass-market brands while Timothy thought the focus should be on the Mondavis' finest wines. Meanwhile, the ageing Robert would publicly humiliate his children whenever anything was found wanting.

Success came to a head. The market was confused—there were too many types of wines from the Mondavis in the market. Some wine got bad reviews. The company also made too many bad investments, and the value of stocks of the company, which in the meantime went public, crashed.

Taking advantage of the situation, and playing the siblings against each other, the Mondavi board forced the family to hand over power to them. It was not so long afterwards that the company was sold, to Constellation Brands.

The Mondavi family, after years of internal battles, lost total control of the empire which they had started only a generation back.

Robert Mondavi, when he breathed his last at a ripe age of 94, would have died a sad man, experiencing his own rise and fall during his lifetime.[15]

The Mondavi story is a clear instance of how values of organizations are destroyed by entrepreneur-fathers who force their children to perform within the same space in the face of stomping rivalries. Had there been clear and distinct roles for the children, and a sense of appreciation of each other's strengths and weaknesses, the sad story of the Mondavis would have rolled out differently.

In another famous sibling bickering, India's billionaire brothers, Mukesh and Anil Ambani, fighting over family fortune, have been satisfying the common man's desire for melodrama.

Time and again, the feud between the two brothers kept flaring up after the enormous Reliance industrial conglomerate in India, created by their father, Dhirubhai Ambani, was split between them in 2005. The patriarch died in 2002 without leaving a clear succession plan. Problems brewed therefrom. Dhirubhai's wife, Kokilaben, brokered an agreement to carve out the empire between her two sons. In spite of enormous wealth, the slugfest between the brothers was all about controlling the wealth.

The Ambani sibling wrangle has knocked off significant enterprise value especially for the younger brother Anil. The elder sibling, Mukesh, became Asia's richest man in 2018, toppling China's Jack Ma, after driving a telecommunication revolution with Reliance Jio that propelled his petrochemical conglomerate, Reliance Industries, into the $100 billion club. His net worth swelled to $43 billion, reported Bloomberg Billionaires Index.

On the other side of the spectrum, Anil Ambani shrunk his personal wealth to $1.5 billion, according to the index. To top it all, **Reliance Communications**, once Anil's flagship company, went bankrupt in 2018. Who would have ever thought that an Ambani (Reliance) company can some day run out of money? It has all happened post the sibling split. Anil just could not manage his allocated empire.

While peace has been brokered of late between the brothers, the outcome still remains uncertain.[16]

Tailpiece

The family patriarch is generally responsible for feuds between the siblings, if proper delineation of business or responsibilities is not done. The problem multiplies if the mother has a favourite child. The situation becomes more complicated with the spouses coming into the picture, with each spouse having obviously more stake on their respective partner's career and power. The Ambani-brother feud in the Reliance Group is a reflection of the desire to control wealth and power, especially when their ambitious wives pulled their respective personal strings.

Poking One's Nose

Family businesses often turn to professionals to run their businesses. Either because they do not have enough skill base or because there is not enough talent within. But when the family keeps poking their nose into the business after handing over to professionals and wants to yet micromanage the affairs, disaster strikes. Once a professional driver is appointed to drive the business car, many families find it difficult to keep their hands off the steering of the business which they were so used to navigate.

A similar mistake was committed in 2014 by Italy's richest man, Leonardo Del Vecchio. At the ripe age of 79, he decided that it was time to take back control of the well-run company **Luxottica** he had started 50 years earlier. The owner of the well-known eyewear brands of *Ray-Ban* and *Oakley* decided that he needed to re-run the enterprise after a decade of absence. The market was stunned.

After decades of running the group, Del Vecchio had handed it over in 2004 to Andrea Guerra, a professional manager. The entrepreneur was commended for handing over his company to a trained professional, to avoid the usual trap of succession-related discord. To the credit of Guerra, during his decade-long leadership, the turnover more than doubled to over €7 billion ($10 billion).

But Guerra could not continue when Del Vecchio decided to come back abruptly in 2014, pushing out Guerra unceremoniously. Del Vecchio felt that Guerra's views on the firm's strategy had 'diverged' from his own. Strangely, this is in spite of Guerra having expanded Luxottica globally and having doubled its profits.

The entrepreneur's return to day-to-day management led to instability, with three chief executives leaving in as many years, needlessly muddling the otherwise well-oiled enterprise.[17,18] (Luxottica has since merged in 2018 with the French lens maker Essilor to form the $50 billion eyewear behemoth global group—EssilorLuxottica.)[19]

Exceptions are everywhere.

Hermès, a French luxury goods house, fell back into family control in 2014. The sixth-generation Axel Dumas took sole command of the luxury house founded in 1837 after eight years under non-family chief executive Patrick Thomas.[20] It was family to professional and back to family—but with a relatively smooth transition, one of the rare stories of rollback in business control.[21]

Tailpiece

Families will ultimately run out of their own skill bank. Blending family-controlled enterprises with professionals at important positions is a common practice followed by most large organizations.

The professionals need to, however, play the game well by maintaining good relations with the family members, understanding their vision and keeping them informed of the progress in business—and yet keep the personal issues of the family members and that of the business at arm's length for best results. This will help in keeping household members away from frequent incursion. Not doing so would be a mistake on the part of the experts running the business.

Family Values

Values of a family can make or break its history and ambitions. Not all families bond together, neither every family is at war; not everyone is in a state of charity, nor all are miserly and self-focused. Some are virtuous, while others are shrewd, and a blend is rather common.

Family businesses are different from other forms, as all or many of its directors, managers and employees would normally belong to the same household. Family values, behaviours and ethics would typically flow into their business.

In some cultures, families are large, such as in Asia, in the Middle East and in Latin America, while in others these are compact. Extended and large families will have their kinship but could have dollops of jealousy, distrust and animosity. It would be a mistake for the family head not to recognize the undercurrents of family ethos and to drive it suitably towards oneness of purpose.

Family firms riding on waves of success, cold-shouldering changing environment and potential risks, could be calamitous.

The **Guinness family**, once Europe's brewing powerhouse, lost its position of leadership by not recognizing talent but placing family members in important positions only because they were born in the Guinness.[22] While you can still enjoy the iconic Irish Guinness stout drink, the Guinness family does not control it any more. The famed brewer has been taken over by the British alcoholic beverages multinational, Diageo, to drive Guinness's onward journey.

Similarly, the heady performance of **Seagram**, headquartered in Canada and founded in 1857, is a lesson in poor management, substandard corporate governance and playing strategic roulette, leading the Bronfman family to lose control over its long-nurtured business. Once, Bronfman was placed on the same pedestal for alcoholic drinks as Henry Ford was to automobiles and J.P.Morgan to banking, but ultimately Seagram had to be broken into pieces and sold after almost 150 years of its existence due to poor leadership and improper foresight of its successive generations.[23]

It is difficult to define family values. It is all encumbering—it is a way of life—it is an 'organizational culture'.

Some families run their businesses with consensual decision-making, whereas many are dictatorial with very little regard for opinions and views; some families are highly ethical, while others may think that good governance is a burden.

Values are what families stand for; vision is the shared sense of what they would collectively like to achieve. Together, they provide the path to progress. Not articulating values and vision in clear terms would not auger well for long-term sustenance of any business, be it family or otherwise.

Look around, and you will find umpteen instances of contrary business morality. The real-estate business in India is essentially run by families. Construction of some well-known builders stands on quality, while several others do not care much for excellence. While the former would command a premium pricing, the latter attract those looking for cheaper options. It is no rocket science to understand which type of builders will create value in the long run!

Tailpiece

Time only proves what the best lasting value system is. Families commit grave errors in believing there are shortcuts to success. It takes a lot to build businesses on conscientiousness, mutual trust and ethics. Giving short shrift to a sound family value system is hara-kiri.

Long Term vs Short Term

Debates will perhaps never settle the ever-contentious business strategic position—long–term tactical play is better or focus on short term yields superior results? Family businesses many a time go through this quandary during their business life cycle.

It is a common impression that families are more focused on long termism, have the ability to take risks, and are decisive and un-bureaucratic. Professional managers, on the other hand, are believed to be more process oriented, engaged on quarterly results, annual appraisals and bonuses.

Of course, sometimes 'long-termism' takes to extreme outcomes in family endeavours. In a bizarre instance, Danish businessman Mærsk Mc-Kinney Møller, the main shareholder of the world's biggest container shipping line **AP Møller-Mærsk**, ordered at his ripe age of 94 a new personal yacht for delivery in two years—a real long-term and optimistic view taken by the family patriarch. Møller ultimately died, aged 98 in 2012. The luxury sailboat was put on sale, a year after Møller's death. The long-term view of the shipping magnate ended with a short-term action!

Taking a long-term view, the group invested in all sorts of assets since the 1960s—shipping and oil drilling, with supermarkets and airlines also being explored. The idea was to build a hedge against falling freight rates and spurts in oil prices. When fuel was dear, reducing container shipment business profits, it was thought that drilling for oil and gas would keep it afloat. But since 2014, oil prices halved and freight rates plummeted due to weak global trade and overcapacity, leading both the shipping and energy units into a sea of turmoil.

With the container shipping line collapsing, the family moved in and tried to heal the wounds of trade vagaries. The family decided in 2016 to break Mærsk into two—a new transport arm which will centre the group once again in the world's largest container shipping business, Maersk Line, and an energy unit that could be jettisoned in due course through spin-off, sale or joint ventures.[24]

The breaking up of the company was, again, a very long-term decision likely to impact the group for the next 100 years. Ane Uggla, the daughter of Møller who serves as Mærsk vice chairman and chair of the main family foundation, disclosed in 2013 this long-term mindset of the group stating: 'Of course, 10, 15, 20 years is a long time to look ahead for a company but in the foundation it is not very long. I like to look 100 years ahead: that is the long-term goal, which is most important for the foundation.'

Whether the long-term strategy works or not for Mærsk, only time will tell. In the meantime, the group is struggling to keep its profit nose above water.[25]

The good news is that due to its sheer nature of holding structure, family firms tend to take somewhat a longer-term perspective while deciding on business issues. However, professionally run organizations like non-family-controlled public companies or companies owned by private equity firms may tend to be obsessed with meeting the demands of investors to maximize short-term profits. Quarterly results often become more imperative, and may be sacrificed at the altar of long-term strategic vision, especially when investors want to sell their holdings with juicy profits within a few years of their investment.

Family firms score high on employee relations but lag on innovations and, more often than not, are internally focused, reckons a McKinsey study. Employee motivation and leadership are long-term strategies, but lack of proper qualifications and experience at the controlling level of family businesses perhaps provides brakes on innovative spirits.

Family companies are known to take big bets and big risks. If a majority of these bets fructify along with their entrepreneurial zeal, many families are able to turn out performances which beat public and professional companies.

Conventional wisdom says that the unique ownership structure of family businesses gives them a long-term orientation, which public firms and professionally run organizations often lack. But studies have not been conclusive to prove that they outperform other businesses over the long term.

Nicolas Kachaner, George Stalk Jr and Alain Bloch studied the implications and published their findings in the *Harvard Business Review*. They studied 149 firms in the United States, Canada, France, Spain, Portugal, Italy and Mexico and concluded[26]: During good economic times, family-run companies do not earn as much money as companies with a more dispersed ownership structure. But when the economy plummets, family firms far outperform their peers. And when researchers studied across business cycles from 1997 to 2009, they observed that the average long-term financial performance was higher for family businesses than for non-family businesses in every country they examined.

Tailpiece

Family businesses face several hiccups as they trot along. But one good news is that they tend to focus more on resilience than on performance. They generally forgo the super profits available during good times in order to protect themselves during bad times. Family businesses often invest with a decade or two in mind, focusing on what needs to be done today so that tomorrow's generation can benefit.

What Makes Success Speak?

It is rather common to encounter a family business grown through its first generation, stability brought in it by the second generation, and ultimately destroyed by the third.

But when you bump into examples of fifth generation and there-after, seamlessly managing and growing the business, the heart starts singing.

An apt example is the well-known *Swarovski* Group, now run by the fifth generation through a 'collective responsibility' format.

While travelling through the airports, you would have encountered the dazzling Swarovski outlets selling exquisite crystal jewelleries and figurines. They have 3,000 such stores across 170 countries with revenues of $3.5 billion.[27]

In spite of daunting competition from Chinese, Egyptian and Czech companies producing fine crystals at a fraction of Swarovski's cost, there is no sign of Swarovski withering. Wattens, a small touristic town in Austria, lives on Swarovski, its main employer, and it has been like this for over a century.

The storied family-run enterprise has been making changes with time. Currently, it is slowly but surely transitioning into the cutting-edge luxury and technology organization.

The five-member board who run the company are all direct descendants of Daniel Swarovski who set up the factory in 1895. But the best part is that there is no group CEO, and the chairman of the board is nominated by rotation. Individual businesses of crystal, precision cutting tools and optical tools are run as separate companies. But the big decisions are always taken collectively. While the family tries to take all the board decisions unanimously, sometimes a majority opinion prevails, thus often delaying the decision-making process—the consultative method of management is inherently time consuming. The harmony and close ties among the five cousins in the board are the harbinger of Swarovski's continued success.

It is the grit behind the glitter which is keeping Swarovski gleaming. It is this amity and assonance that make families resonate for generations.

The secretive world of family business has a lot to teach to the world of business. One, most businesses in any region belong to families. Two, most of today's large businesses had their roots in a family business. And three, large businesses have a lot to learn from family businesses, as every business has some family-ness to bond human effort. Ignoring family businesses will be only at one's own peril—to make it tick through time will only add to human wealth and well-being.

Historical evidence shows—the first generation builds the business, the second allows it rot and the third dissipates it. The big question is: *What* should family enterprises do to keep their clan flag flying high?

- *Successful succession:* Planning for the future and passing the baton to the best-fit person in the next generation is the cornerstone on which businesses flow from one generation to the other. It is, of course, the toughest task to do. No wonder only 30 per cent survive the second generation with 1 per cent left for the fifth.

    Identifying the right successor, who may not be the eldest son of the family, and handing over the reins, first through management transfer and then through ownership, are the keys for bolting the lock firmly on a family edifice. Bharti, Bajaj, BMW, Fiat and Ford have done it down the ages.

- *Business is not family:* Sometimes household businesses implode where families treat their businesses as their home affair. Businesses ought to be treated differently and cannot be linked with personal whims, fancies and interests of the controlling family and their relatives. De-blend work and family—keep the two worlds separate.

    The families that do best to continue their legacy are those which understand that their own interests and those of their business can deviate. They need to put in place processes to manage the consequences of these differences.

- *Coach the gen-next:* Families need to train the next generation to take over the reins. Some families are more adept at training the next generation to work in the family firm than others are.

    Look at the most powerful company in the Philippines—*Ayala*. The empire has been run by the Ayala-Zóbel dynasty for over 180 years. Today, two brothers from its sixth generation run the holding company that sets the strategy. Three children from the eighth generation are working their way up the corporate hierarchy.

- *Professionalize management:* Sometimes children do not want to join the family business, or may turn out not to possess the genes of their business-parents. The best option is to turn to professional managers, rather than handing the keys to incompetent or unwilling descendants, though the family could still hold ownership control. Turning to professionals earlier than later has shown to have enhanced a firm's longevity.

Many good talents love to join such organizations, expecting one day to get the top job, rather than join family firms where there is little or no chance to occupy the corner room.

The *Economist* reported from a PWC-led family firms' interview study that around 40 per cent of the family businesses said that professionalizing their business was among the main challenges they face in the next five years.

A classic example of a family business not afraid to appoint professional managers is Sweden's enduring business dynasty, the Wallenbergs. By the late 1990s, the family controlled almost 40 per cent of the value of the companies listed on the Swedish stock exchange. Their interests ranged from AstraZeneca, a pharmaceuticals company; Electrolux, a white-goods manufacturer; and ABB, a global engineering giant. Very little happens in Swedish business without the involvement of the Wallenbergs. The family's secret of success has been not to be afraid of change and to appoint professional managers—and the family is poised to hand over the reins to the sixth generation.

- *Relatives are no panacea:* 'You trust your blood—that is given,' remarked an entrepreneur. And that is the problem! Just because there is a blood strain, it does not mean that the relative will be good to go. Just because a relative needs a job or the family scion is available for drafting into the business, it should not be their birthright to join the business and that too at a higher echelon. The unwritten assurance to relatives that 'there is always a place for you in our business' is strictly avoidable.

The fifth-generation-run *Ford Motor Company* does not guarantee a job to their family members. Ford family members who join the company start with relatively low-level salaried jobs. A Ford spokeswoman said in 2013 and reported in the *Wall Street Journal* that family members are not exempt from the standard hiring process. 'There are no guarantees for any of them,' says Ford Chairman, Bill Ford Jr.

- *Prudent processes profess proficiency*: Process-driven family businesses thrive better. When families delineate standard operating systems for managing their businesses, it helps them to flourish.

A few good family business practices could include the following: have a board where outsiders, preferably a significant proportion, are members; lay down a minimum number of board meetings per year, say four; and have structured family meetings for briefing and strategizing business. These would go a long way towards business adeptness and continuity. The Mahindra Group in India does well in running its businesses proficiently through laid-down processes.

- *Eliminate bloodline silos:* A tunnel-vision mentality where certain departments or sectors do not share information with others in the same organization is a value destroyer.

Families in the same line, like father and son, often follow this silo approach by specializing or focusing on the same discipline like manufacturing or marketing, at the cost of ignoring some crucial ones. This creates a leadership vacuum as the next generation may not get exposed to other disciplines of running a business. Family silos need to be dumped.

- *Family councils facilitate:* The heart of success of any business is its professionalism and objectivity. Outside expert help is often sought to provide this support. A good way is to have a family council, which could meet regularly to discuss matters of business, succession and disputes, if any. They would also lay down rules of engagement of family members as to who can join the business based on merit, capability and experience.

  Dabur India Ltd has the Burman family council, meeting once a quarter to review business performance and strategy. This has worked well for the group.

- *Strategizing strategy:* Sometimes family businesses are run as a fiefdom of the entrepreneur. Ego, whims and fancies prevail. Strategies are adopted based on kneejerk reactions. These are all recipes for a disastrous outcome.

  The family firms should lay down their strategy—what to make and when, a financing game plan, a manning approach, and a sales and marketing tactic, just to name a few.

In Closing

Family businesses have generally been outperforming professionally driven enterprises. Credit Suisse, tracking the share price movements of more than 1,000 family-owned businesses where family shareholding is over 20 per cent with a market capitalization of $250 million and more, found that they have outpaced non-family-owned companies since 2006. The 2018 survey reflected that family-owned companies have a greater focus on long-term quality growth than non-family-owned companies.[28]

The success of family businesses occurs in spite of the battles they often have among themselves, and these skirmishes are unlikely to ever end. It, however, does not mean that the scuffles will bring down businesses built through blood and sweat, like the house of cards.

For success in family businesses, it is best to no longer leave enterprise management solely to the genes. Having too many useless family members without a clear chain of command and succession plans, with feuds preceding collective decision-making, without plans for professionalism to substitute for lack of internal talent is an avoidable serving on any plate of family business.

References

1. Stalk G Jr, Foley H. Avoid the traps that can destroy family businesses. Harvard Business Review [Internet]. 2012 Jan–Feb. Available from: https://hbr.org/2012/01/avoid-the-traps-that-can-destroy-family-businesses

2. Narayanan C. What does it take for family businesses to last generations? The Hindu Business Line. 2018 Jan 31. Available from: https://www.thehindubusinessline.com/specials/people-at-work/what-does-it-take-for-family-businesses-to-last-generations/article22612817.ece

3. Cadbury SA. Family firms and their governance creating tomorrow's company from today's. Egon Zehnder International [Internet]. Available from: http://www.ecseonline.com/PDF/Cadbury%20-%20Family%20Firms%20and%20their%20Governance.pdf

4. CPPLuxury. Giorgio Armani to transfer stake of his company to his foundation. CPPLuxury [Internet]. 2017 Oct 23. Available from: https://cpp-luxury.com/giorgio-armani-to-transfer-stake-of-his-company-to-his-foundation/

5. Barry C. Giorgio Armani outlines succession plan to keep house intact. Financial Post [Internet]. 2017 Oct 23. Available from: https://business.financialpost.com/pmn/business-pmn/giorgio-armani-outlines-succession-plan-to-keep-house-intact

6. The Economist. Keeping it in the family. The Economist [Internet]. 2014 Sep 6. Available from: https://www.economist.com/business/2014/09/06/keeping-it-in-the-family

7. PWC Global. 2016 Family Business Survey: The 'missing middle'—Bridging the strategy gap in family firms. PWC Global [Internet]. Available from: https://www.pwc.com/gx/en/services/family-business/family-business-survey-2016.html

8. Wendel. Industrial and family roots. Wendel. Available from: https://www.wendelgroup.com/en/industrial-and-family-roots

9. Chicago Tribune. Fortune's fate: Pritzker family agreement to divide billions in wealth comes to a close. Chicago Tribune [Internet]. 2011 Dec 18. Available from: https://www.chicagotribune.com/business/ct-xpm-2011-12-18-ct-biz-1218-pritzkers-mainbar-20111218-story.html

10. The Guardian. Karmann goes bankrupt as Daimler car workers stage protest. The Guardian [Internet]. 2009 Apr 8. Available from: https://www.theguardian.com/business/2009/apr/08/daimler-workers-protest

11. Ruppert J. Obituary: Wilhelm Karmann. Independent [Internet]. 1998 Nov 2. Available from: https://www.independent.co.uk/arts-entertainment/obituary-wilhelm-karmann-1182239.html

12. Financial Times. Walter Kwok, property developer, 1950–2018. Financial Times [Internet]. 2018 Nov 2. Available from: https://www.ft.com/content/6e500870-dd10-11e8-8f50-cbae5495d92b

13. The New York Times. Lohr S. I.B.M.'s computing pioneer, Thomas Watson Jr., dies at 79. The New York Times [Internet]. 1994 Jan 1. Available from: https://www.nytimes.com/1994/01/01/obituaries/ibm-s-computing-pioneer-thomas-watson-jr-dies-at-79.html

14. BBC. Who are the Koch brothers? BBC News [Internet]. 2018 June 10. Available from: https://www.bbc.com/news/world-us-canada-44385053

15. The New York Times. Grapes and power: A Mondavi melodrama. The New York Times [Internet]. 2007 Jun 20. Available from: https://www.nytimes.com/2007/06/20/dining/20pour.html

16. Shrivastava B. The $41 billion wealth gap that divides the Ambani brothers. Livemint [Internet]. 2018 Oct 22. Available from: https://www.livemint.com/Companies/w87CrNEJfCBPGDD4zHZgkI/Mukesh-Ambani-net-worth-Anil-Ambani-Reliance-Jio-RCom.html

17. The Economist. Keeping it in the family. The Economist [Internet]. 2014 Sep 6. Available from: https://www.economist.com/business/2014/09/06/keeping-it-in-the-family

18. AFP Relaxnews. Luxottica and Essilor merger: How Leonardo Del Vecchio grows the success of his frame-making business. Luxuo [Internet]. 2017 Jan 27. Available from: http://www.luxuo.com/the-lux-list/super-rich/luxottica-and-essilor-merger-how-leonardo-del-vecchio-grows-the-success-of-his-frame-making-business.html

19. Financial Times. Luxottica and Essilor agree €50bn eyewear merger. Financial Times [Internet]. 2017 Jan 16. Available from: https://www.ft.com/content/a4b43936-db78-11e6-9d7c-be108f1c1dce

20. Adams S. Inside Hermès: Luxury's secret empire. Forbes [Internet]. 2014 Sep 8. Available from: https://www.forbes.com/sites/susanad ams/2014/08/20/inside-hermes-luxury-secret-empire/#752b91572ad2

21. Financial Times. Lunch with the FT: Axel Dumas. Financial Times [Internet]. 2015 Mar 27. Available from: https://www.ft.com/content/ 75d8a0da-d228-11e4-a225-00144feab7de

22. Siggins L. The Guinness business. The Irish Times [Internet]. 1997 May 17. Available from: https://www.irishtimes.com/news/the-guinness-business-1.73356

23. The New York Times. Whiskey chasers: Book review. The New York Times [Internet]. 2006 Jun 25. Available from: https://www.nytimes. com/2006/06/25/books/review/25prial.html

24. Maersk Group. Progress update on strategic review. Maersk Group [Internet]. 2016 Sep. Available from: http://investor.maersk.com/ static-files/d941a945-9407-4f98-b5bf-44c2f08e83d2

25. Maersk. Interim report Q3 2018. Maersk [Internet]. 2018 Nov 14. Available from: https://investor.maersk.com/news-releases/news-release-details/interim-report-q3-2018

26. Stalk G Jr, Bloch A, Kachaner N. The long-term view of family-business performance. Harvard Business Review [Internet]. 2012 Nov 1. Available from: https://hbr.org/search?search_type=&term=Nicola s+Kachaner%2C+George+Stalk+Jr+and+Alain+Bloch+&searchtype=s ubscriber-search

27. Swarovski Group. Fact sheet 2018. Swarovski Group [Internet]. 2018. Available from: https://www.swarovskigroup.com/S/aboutus/Facts. en.html

28. Credit Suisse Research Institute. The CS family 1000 in 2018. Credit Suisse Research Institute [Internet]. 2018 Sep. Available from: https:// www.credit-suisse.com/media/assets/corporate/docs/publications/ research-institute/the-cs-family-1000-in-2018-en.pdf

DISPUTES SPELL DOOM

In the midst of attractive Black Sea beaches and Balkan peaks, two banks in quick succession in Bulgaria—Corporate Commercial Bank (KTB) and First Investment Bank (FIB)—had a run on their deposits. Depositors panicked and stood in long queues to withdraw their savings almost overnight. KTB shut its doors to its depositors in July 2014.

Panic-stricken depositors were alarmed by a dispute between Delyan Peevski, a media mogul and a Member of Parliament, and his former business partner, the financier Tsvetan Vasilev. Both fought bitterly. The animosity was so intense that Peevski withdrew his money from KTB, which was under the control of Vasilev.[1]

Spurred by this news in the media, depositors queued up to withdraw almost a fourth of the bank's assets—$1 billion from KTB.[2] The panic then spread to FIB and customers withdrew about $550 million after rumours of a bank-run spread through the social media.[3]

The worst banking crisis in Bulgaria since the 1990s[3] arose due to strife and rivalries. Mistrust and collision between the key stakeholders can ruin good work done in any organization. The two banks here became a testimony of such an eventuality.

Conflicts between individuals are an inevitable part of working life. But when conflicts are left unmanaged, they can harm individuals, severely damaging any team or organization.

Dispute Destroys

Combats, clangs and clashes are inevitable parts of a business. They are mostly overwhelming, exasperating and financially draining.

Most managers dread disputes and litigations, but, unfortunately, it is not going to ebb, harming relationships and smudging reputations.

Bickering and brawls could be all pervasive—it has the potential to engulf every aspect of a business.

The Indian corporate world perhaps had the most celebrated conflict between Nusli Wadia, chairman of **Bombay Dyeing**, and **Reliance's** Dhirubhai Ambani, the man with the right connections.

The fight was on dimethyl terephthalate (DMT), a vital raw material for synthetic fibre and yarn which Reliance made, but Bombay Dyeing sought government licence to manufacture it. While Wadia had to contend with bureaucratic delays, Ambani, with the right connections in Delhi, continued operations—when Wadia floundered, the Ambanis (of Reliance-company fame) kept marching on.

Family-related disputes are, however, not discussed in this chapter, as these have already been dealt with in the Chapter 'Family Business Fallacy'.

Contract Conflicts

Businesses buy, produce, service, market and sell their wares. Agreements are entered between parties in business to jot down the intent of the arrangement and the ways to execute it. Any party could either interpret the contents differently or fail to deliver the intent of the arrangements entered. Disputes may arise.

Contract terms may be dishonoured—with or without adverse intent. What is important to understand is whether the breach is material or not. A material breach usually harms the affected party, and damages can be sought.

It is always good to get disagreements settled outside the four walls of a magistrate's office. Due to heavy loads, courts are notorious for their delays.

Even **Microsoft** and **Samsung** kissed and made up in 2015.[4] Microsoft sued Samsung, claiming it failed to make timely royalty payments related to their patent licensing deal. Microsoft has long claimed that Google's Android operating system violates a number of Microsoft patents, and sought a licensing deal with Samsung using the software. Samsung contended that Microsoft's decision to acquire the mobile handset business of Nokia—a direct competitor of Samsung—violated the patent licensing agreement between Microsoft and Samsung.

As the dispute was going nowhere, hands were shaken outside the court, with the terms of settlement remaining private.

Tailpiece

When businesses sign a contract, it is expected that terms of the contract will be honoured. Some contracts could be complicated, involving large sums of money. Whether it's a contract to deliver or advertise for goods, it is important to read through the agreement properly and understand its terms and conditions. It is good to have an 'escape' clause should anything go wrong. No one knows the future; hence, not planning for it is a miscalculation.

Intellectual Property Quarrels

You will often see Chanel, Gucci or Dior branded handbags hanging in shops in numerous geographies—and many could be fakes. Should these companies, spending millions of dollars to develop the styles and designs, not be able to protect their rights to sell their own creations and innovations? Generally speaking, these rights include trademarks, copyright, patents, industrial designs, and are popularly known as IPRs. An intellectual property right protects the developer or inventor from others copying or duplicating their creations.

'Infringements' of patents, copyright and trademarks and 'misappropriation' of trade secrets are possible breaches. Needless to mention, numerous disputes emanate from this arena.

It is obviously mistakes of businesses to allow others to breach IPRs. Hence, actions should be taken to protect these by those who possess the rights.

Should **Kellogg's** have the right to market pillow-shaped shredded wheat? A famous IPR-related battle emanated. After Henry Perky, the inventor of the first pillow-shaped shredded wheat cereal, died in 1908 and his patents on his product expired in 1912, Kellogg's started making similar pillow-shaped cereals.

In 1930, the **National Biscuit Company (Nabisco)**, the acquirer of Perky's company, filed a lawsuit against Kellogg's arguing that the new shredded wheat was violating trademark. In 1938, the Supreme Court decided in favour of Kellogg's saying the term 'shredded wheat' cannot be protected as trademark and its pillow shape was functional.[5]

In this instance, Nabisco was under a mistaken notion to implement a trademark right which had expired long back. It is good to know one's legal rights before commencing the fight to get legitimacy.

An interesting copyright tussle emanated in the Indian biscuit sector in 2017—between **Britannia**, the market leader with 66 per cent share, and **ITC**, holding a lowly 2 per cent in the ₹26,000 crore ($4 billion) biscuit market.

Britannia launched its 'Nutrichoice Digestive Zero' biscuits in a yellow-blue combination packaging. ITC, which had launched 'Sunfeast Farmlite Digestive—All Good' biscuits sometime before in mid-2016, accused Britannia of copying its colour and design scheme. ITC contended that Britannia should be desisted from selling biscuits in the yellow-blue packaging. The court ordered that it would not be easy for a person to claim exclusivity over a colour combination particularly when the same has been in use for a relatively short while. It was established that if the colour combination has become distinctive of a person's product, only then an order may be made in his favour.[6]

ITC failed to stop Britannia from launching a rival product with a somewhat similar colour scheme as it was not being used for long.

Deceptive similarity claims where someone's goodwill gets misrepresented and hijacked could not be established.

Tailpiece

Spending millions on fighting competition is a business necessity, but every effort should be made to ring-fence inventors and creators and not to make the lawyers richer. If disputes happen—try to settle it outside the court walls.

Employment Squabbles

Hiring and firing are parts of a business. But employees need to be treated fairly and squarely. Discrimination, harassment, inappropriate working conditions, different salary expectations or unfair dismissals could fuel conflicts with employees. It is business disruptive as more often than not, employee disputes could lead to imbroglio with government agencies and labour departments.

Simmering labour unrest could be fatal. An argument between workers and a supervisor over work conditions turned violent at a **Maruti Suzuki India** plant in Haryana in 2012. A manager was burnt to death when protesting workers set fire to the factory floor, leading to a month-long shutdown. Apparently, there was also seething anger over the use of lower paid temporary workers.[7] It is a big mistake if fair treatment to workers, whether permanent or temporary, is not meted out.

In another instance, in Britain, 'self-employed' couriers who transported blood and pathology samples embarked, in early 2017, on a fight to be classed as 'employees'.

They claimed their everyday working lives were like those of employees: they worked regular shifts, wore uniforms and worked exclusively for an employer. However, they are classed as self-employed, which means they do not receive holiday pay, sick pay or other employee rights.

Self-employment has been propelled into the limelight by a string of similar legal fights. *CitySprint,* the courier company, and *Pimlico*

Plumbers, the plumbing company, have both lost similar employment tribunal cases recently after courts ruled that they should class staff as 'workers', not 'independent contractors'.

These are instances where there were no employment contracts, but the so-called self-employed were asking for it.

Employers the world over need to be cognizant of such risks, taking into consideration local prevalent labour laws.

Tailpiece

There are millions employed. Extricating from crummy employment stories or toxic bosses is not easy with employment contracts often being one-sided, and compensations often deemed unfair. But these are often the realities of employer–employee relationships in the real world, and not recognizing it will be a snafu!

Entangled Partnership Tangle

Nancy and Peter's travel business was going very well. However, their relationship of 15 years soured, resulting in their partnership business hitting serious bumps. They did not have a written partnership agreement to fall back upon to guide the way forward should anything go south. The carefully nurtured business of many years collapsed.

It is common sense that two heads are better than one. Getting into business together with someone else is much better than running around with singular effort. Collaborations multiply effort.

But disturbing developments can arise. When partners in business cease to see eye to eye, it can cause business failures and is highly disruptive. Differences usually arise when tough times come—who will bear liabilities, what cash is to be brought in and how will dividend be distributed among partners. Who can be hired and how should the business be run are other common areas of dispute.

A written agreement, either operating or partnership, goes a long way in helping resolve disputes. Not having a written agreement is a serious mistake.

To cite an instance of the power of partnership, some of the most admired businesses have been started with two partners. To name a few—Apple's Steve Wozniak and Steve Jobs, Google's Larry Page and Sergey Brin, Hewlett-Packard's Bill Hewlett and David Packard or Flipkart's unrelated Sachin and Binny Bansal.

Partnerships have made great success stories. But why do so many fail? It looks easy to run a partnership, but it is incredibly difficult to make two or more humans work in symphony like an orchestra. Any false note, unless rectified swiftly, will completely jar the outcome.

In a classic instance where the partnership went sour even when it had perhaps the best pair was when Jamie Dimon and his former mentor, Sandy Weill, together built the highly successful businesses, the Travelers and the Citigroup. Dimon was fired by Weill shortly after the two companies were merged in 1998, suddenly ending a 15-year partnership that saw them create one of the most successful financial service empires. Everyone had expected that Dimon (who is now the boss of J.P.Morgan Chase) would be Weill's successor. But Weill sacked Dimon. Weill, later in 2014, lamented that one of his two greatest mistakes was not making up with one-time protégé Jamie Dimon and the choosing of Chuck Prince to succeed him as the Citigroup boss in 2003, which led to many top-level executives' departure.[8] Two immensely talented personalities with prodigious business acumen could not work together for long. When the mistake was acknowledged, it was too late to rectify the damage done.

When partners have differences, not the daily niggles, but major disagreements, it affects not only the business but also the partners' personal lives.

What should be done? When partners fall out, many are the ways to wriggle out of the thorny situation.

- Sit across the table, have a heart-to-heart chat, keep aside egos, which usually challenges partner behaviour—talk–listen–understand. Pain points may get sorted out.

- If this fails, divide the work among the partners and have trust in each other to deliver the areas allocated.

- Partners may need to step back and appoint an experienced external candidate as CEO. This sometimes helps to salvage the situation in the midst of crumbling relationships.

- The exit of a partner by selling the business interest to another often provides salvation.

- If resolution efforts do not work, divide the empire and compensate the partners taking lesser valuable part of the business.

- Disposing of the business to a third party may be a way to salvage the business if other solutions become ineffectual.

- If nothing else works, liquidate the business for partners to take away the crumbs.

Tailpiece

There is no one-size-fits-all solution for untying the knotty knots when partners are at odds with each other. While legal ways are often preferred, it is best to redeem the situation among the partners without enriching the lawyers.

B-to-B Bickering

Business-to-business tussles may or may not result from explicit contracts. There could be either unwritten practice of delivering promises or past custom, and it could be broken and unkempt.

Facebook and **BBC** are in dispute over claims that the world's largest online social network is failing to police offensive and illegal content on its site. BBC accused Facebook in 2018 that after decades of ethnic and religious tensions and sudden explosion of internet access in Myanmar, Facebook kindled hatred by having trouble identifying and removing the most hateful posts.[9]

Facebook is facing increasing pressure over its role in politically sensitive issues, such as the spread of fake news and recruitment of terrorists. BBC criticized Facebook after it emerged that the company had known for years that the political data firm Cambridge Analytica had harvested data from about 50 million of its users, but had relied on self-certification by the consultancy firm that it had deleted the information. Apple's Tim Cook blamed Facebook saying that it is an 'invasion of privacy' to traffic in users' personal lives (Note 9).

The public spat with the broadcaster and others is a setback for Facebook as it tries to convince critics that it is meeting its social responsibilities.

Corporate squabbles, especially in the public domain, can set back goodwill and brand image earned over years; hence, it is a blunder not to avoid it.

Disputes not handled properly can even mean the axing of the CEO.

An instance applied to a deal in 2008 between two telecom giants—**NTT DOCOMO**, the Japanese company that agreed to buy 26 per cent of **Tata Teleservices** at $2.7 billion, an Indian company. DOCOMO got a guaranteed exit route—a 'put option'—from the Tata Group in case the investment turned sour—at half the investment value in 2014 if performance targets were not met and no other buyer could be found.

By 2016, the agreement descended into lawsuits and bitterness. DOCOMO sought to enforce a $1.2 billion arbitration award, obtained from London, in its favour. The Indian central bank refused permission to remit because the put option was designed only to offer 'downside protection'.

DOCOMO howled back, publicly accusing Tata of having mis-represented the situation to the central bank in order to secure a prohibition on the payment.

The dispute struck a discordant note between India and Japan and sparked divisions at the highest levels of the Tata Group's governance structure.

As the saga dragged on, Ratan Tata, holding 66 per cent of the holding company Tata Sons, grew unhappy with the handling of the situation. This became one of the reasons for Ratan Tata to sack his successor, ex-Tata Group chairman Cyrus Mistry in November 2016. (The DOCOMO-Tata dispute has since been settled where NTT DoCoMo received $1.2 billion from Tata Sons, after a new leadership took charge of the Tata Group.)[10]

Tailpiece

Disputes and conflicts, if not handled properly, result in immitigable damages to many—not only to the disputing parties but also to its managers. It is a gargantuan gaffe if corporate rows are not handled seriously and with appropriate sensitivity.

Business Rivalries

The business world is full of stories of race, rifts and recriminations. These are not disputes leading to the warring factions ending up in courtrooms, but the intensities with which they are fought could be several times bigger. Rivalries are healthy outcomes of competition. But in many rows, errors are often committed and fumbles encountered.

Think of intense rivalries in Rafael Nadal vs Roger Federer in tennis, India vs Pakistan in cricket, Mohammad Ali vs Joe Frazier in boxing, Barcelona vs Real Madrid in football and Phil Mickelson vs Tiger Woods in golf. And, of course, such passionate battles lead not only to bring the best in them, but also often to committing grave mistakes, as Tiger Woods did while playing at the 2013 Golf-Masters Tournament by surreptitiously moving his golf ball.

Similarly, in the world of business, who has not heard the stories of **Adidas** vs **Nike** hostilities or **UPS** vs **FedEx** combats or **McDonald's** vs **Burger King** duel or **Vodafone** vs **Airtel** animosities? Some have made the rivals stronger, while others have scarred enterprises. Rivalries need not involve dirty tricks, but competing behaviour may leave many healing their wounds, with some learning a lesson or two. It will be a big bungle attempting to sweep business rivalries under the carpet. Big names commit hefty slip-ups. Dirty market-share wars between rivals include the murky practice of calling names.

The duel between **Coke** and **Pepsi** for over a century to gain additional stake in the consumers' share of throat is long regarded as among the most bitter fights in the business world. The feud has often gone personal. Coca-Cola has called Pepsi names such as 'the Imitator' or 'the Enemy'. Both companies have made errors while on their way to trample each other in the marketplace, and have taken millions of dollars hit in costs.

Battle through advertisement is plenty. Comparing competitors' products and showing it in poor light or making unsubstantiated claims are rather common mistakes businesses make.

Multiple complaints have been made by **Sainsbury's** about **Tesco's** advertising—the Advertising Standards Association is perhaps tired of handling the pair fighting. In another instance, **Heinz** India's, maker of *Complan*, claim in its advertisements that its drink has 100 per cent milk protein and hence is much better than other malt-based drinks like **GlaxoSmithKline's** Horlicks, was found misleading.[11]

To fight the rivalry battles, businesses sometimes involve the pathetic act of corporate espionage.

Unilever and **Proctor & Gamble** (P&G), two global fast-moving consumer goods (FMCG) giants, have fought bitter battles over decades. P&G had hired espionage agents in 2000 to spy on Unilever and get information on the hair-care business. Not long after, the agents were caught that P&G made a pay-out to Unilever of $10 million. P&G had confessed at one point, looking through Unilever's trash cans for information on their strategy and proba-ble new launches.[12] What a sordid act on the part of such a famous name like P&G!

Bruising business rivalries can sometimes lead to sickness and bankruptcies among the competing players.

A classic case of intense sectorial distress emerged in the Indian mobile-telecom sector in 2017. The oil refining giant, Reliance Industries, diversified and launched **Reliance Jio** in September 2016. It swept the then 12 competing players off their feet. Jio upset rivals by offering its services free for seven months after its launch, and then offered free voice calls and mobile data at prices far below levels previously seen.

The result: **Aircel**, India's fifth-largest private mobile operator with 85 million subscribers, filed for insolvency in February 2018; **Reliance Communications**, controlled by billionaire tycoon Anil Ambani, succumbing to the Jio-led price war, headed for bankruptcy in mid-2019; and several smaller players such as **Idea Cellular**, **Tata Teleservices** and Norway's **Telenor** agreed to merge with larger firms **Vodafone** and **Bharti Airtel**, to save themselves from extinction.

Such was the impact of the shake-up post-business-rivalry episode that it left India with just three private-sector mobile operators accounting for over 90 per cent of the market, and two state-owned businesses collecting the morsels.

Tailpiece

Business-rivalry impact cuts both ways. Some fly; many flunk. When *Uber* fights *Lyft* in the United States, or *Flipkart* battles *Amazon* for the Indian share of the retail wallet, or Elon Musk's *SpaceX's* reusable rockets combat with *Blue Origin* developments for space business, or *YouTube* fights *Facebook* for our attention in the internet space, a lot of cutting-edge contending conduct will continue to develop, but some black eyes will also emerge. However, ignoring the fallouts of corporate rivalries will be improper.

Bickering Bloopers

Every manager knows that disputes are avoidable. They are not value accretive. They suck out time, sweat and money. Hence, the best way is to settle it. But in our enthusiasm to settle business rows, loads of blunders are committed. Let us look at some such cases:

- *Not knowing which terms apply:* Knowledge is power and lack of it is calamitous. In a dispute, make sure you know what contractual terms are applicable and whether it was agreed to by the other party. Often long contracts are entered into, which most do not even read, except perhaps the lawyers who got paid to make it. In addition, there could be several contracts entered in the past, with the earlier ones superseded by the later versions. Managers are often not aware which one to refer to when squabbles strike.

- *Not having signed the contract:* Very often, managers enter into arrangements before final terms are agreed upon. For instance, procurement of goods take place before the formal Purchase Order is raised. If transactions take place before final agreements are signed off, you are on slippery ground.

- *Not tracking the intent:* Contracts are entered into after negotiations and exchange of communications. Not retaining emails and letters exchanged would be a faux pas. If the contracts are not well drafted, circumstantial evidence often prevails.

- *Not dealing with authorized persons:* The other side, who has signed the contract, must be an accredited person. Make sure he was authorized to do so. Trust is good, but do not get taken for a ride just because you trusted too much.

- *Not settling on time:* Time-barred is an oft-repeated term in the legal world. It means you should not sit too long on a dispute. Take action. Write a letter. Forward your claim or point of view. Three years is often taken as a limitation for legal purposes—exceeding this period would be a booboo.

- *No handing over from the earlier negotiating person:* The manager who knew the background, or negotiated the deal or signed the contract, may leave. Employee turnover is a risk in any organization. Make sure that every leaving manager does a proper handing over to another person—or else, it will become a howler.

- *Not taking legal opinion:* Leave legal wrangles for lawyers to explain and deal with. Every one cannot be master of everything. Avoiding specialist intervention when dispute fever rises, will be a clanger.

- *Not exploring different avenues:* Alternative remedies pay. Arbitration or mediation works better. More so, enter into a dialogue with the adversaries. They may see reason. No one wants a legal dispute. It costs both time and money. Remember, courts are no dream destinations!

Rules to Reduce Rows

Confrontations, controversies and clashes are part of business. They cannot be eliminated but they need to be resolved quickly. Delayed settlement could cost a business dearly. Justice delayed is justice denied. Let us look at some steps that businesses could take to avoid or reduce discord:

- *Practise standard operating practices.* Institute policies and procedures meant to conduct day-to-day business exchanges and dealings in order to reduce the possibility of disputes. For instance, standard contract forms can help to ensure that agreements follow set procedures and include standard clauses for easy enforcement.

- *Do not overpromise product performance.* Obtain waivers from customers and clients, or ensure that products clearly demonstrate all necessary warnings and information. It will help limit liabilities and ensure customers are informed of what they are procuring.

- *Lay down processes for hiring and firing employees.* Standard employment contracts, pre-employment verification and employee-related policies will help avoid or refute claims of inequity or unreasonableness.

- *Written words are better than spoken promises.* Put things in writing. While friendly arrangements sound attractive to start with, undocumented business measures frequently lead to turbulences down the road.

- *It is good to think through what happens, if disputes arise.* Magistrates take a long time to resolve, plus it is expensive. Out-of-court settlements are desirable. Plan for appointing mutually acceptable arbitrators or mediators or having alternative dispute resolutions for deciding on quarrels—a better way to avoid the dull walls of the courts.

In Closing

Human behaviour gives many a blow, with some landing knockout punches. The mortal mind is often unpredictable and complex. It is, therefore, hard to enumerate every type of dispute or conflict. This chapter provides a glimpse of a few oft-repeated ones, trying to advance a few lessons. A lot of bad behaviour comes from insecurity and ego. Mistakes and fiascos get committed all the time, and the solution to each type of conflict varies from one situation to another. Awareness helps. Planning for the worse lessens pain. Communication resolves many an unresolvable mystery.

References

1. The Economist. Why the run on banks? The Economist, Bulgaria [Internet]. 2014 Jul 2. Available from: https://www.economist.com/eastern-approaches/2014/07/02/why-the-run-on-banks

2. Kantchev G. E.U. Banking watchdog warns of legal breach by Bulgaria. The New York Times [Internet]. 2014 Oct 21. Available from: https://www.nytimes.com/2014/10/22/business/international/eu-banking-watchdog-warns-of-legal-breach-by-bulgaria.html?searchResultPosition=8

3. Kantchev G. Caught in indecision, Bulgarian government is urged to solve banking crisis. The New York Times [Internet]. 2014 Aug 4.

Available from: https://www.nytimes.com/2014/08/05/business/international/Bulgaria-Under-Pressure-on-Corporate-Commercial-Bank.html?searchResultPosition=6:

4. Reuters. Microsoft, Samsung settle contract dispute over patents. Reuters [Internet]. 2015 Feb 10. Available from: https://www.reuters.com/article/us-microsoft-samsung-elec-settlement/microsoft-samsung-settle-contract-dispute-over-patents-idUSKBN0LD2LA20150209

5. United States Supreme Court. Kellogg Co. v. National Biscuit Co. United States Supreme Court [Internet]. 1938. Available from: https://caselaw.findlaw.com/us-supreme-court/305/111.html

6. India Today. SC gives Britannia, ITC chance to settle dispute out of court. India Today [Internet]. 2017 Jul 11. Available from: https://www.indiatoday.in/pti-feed/story/sc-gives-britannia-itc-chance-to-settle-dispute-out-of-court-996299-2017-07-11

7. Business Today. After Maruti Suzuki, labour unrest grows at Honda Manesar plant. Business Today [Internet]. 2012 Sep 4. Available from: https://www.businesstoday.in/sectors/auto/trouble-brews-at-hondas-manesar-facility/story/187762.html

8. CNBC. Jamie Dimon breakup one of my big mistakes—Weill. CNBC [Internet]. 2014 Apr 30. Available from: https://www.cnbc.com/2014/04/30/no-gotcha-oversight-regulators-too-adversarial-weill.html

9. BBC. The country where Facebook posts whipped up hate. BBC News [Internet]. 2018 Sep 12. Available from: https://www.bbc.com/news/blogs-trending-45449938

10. Business Today. Tata, DoComo agree to settle $1.17 billion dispute: Here's all the twists and turns in the case so far. Business Today [Internet]. 2017 Mar 22. Available from: https://www.businesstoday.in/current/corporate/tata-docomo-agree-to-settle-1.17-billion-dispute-heres-all-the-twists-and-turns-in-the-case-so-far/story/247110.html

11. The Economic Times. Kraft Heinz to recall Complan ad 'disparaging' Horlicks. The Economic Times [Internet]. 2017 Nov 27. Available from: https://economictimes.indiatimes.com/industry/cons-products/food/kraft-heinz-to-recall-complan-ad-disparaging-horlicks/articleshow/61788694.cms

12. The New York Times. P.& G. said to agree to pay Unilever $10 million in spying case. The New York Times [Internet]. 2001 Sep 7. Available from:https://www.nytimes.com/2001/09/07/business/p-g-said-to-agree-to-pay-unilever-10-million-in-spying-case.html

M&A IS A MUG'S GAME

The world of business is rather bizarre. Globally, over $2 trillion worth of transactions chase the mirage of mergers and acquisitions (M&As). Believe it or not, three out of four transactions fall on their faces.

M&A is a seductive strategy to jump-start growth, to fulfil ambitions, to showcase corporate stature or to boost performance. Take the example of the auto sector in the United States. There were over 270 car producers in 1909. By the 1950s, the sector consolidated and led to the creation of the current oligopoly of GM, Ford and Chrysler. But the same sector has done very badly in the M&A space, failing numerous times in their combination endeavours, like the DaimlerChrysler fiasco.

Most mergers meet with abysmal failure in their quest to achieve quick success.

To cite an example, **Microsoft** learnt a $8 billion lesson when it acquired **Nokia's** mobile business in 2014, only to jettison its plans a year later.[1] Microsoft committed a huge mistake by wanting to build a third ecosystem within the smartphone business, apart from the other two well-established global duopolies of Google–Apple dominating 'software' and Samsung–Apple dominating 'hardware'. Microsoft's dream—to have a single platform that ran on PCs, laptops, tablets and phones, and to be able to sell applications that run Windows—was botched.

Even the investment guru **Warren Buffet** made mistakes in his acquisitions. He had an expensive failure recently when he took a loss of over $870 million on $2 billion of debt in **Energy Future Holdings**, a Texas energy company. The company is struggling with bankruptcy unless natural gas prices go up a lot. Acknowledging his mistake, he said that he did not consult his long-time investment partner, Charles Munger, before taking on the debt. 'Next time I'll call Charlie,' Buffett said.[2]

A comprehensive research throws more light on the dismal outcome of M&As. The S&P Global Market Intelligence August 2016 report on mergers and acquisitions found that among Russell 3000 companies (benchmark of the US stock market) making significant acquisitions, post-deal returns generally underperformed those of their peers.

Studying 9,000 American companies acquisition transactions between 2001 and 2016, the research study found a $1,000 investment in the Russell 3000 Index would have grown to $3,000. The same investment in an index of Russell 3000 companies that made M&As of the type examined by the researchers would have become a measly $1,670. This study showed that M&A companies lagged significantly behind the pack of the universe of research companies.

M&A Botches and Bungles

'M&A synergies' is the term you will often hear in the corridors of corporate offices. But you will be surprised to know that in most cases, profit margins, earnings and return on capital, all decline relative to peers, post M&A. And the worse is that interest expense increases as debt soars, and other 'special charges' escalate when you examine a post-M&A profit and loss account. M&A tends to be dilutive to earnings growth over an extended period. In short, the sum of the parts in the M&A promise does not usually add up to the whole!

Let me cite an instance of one of the biggest business blunders ever committed—which happens to be in the arena of M&As.

It was the merger of the internet giant America Online (AOL) with the media conglomerate Time Warner, in 2001. The titanic **AOL–Time Warner** deal of $165 billion had gala visions—synergies in technological infrastructure, consumer reach and operations. The merger was supposed to give Time Warner's movie and TV content,

AOL's internet access by digitizing it and reaching out to a new online audience. AOL, which got rich through dial-up internet service in return, was supposed to get access to Time Warner's broadband cable systems, giving additional content to its 30 million subscribers.

The merger was such a disaster that in the following year, the merged entity declared a massive financial loss and nine years later, the merger fell apart with companies demerging.

This merger has become a case study for business schools, with its strategy and structure ripped apart to unveil the genesis of the failure.

Though spun as a merger, in reality, AOL with its more valuable stock was acquiring Time Warner. AOL would own 55 per cent of the new company and Time Warner the rest. But the new board would have an equal number of AOL and Time Warner directors—the harbinger of the fiasco. Though hailed as the merger of equals, everything which could go wrong went wrong.

The mutuality of benefit-sharing was missing. No 'give-and-take' philosophy existed post-merger. The cultures too were different, and the employees at the two companies resented one another. The situation became worse by a rather rickety management structure, with both companies fighting over top management positions, leading to four individuals taking the coveted chief financial officer spot within a space of three years. And, to top it all, the Time Warner CEO resigned just after a year of the merger.

The dotcom internet bubble started to show its ugly face from May 2000. This added fuel to the fire as online advertising began to slump. This made AOL's financial targets difficult to be met, the logic on which the deal was based. The world began to move to high-speed internet access, putting AOL's permeating dial-up service in peril. In 2002, the AOL division suffered a massive loss of $99 billion. And during those tough days, the hatred between both the sides prevented them from implementing growth strategies that the merged entity needed to work upon.[3]

And the icing on the catastrophic cake was the detection of a financial fraud. You will not believe that such a humungous transaction was backed by due diligence by their respective lawyers more or less over a weekend. No wonder skeletons hidden in the cupboards remained unknown. AOL had been improperly inflating its advertising revenue, and stories emerged within sections of the media in 2002 prompting investigations by US officials. Eventually, the fraud was caught, and the company was asked to pay hefty fines.

The enduring deliberation is whether the deal malformed as the concept was blemished from the start, or because the cultures did not fit. I believe this to be a classic case where two large organizations priding themselves to be individually successful, could not bury their arrogance and lacked a give-and-take approach to create a successful enterprise. The resultant outcome was the dreamboat sinking as soon as it was put to sail.

Tailpiece

Despite the oft-repeated assertion that M&As help businesses to grow better and faster, companies with M&A undertones are more likely to destroy value than benefit from their acquisitive-bent of strategy.

M&A Musings

Heavy-deal companies (those doing frequent or large M&As) do not perform well and should ideally be kept at arm's length. An S&P Global Market Study 2016 found that acquirers with the highest one-year spending on buyouts underperformed their peers by 2 per cent in the first year post-closing, and by 9 per cent after three years. In essence, post-M&A, acquirer returns have underperformed peers in general.

Business combinations fail due to a myriad reasons. Usually, there is no one reason that derails the train of hope and optimism.

M&A synergies get overstated. Anticipating dis-synergies such as loss of customers is often underrated. One-time likely costs are underestimated. Assumptions go haywire on post-M&A market share numbers, end-product pricing and potential cost savings. More importantly, M&A deal decisions are taken based on available information, which could be sketchy, and with limited pre-transaction target company management interaction. These are all common errors and routine mistakes but often ignored, ending in pain and peril.

Let us look at few of the lessons learnt from the numerous M&A transactions that have tanked or faltered.

One-Plus-One, Not Always Two

Like the romance of Romeo and Juliet, many a corporate marriage begins with a lot of passion, paroxysm and promise—only to end in a fiasco, especially when both sides are fairly comparable and commensurate.

When equals get together, one plus one is supposed to be two-plus. Unfortunately, in many cases, the stress and tension of two equals combining, supersedes the benefits it is supposed to provide. When two so-called equals want to go ahead with cooperation logic, many a time either the talks fail or the deals end in disaster.

When two companies are perceived to be alike in terms of size, scale and market relevance, key tasks involve aligning the management, culture and strategy. Markets do not often encourage equals to be merged. Hence, both companies must convey the story about how one plus one will be greater than two—including enhanced revenue, cost savings or marketing advantages.

The challenge of who is to be subordinated or who should call the shots in the merged entity becomes too complicated to be resolved with equanimity.

Let us turn our attention to an instance of corporate disaster when equals came together but unequal outcome results.

In the so-called merger of equals, disasters struck sooner than later. **Daimler** Germany announced that they were creating a 'merger of equals' when it paid $36 billion to unite with **Chrysler** in 1998. The promised synergy between the companies never developed, and the marriage made in heaven turned out to be a hell of an outcome. Daimler ultimately had to 'pay' Cerberus Capital Management, to hand over a majority stake nine years later.[4]

The DaimlerChrysler combination tumbled due to clashing corporate cultures, strategic missteps and worse, the spraining changes in the American auto industry. High oil prices drove Americans to smaller, more fuel-efficient vehicles. But DaimlerChrysler continued to churn out gas guzzlers like sport utility vehicles and minivans.

In M&A deals, one plus one need not be two!

Failed Cost Savings

There is no shortage of literature preaching M&As take place on the premise of effective synergies leading to cost savings. Many are overstated; most lack credible calculations and some are based on botched-up assumptions.

Many M&As flounder to reach the targeted cost optimization. The botched takeover of **DaimlerChrysler** to abortive alliances of **VW–Suzuki** are all instances of partnerships that sought massive cost savings but failed to deliver.

The *New York Times* had to sell **Boston Globe** for $70 million in 2013, a massive drop from the price it paid two decades ago of $1.1 billion. Cost-saving ideas which drove the original transaction remained on paper.[5] As both were news bearers, the reporters and printing necessarily needed to be kept separate. Administrative cost savings of finance, human resources and marketing were a trifle. The deal went sour, though it had to be kicked in when the media world faced unsettling times.

Most deals overvalue synergies and ride on the dream of cost reduction—a mistake commonly made but yet often repeated.

Botched-up Due Diligence

One of the biggest cases of buyer's remorse in recent memory was when **Hewlett-Packard** (HP), a computer maker, acquired the British data-intelligence software maker **Autonomy PLC** for $11 billion in October 2011. But the deal was mired by accounting loss recognitions, controversies and accusations ever since. In 2012, HP wrote down the value of Autonomy by $8.8 billion, wiping out almost the entire investment value.

HP blamed that some $5 billion of the write-down stemmed from wilful misrepresentation by Autonomy's management of the company's financial performance. Expectedly, Autonomy disagreed, and the two sides headed for a legal recourse. (In November 2018, the US government charged Mike Lynch, the former chief executive of Autonomy, with fraud for alleged wilful inflation of financial statements to make Autonomy look more attractive to a potential purchaser.)[6]

The moot question is how did HP buy a company paying a whopping sum without adequate due diligence? How could the auditors and lawyers not find such a large hole in Autonomy's accounts when they were reviewing Autonomy before the takeover? Or was it HP's sheer inability to extract value from the large acquisition resulting in losing value almost overnight? (SEC in the United States has observed that Autonomy fooled HP by cooking numbers.)[7]

Another instance of horrible due diligence: when Japan's **Daiichi Sankyo** acquired 64 per cent of **Ranbaxy Laboratories**, India's then largest pharmaceutical company, for $4 billion in June 2008. Just a few months later in September 2008, US drug authorities banned Ranbaxy from exporting 30 generic drugs to the United States due to lapses observed in manufacturing practices at two of its plants. Ranbaxy, later in 2013, did agree and pleaded guilty for its export of subpar drugs.

The moot question is how did Daiichi not realize during their due diligence process that Ranbaxy was under the radar of the US drugs administration? Ranbaxy must have been discussing the potential blacklisting and ban for quite some time since this was an eight-year-old dispute. It seems to be a basic failure of Daiichi's due diligence process—a mistake which became costly for the company as it had to exit six years later when their investment had lost almost 40 per cent of its value.

It is common sense—buy only after you have inspected and ensure what you are getting into. Blind faith, trust or love does not have space in the corporate world.

Chalk-and-Cheese Merger, Miscarry

Companies often venture into unrelated areas. Some work. Many fail. M&A obviously is an attractive mode to enter uncharted waters and hoping fishing will be fruitful.

Intel's $7.7 billion deal in 2010 to buy the security firm **McAfee** was such a gamble. Mobile devices are the chip industry's bread and butter, and Intel was floundering. It hoped to bet that combining McAfee's security software with its hardware would give it the desired push. But the chip maker has not been able to pull it off. (Intel took a big haircut when it sold its 51 per cent stake in McAfee to TPG, a private equity firm, for $1 billion in September 2016.)[8]

Just imagine integrating Intel's engineers of intricate devices made in super-clean offices with the technologists at McAfee who figure out how hackers break software security. Intuitively, both couldn't have integrated.

Hardware and software makers could be treated as chalk and cheese. It's an error to assume both can always be nurtured seamlessly!

Terrible Timing

In life, it is all about timing—you need to be in the right place, at the right time to grab a great opportunity. For the perfect down the line tennis shot, the racket must contact the ball at the right time. Not getting the timing right may not be a mistake, but it will definitely be an opportunity lost.

The 2016 S&P Global Market Study revealed several causes for the big bad world of M&A fumbles. Wrong timing is one major cause. M&As often gain traction when the market is heated up, with the future looking not so bright. Then the inevitable happens. The business cycle takes over. Markets fall as things cool down, and valuations look exaggerated.

While cash is the king, excess cash in the balance sheet could lead to poor acquisition timing. It can cause delirium to its management and can prove detrimental for M&As, due to probable lack of discipline in deploying that cash—resulting in a probable bungled acquisition.

Tata Steel, India's premier steel company, acquired the Anglo-Dutch major Corus Group for $12.2 billion in 2007, Europe's second-largest steel producer, to fulfil Tata's ambitions of becoming a truly global steel player. But the deal, just before the financial crisis of 2008, was ill-timed. Since the acquisition, there was a waning global demand for steel, which led to the demand for steel in Europe and the United Kingdom shrinking by a third, everyone wanting to export into Europe, and currency becoming volatile. The lesson—no one can time the market, even the Tatas could not: a wretched outcome of an utterly wrong M&A timing.

Another topic related to timing in the M&A process is not to keep it dragging on. If that happens, there is a likelihood that the deal may die or the terms may get worse. Both the buyer and seller, including their lawyers, must have a sense of urgency, responding to due diligence requests and turning around mark-ups of documents fast. Not focusing on transactions for quick closure will be an avoidable glitch.

Timings would also include assumptions of savings—the so-called M&A synergy. How quickly can it accrue and in what periodicity? But not getting the synergy benefits on time and in accordance with original assumptions made, will be a great minus.

Is timing, efficiency or providential? Does luck play a part in getting your timing right? It is said that the only thing that overturns hard luck is hard work!

Inability Sucks

Yahoo, formed in 1995, acquired over hundred companies of various hues and sizes, and yet it failed to take off. Chief executive Marissa Mayer blamed her own company for the fiasco, saying 'we did not have the talent base'. The once-vaunted internet colossal came down into shambles. Between 2012 and 2016, Marissa led Yahoo through an M&A binge, gobbling 53 companies and spending over $2 billion. She announced in 2015 that her objective was to acquire companies from mobile, video, native advertising and social sectors. Her strategy was to unlock values engrained in the smaller outfits, get the requisite talent and put it together to lead the internet world. But nothing worked. Unable to save its skin in spite of all the acquisitions, the web-pioneer Yahoo had to sell its internet business to Verizon in 2017 for $4.5 billion.[9]

It was a classic example of management failure to integrate the dozens of companies acquired and put them into one common platform.

Lack of ability on the part of the management to make a business combination work is a potent reason for abysmal failures in the field of M&As.

Culture Shocks

Businesses are not made of bricks and mortar. They consist of human beings. Business combinations survive only when the humans within are motivated to make it work. I am testimony to an instance where an European takeover by an Indian corporation failed to take off when a conference call was fixed for the Christmas Eve, which the European managers refused to honour. The Indian company felt short changed, and mutual trust cracked.

In an Aon survey, cultural integration was observed to be the number two driver of a deal failure.

Let me cite a few instances where culture concerns played a big spoiler.

In the advertising trade, mom-and-pop shops often come up with catchy phrases and hummable jingles and take away chunks of ad revenue. But when two ad giants, **Publicis** and **Omnicom**, announced in mid-2013 to form the world's largest ad company, it created quite a flutter. The business objective was to face the competition from technology companies such as Google and Facebook, which were using their huge repositories of user data to place ads. A mix of clashing personalities, disagreement over who will run the company, and some legal issues derailed the plan within nine months of the announcement.[10]

Believe it or not, it ultimately boiled down to which camp will appoint the chief financial officer (CFO) or the general counsel, as there could only be one and not two of them. Each side thought it would be in charge and it could not agree where and how would the merged entity function. Culturally, they just could not adjust with each other.

Even product formulae could create heartburns between two players. The Japanese drinks group **Suntory** (known for its *Yamazaki* and *Hakushu* whiskies) acquired US spirits maker **Beam** in 2014, but the integration has been bruised by Suntory's suggestions of tweaking the way the United States-based group produces its Jim Beam bourbon.

You will be surprised to know that the Japanese company is suggesting only minor modifications to the water purification process and adoption of the Japanese 'kaizen' continuous improvement philosophy. But it is seen by the American Beam team as an insult to the formula perfected by the Jim Beam family over two centuries. The $16 billion merger, combining the Japanese and American corporate cultures, is proving to be a headache.[11]

In recent times, Chinese players have been very active in the outbound M&A space. But they too faced a similar dismal experience—70 per cent of overseas M&As by Chinese companies ended up unsuccessful, reported *Shanghai Daily* in November 2013.

A clash of cultures has been observed as the most important impediment in M&As. Culture is a delicate concept. It is a set of largely implicit influences that is difficult to conform to and comprehend completely. It encompasses shared values, beliefs and assumptions that influence behaviour and attitudes within a group in a business or society. Culture inhibits or encourages human endeavours. It has been observed that in almost one-third of cases, culture became the cause for failed M&As.

Regulators Regulate

M&As typically impair competition through business combinations with a likelihood of pushing price upwards. M&As are also sometimes planned to save tax by locating portions of the entity post deal in low-tax regimes—in business parlance known as tax inversions. Regulators do not like either.

The planned $6 billion merger of **Staples** and **Office Depot** was not allowed in 2016 by a US federal judge, setting back beleaguered retailers, who braved years of dropping sales and increased competition from Amazon and other rivals. Combining the two companies would have effectively created just one dominant retailer focused on pens and papers, which the court did not like.[12]

Governments obviously do not like tax savings or, shall we say, tax avoidance deals. Let us take an example. For several years, **Pfizer** was seeking to escape the high US corporate tax rate with its enormous profit of $125 billion. It planned to merge with **Allergan** so that its address could be shifted to low-tax Ireland, where Allergan is domiciled. A $160 billion merger was planned, but in April 2016 it had to abandon the proposed largest tax inversion deal in history.[13] This marks a watershed victory for an interventionist US government.

The regulators could have other reasons for not being comfortable with a business combination. For instance, a proposed merger between South Africa's **MTN** and India's **Bharti Airtel** failed in 2009 because the Indian regulators did not allow a dual listing, and the South African regulators would not allow the deal to go ahead without one.

Tailpiece

Regulators do not like too few players controlling too much of the market, which may be dubbed as anti-competitive. Tax inversion deals are disliked by most governments, and rightly so. Only time will tell whether the regulators will ultimately be happy to be flexible in these areas to encourage more M&As. But my feeling is things may get more stringent as consumer activism will enhance as times go by. Not heeding these warnings would be unwise.

'Acquirer's' Loss Is 'Target's' Gain

British American Tobacco (BAT), best known for the *Dunhill* and *Lucky Strike* brands, acquired in 2017 the balance 58 per cent of **Reynolds American Inc**, which makes *Camel* and *Newport* cigarettes, in a $49 billion cash-share deal to create the world's largest tobacco company by sales.[14] Strangely, BAT re-entered the American market after a decade, having earlier retreated post billion dollar-settlements, at a time when the Americans were smoking much less—only 15 per cent smoked in 2015, compared to 42 per cent in 1965.[15]

Who ultimately benefits from the deal only time would tell, but history suggests that BAT shareholders perhaps would feel wary, while Reynolds shareholders could sense confidence. This is also the message from a comprehensive 2016 S&P study on M&As. It shows that M&A creates value for 'target' company shareholders, but studies on post-M&A results for acquirers, however, do not show such positivity.[16]

This disparity is due to a simple truth: target company shareholders almost generally receive a takeover premium. However, post

M&A Is a Mug's Game

M&A, acquirer returns will depend on fundamental business performance, which can get impacted by several reasons, including value and structure of the deal, debt component, due diligence adequacy, corporate values and management expertise.

Tailpiece

No wonder that studies show that by the third year following an acquisition, a majority of acquirers have underperformed their relative industry benchmarks—stories which the deal makers and its advisors will never talk about.

Spin-offs

While in the entertainment world, spin-offs are the offspring of popular shows, in the business world, spin-offs or demergers are the progeny of established companies. For hit shows, take popular characters and give them a new twist. In business, take a unit and make it a free-standing business. Both are spin-offs, but different strategies with similar intent, to enhance value.

In business school corridors, you will often hear—small is beautiful; focus helps performance. A good way to fulfil the axiom is to do the reverse of M&A and spin off firms from the group they belong to—either as new, stand-alone enterprises or under the control of new parent companies.

The rationale varies for spin-offs. Some want to get rid of a weak link or an underperforming asset. Some want to flaunt their star, which is not believed to be getting reflected in the parent's valuation.

Reasons could be several, but many possess spin-off ambitions. China's famous WeChat app-maker **Tencent**, a $380 billion social media giant, spun off its web music, publishing and search units to incentivize the units' management. **Glencore**, the miner and commodity trader, desires to spin off its portfolio of mining royalties into a new company to attract outside investors with an eye on an eventual stock market listing. The German retailer **Metro** sought higher valuation by splitting it into two—consumer electronics and the wholesale food business, and planned to get rid of 'conglomerate discount'.

Historical evidence shows that whatever is the underlying motivation for spin-offs or demergers, they tend to do well post hiving-off. *Financial Times* quoting data from S&P Global shows that spin-offs outperform their industry peers by 8 per cent in the first year and 22 per cent over three years. This is rather contrary to M&As where post-deals, things normally slide downhill. Not taking note of this reality will be a mistake.

Spin-offs That Spun Out

Just as most spin-offs work, it does not mean all will work. Many spin-offs do not work, as some end up with broken legs.

Oil driller **Kerr-McGee** separated its chemicals unit to form **Tronox** in 2004. But after allegations of environmental damage, Tronox collapsed, leaving Kerr-McGee and its new owner Anadarko Petroleum Corporation to pay out $5 billion in damages in 2014.[17] In **Xerox**, shareholders decided that corporate separation was good for them, only to be denied by the creditors in 2016 as they felt it was at their expense. In recent times, the spin-off controversy has centred on their tax-free feature. **Yahoo** notably abandoned its **Alibaba** spin-off over tax liability concerns raised by the government.

Make Spin-offs Spin Well

While spin-offs usually work, at least from the market valuation angle, a checklist for successful spin-offs is useful or else you may rue the action plan.

– Make the firm stand on its feet after carefully carving it out from the parent;

– The carved-out business should have a good management team;

– The parent should be prepared to free the spun-off asset and not micromanage it;

- The carved-out entity should be financially well backed up to last the transition period—from carving out to full independence and perhaps till a new parent arrives to tender.

Tailpiece

Markets usually love to see a sum-of-the-parts analysis of conglomerates, implying how much a corporate could get from piecemeal sales. Shares in a company made up of diverse businesses often trade at lower forward earnings multiple than those operating in a particular area. Strip them into individual divisions, valuation become easier—not looking at this hiving-off option would entail an opportunity lost.

M&A Fallouts

M&A deal failures often lead to various consequences. Some careers collapse, few get shunted out, while many rationalize. Deal failures often tarnish the image of managers, who have built their goodwill over the years.

Jack Welch of **GE**, just before his retirement and after a long and brilliant career, tainted his reputation when his bid to buy Honeywell failed.[18] Similarly, the reputation of Marius Kloppers, CEO of **BHP Billiton**, sullied with the botched-up deal for its arch-rival Rio Tinto in 2008 for $150 billion. He subsequently wanted to revive his reputation by buying Potash Corporation of Saskatchewan, a Canadian fertilizer company, for an unbelievable price of $39 billion in 2010. This, too, failed to take off. Kloppers had to leave BHP Billiton in 2013.[19]

There is another consequence of a failed takeover plan. In order to prevent takeovers, the target companies often prop up ambitious forecasts. But this leads to difficulties in meeting them.

AstraZeneca, defending itself from **Pfizer's** abortive attack, declared in 2014 that its sales will double by 2023 as new drugs arrive, despite its sales being stagnant when the tall claim was made.[20] (Incidentally, AstraZeneca sales have started rebounding since end 2018, riding on new drugs.)[21]

However, sometime frustrated deals become a blessing in disguise.

ABN AMRO in 2007 was targeted for a takeover for $92 billion by Barclays. Had this happened, Barclays perhaps would have gone under, as was the case with the Royal Bank of Scotland, the ultimate victor who needed to be bailed out by the government. In fact, ABN AMRO's disastrous $96 billion acquisition price proved RBS's undoing.[22]

Tailpiece

Who wants to fail? Surely not the corporate head honchos, backed by a battery of investment bankers and advisors, working on deals to prop themselves up. Unfortunately, most deals fail to deliver. Some do not even take off. A few, the governments do not even allow. Justification starts flowing from the powers that be, in rationalizing failed developments. Strange are the ways businesses function!

Making Mergers Meaningful

A whopping 70–80 per cent of M&As fail to make any difference. It is typically a mug's game. The key question is how to make it work? *What* should be done to get the desired objectives?

The formula to remember is: if you wish to 'give', you win; if you want to only 'take', you are likely to lose out.

You may feel that the recipe is contrary to popular belief of the business world. Most acquisitions take place with the objective to get new technology or obtain access to cash or enhance product portfolio. It could also be a combination of these. It is these 'take' or 'get' strategies that drive most business transactions. And that is what results in the failure of most takeover cases.

The 'give-and-take' principle is also true in our lives. If one believes in only 'taking', relationships are bound to sour. Adam Grant's bestselling book *Give and Take* talks about this philosophy with lucidity and aplomb. The book comments that at work, most people operate as 'takers', 'matchers' or 'givers'. Whereas 'takers' strive to get as much as possible from others and 'matchers' aim to trade evenly, 'givers' are the rare breed of people who contribute to others without expecting anything in return. Adam Grant's research shows that, although some givers get exploited and burnt out, the rest achieve extraordinary results across a wide range of industries. Similar experiences have been noticed in business-combination deals.

Many big mergers failed to deliver on their projected benefits because they lacked the 'give' approach. Look at **AT&T's** acquisition of the **NCR Corporation, Sony's** purchase of **Columbia Pictures, Matsushita's** acquisition of **MCA, Kmart's** acquiring **Sears, Quaker Oats** buying but selling quickly **Snapple** drinks and similarly for **eBay** buying and disposing of **Skype.**

You will notice that if the acquiring company wants to give more to the acquired company than what it plans to take, the combination is likely to work better.

'Give' Approach, the Harbinger

There is a fable in India that when a daughter-in-law arrives, relationships at home are likely to sour, even though both—mother and wife—love and care for the same man. How can this relationship work? Psychologists agree that if both would practise the 'give' tactic, the bond will strengthen and peace will prevail.

Business combinations are no different. A company with an acquisitive mode must make up its mind about its 'giving' approach to the target company. The acquisition should make the acquired company more competitive. It is juxtaposed with the acquiring company that is able to do the same on its own.

There are several ways the 'give' strategy can be implemented. Let us look at some of them to help businesses avoid mistakes during acquisitions.

- *Access to market:* Smaller companies or start-ups have limited market access. They may have a great product, but their ability to spend on marketing or making potential customers know about their products and services could be hindered due to lack of money or depth in market presence. A larger company can provide this benefit. If the acquiring company has the strategy to provide market access to the target company, it is a great recipe for success.

The Walt **Disney** Company was a powerhouse of film production and distribution. **Pixar**, a graphics group, made marvellous computer-generated animated movies. When Disney bought its rival Pixar in 2006 for $7 billion, many people assumed the deal would collapse like most other big media takeovers. It was thought that Disney would trample the innovative spirit of Pixer's animator and its creative culture.[23] The price paid was also a matter of discussion—how could Disney pay so much for a company owning just one small studio and producing only one movie a year?

The Disney–Pixar marriage, however, worked. Disney gave Pixar it's financial and distribution muscle, allowed Pixar to retain its corporate and cultural identity, drawing up an explicit road map of what would not change in Pixar. Disney's respect for Pixar was so great that they even did not change Pixar's nameplate at the gate for long. Disney thus gave Pixar the headroom to remain what it was even within a sprawling corporation. Imagination and inspirational inventiveness thrived, making the merged entity the winner after all.

Tatas, the Indian conglomerate through **Tata Global Beverages Limited**, have been focused on the beverages business. As a part of the strategy, they were looking for drinking water to be added to their portfolio. In 2013, Tatas acquired **Mount Everest Mineral Water Limited**, harvesting natural mineral water sourced from the foothills of the famous Shivalik range of the Himalayas, sold under the premium brand 'Himalayan'.

Just think how on earth can a small company sitting at the foothills of one of the largest mountain ranges bottling spring water, distribute it all across? Tata Beverages gave its distribution network on a platter to their Himalayan experiment. This resulted in a wonderful business combination. Visit any good restaurant in India and you will be served beautifully packaged 'Himalayan' water on your table. A superb case study of how the 'give' approach of one company took the acquired company's products to new levels.

- *Access to technology:* Acquisition's competitiveness can be enhanced by helping the acquired company's technology upgradation.

  Microsoft has purchased over 200 companies. Many faltered. However, their success stories hinge on the 'give' syndrome. Microsoft's acquisition of **LinkedIn** in June 2016 is based on technology sharing—a recipe for success. In another instance, in 1987, Microsoft bought **Forethought Inc**, the PowerPoint software developer. This became the most popular method to create presentations in the business world. Microsoft could add value to the technology platform by making available its Office suite of applications to integrate with the powerful software. Providing a technology platform to enhance the dissemination of the software worked wonders.

- *Enhance pricing power:* Acquisition necessarily means at least one less in the jungle of competitors. If there were four players, and one company merges into another, it would leave three to fight for the market share. It leads to better pricing prowess. However, better profitability will eventually lead to new players coming in, but that will take some time. It may, however, be noted that if the number of competitors is more than five, consolidation may not lead to improved pricing.

  The steel industry goes through serious cyclic pricing pressures. Look at China. It has 1.2 billion tonnes of production capacity, of which more than 400 million tonnes are considered surplus. **Bao Steel** merged with **Wuhan Iron**

& Steel in late 2016, to create the nation's biggest steel company, with an annual production capacity of 60 million tonnes, just behind the world's largest steel producer Arcelor Mittal. It helped rationalize capacity and pushed up sagging steel prices.

Consolidation in the marketplace is, however, bereft with risks with antitrust and competition regulators. They sometime prevail and prevent prospective business mergers.

- *Reduction in costs:* When two companies operate in a similar domain, each will have cost duplication. Each company will have its marketing, sales, human resources, etc., plus two CEOs, two CFOs and it goes on. A business combination is expected to save costs by rationalizing sheer duplicity.

Cost savings can take place through layoffs, selling redundant resources, rationalizing organization structures and consolidating manufacturing or service resources.

When I was the executive director for the leading travel solutions company **Thomas Cook**, we acquired in 2007 **Travel Corporation of India**, a renowned holiday company. Costs could be reduced when we found that both companies had retail outlets on the same street or adjacent buildings. A similar experience was gathered when Thomas Cook acquired a foreign-exchange selling company, **LKP Forex**, a year earlier. Indian airports used to have competing counters facing each other selling forex to travellers. It was a no brainer to close one of them. Saving on the duplicity of efforts resulted in huge savings.

Saved money helps to do many things, which may not have been feasible when the entities were independent. A key reason for the merger between **Sandoz** and **Ciba-Geigy** that created the Swiss pharmaceutical giant **Novartis** in 1996 was to save cost.[24] Saved money was diverted towards enhancing R&D efforts.

- *Access to funds:* Capital is the hub for business growth. Lack of adequate funds straddles many businesses. An investor can bring funds to grow a business. Business combinations with the objective of providing growth capital are a success formula.

When **Oculus**, a start-up that made high-end gear for virtual reality, was acquired by **Facebook** for $2 billion in 2014, its CEO Mark Zuckerberg said, 'We're going to focus on helping Oculus build out their product and develop partnerships to support more games. Oculus will continue operating independently within Facebook to achieve this.' This was made possible by Facebook funding Oculus's efforts. Note the scenario just after few years of acquisition. Ask someone from the VR industry what brought virtual reality from a concept discussed by basement gamers to a product hawked by the world's largest technology companies, and most will say Facebook's buying and funding of Oculus changed everything.

Mahindra & Mahindra, the Indian multinational automobile company, had carried out over 60 M&A transactions valued over $5 billion. Many of them are small companies where the Mahindra Group turned them around through fund infusion.

- *Access to managerial bandwidth:* Many companies, mostly smaller in size, lack management skills, business processes and organizational capabilities. An acquisition can help bridge these gaps.

When **ArcelorMittal** went to Kazakhstan to acquire a steel plant, they found that there were huge weaknesses in their purchasing, logistics and financing capabilities. The London headquarters sent in 20 managers to take charge of the Kazakh commercial operations from the day the company was bought. Kazakhstan became one of the most profitable operations in the ArcelorMittal portfolio.

Typical instances of management bandwidth contribution happen when PE or venture capital funds invest. Their objective generally is to add value to their invested companies and exit in due course at a higher value. The most important contribution is through managerial focus, systems, procedures and controls. Warren Buffet's Berkshire Hathaway, holding investments in Coca-Cola and Wells Fargo, among others, is globally renowned for their focused managerial inputs to maximize value in their invested companies.

- *Access to central resource sharing:* Larger corporations have established business processes, adequately trained departments such as purchasing focused on key tasks and business experience of a host of key personnel. In case of takeovers, the acquired organizations can hitchhike on these central skills and capabilities.

ArcelorMittal, the world's largest iron and steel company, has grown into a multinational giant through acquisitions. It has never set up a green-field site. The steel baron Lakshmi Mittal, chairman of ArcelorMittal, has grown by acquiring steel plants across the globe. He bought ailing plants—Mexico, Romania, Algeria, Czech Republic, South Africa, the United States—and converted them into profit centres. One of the key contributions to the acquired companies is to make available their central resource base. The sheer size of its huge purchasing power over coal and iron ore benefits the acquired companies. I was responsible for and have been a witness to this benefit when ArcelorMittal acquired the large 3 million tonnes Romanian steel company, now renamed **ArcelorMittal Galati**, situated on the banks of the river Danube. The central teams in London office helped immensely to source coal, iron ore, engineering and capital items. Millions of dollars saved within a very short span!—a definitive advantage for the acquisition.

'*Athithi Devo Bhava*', the Sanskrit verse meaning 'guests are Gods', applies equally to business acquisitions. Like welcoming a bride home, an acquisition brings into the arms of a business family, another entity. The acquired company is the guest or the new bride coming home. 'Give' it what you can, and you will find the relationship flourishing. Not following this simple formula would be an error.

'Give' and 'Take' Is Mutual

Success possibilities in business combinations increase manifold when there is a 'give' objective prevalent between the acquirer and acquired organizations. However, it does not mean that the acquirer will not benefit from the deal. No company ever will pay to acquire another company only to 'give', but not to 'take'. These are corollaries to each other. Especially when a merger takes place, where the organizations are perhaps more equal to each other before the deal, the give-and-take formula works wonders.

Acquisitions are ultimately done either to improve the current performance or to reinvent its business model. Hence, every M&A must provide something in return after the deal takes place.

For iPads, **Apple** considered its heart to be the fingernail-sized chip. For device makers, usually they buy their primary chips from specialized microprocessor companies. But for the iPad, Apple chose to design its own—creating a unique bond between the chip and iPad's software. The do-it-yourself approach makes Apple faster, more battery-friendly than rivals and retains secrecy.

To fulfil its business strategy, Apple forayed into the chip business in 2008, acquiring the 150-employee start-up **PA Semi**. That company had been working on chips that could handle large volumes of data while consuming very less power.

It was a give-and-take working in perfect harmony. Apple gave Semi a captive market to sell its chips. Semi gave Apple captive source of specialized chips that a company making music players, laptops and phones would want.[25]

A buyout which shook the world in 2000 when **Tata Tea** (now Tata Global Beverages), the Indian $110 million minnow bought the global sharks, three times its size, United Kingdom's **Tetley** for

$450 million.[26] Tetley was suffering from a shrinking UK market and profits were dipping. Tata Tea was facing intense domestic competition from the likes of Brook Bond and Lipton tea.

The acquisition of Tetley had several years of initial teething trouble. But things turned out rather well with **Tata–Tetley** now commanding over 35 per cent market share in the United Kingdom being sold in over 40 countries.

Both Tata Tea and Tetley followed a give-and-take policy.

Packet tea formed the backbone of Tetley before the merger. Tatas were primarily a bulk tea company and had 40 per cent of its business in packet tea. Tetley's were fully dependent upon outsourcing its entire requirement from more than 30 countries, but Tatas were sourcing its requirement in-house. The merger gave Tetley's a great source of quality tea leaves from the hills of south India, de-risking its procurement from too many sources. Post-acquisition, Tata Tea—the India-centric company—got access to the British and American markets—the give-and-take doctrine working in perfect harmony.

Tailpiece

Businesses are getting remixed and rejigged, spending trillions of dollars each year, but with an obscene failure rate. Mergers, acquisitions, joint ventures, alliances, multi-party consortia and partnerships are taking place daily by the dozen. It is all about mixing and remixing of assets, capabilities, humans and markets to make things work differently, with the hope of doing better business. This may go through some ups and downs as economic cycles do, but the trend will continue, fuelled by managerial ambition, desire for incentives, need to act differently, challenging the status quo, providing kickstarts and fulfilling egos.

M&As are like marriages, two compatible people coming together and dealing with their incompatibility. There are hundreds of theories on how to make M&As work—but following the simple time-tested formula of 'give and take' should normally lead to success. Ignoring it will be at your own peril.

In Closing

I have completed over a dozen M&As. Every transaction is different even when you feel you know it all. Hundreds of seminars take place each day all across the globe; many management education businesses survive by teaching the theme. Reams of papers are filled with the theory of M&A success and failures.

But still we know little of how to make it work! What is common to find is that acquirers usually pay more; deals carried out using stocks often perform better; ego satisfaction is a big driver; business heads often fall in love with deals and do not pull the plugs when they should; and integrating organizations are usually difficult, with even the seasoned frequently slipping.

Everyone is attempting to deploy the same trick—identify an undervalued asset and acquire it. But how easy is to identify these bargains? By the time you buy, will there be any incremental value left beyond the price paid for you to enjoy?

Getting the right recipe in M&A is never going to be easy. It is a mug's game and will remain so. Many will keep searching for the hidden pearls in the depths of the ocean; some will find it but only a handful will be able to treat, polish and enjoy its lustre.

References

1. Day M. Phone deal with Nokia became Microsoft's $10 billion mistake. The Seattle Times [Internet]. 2016 Mar 25. Available from: https://www.seattletimes.com/business/microsoft/phone-deal-with-nokia-became-microsofts-10-billion-mistake/

2. Omaha World Herald. Investment in Energy Future Holdings 'a big mistake', Buffett says. Omaha World Herald [Internet]. 2014 Mar 1. Available from: https://www.omaha.com/money/investment-in-energy-future-holdings-a-big-mistake-buffett-says/article_9bbff0bc-089a-55be-b9cc-f64b615a44f4.html

3. Arango M. How the AOL–Time Warner merger went so wrong. The New York Times [Internet]. 2010 Jan 10. Available from: https://www.nytimes.com/2010/01/11/business/media/11merger.html; Grocer S. What happened to AOL Time Warner? New York Times [Internet].

2018 Jun 15 [cited XXXX Mar XX]. Available from: https://www.nytimes.com/2018/06/15/business/dealbook/aol-time-warner.html

4. Bunkley N. Daimler reaches deal to unload Chrysler stake. The New York Times [Internet]. 2009 Apr 27. Available from: https://www.nytimes.com/2009/04/28/business/28chrysler.html

5. Haughney C. New York Times Company sells Boston Globe. The New York Times [Internet]. 2013 Aug 3. Available from: https://www.nytimes.com/2013/08/04/business/media/new-york-times-company-sells-boston-globe.html

6. Woo S. U.S. charges autonomy founder with fraud over Hewlett-Packard deal. The Wall Street Journal [Internet]. 2018 Nov 30. Available from: https://www.wsj.com/articles/u-s-charges-autonomy-founder-with-fraud-over-hewlett-packard-deal-1543582883

7. Ciesielski JT. How Autonomy fooled Hewlett-Packard. Fortune [Internet]. 2016 Dec 15. Available from: http://fortune.com/2016/12/14/hewlett-packard-autonomy/

8. Cohan P. Has McAfee's value grown since Intel sold 51% to TPG? Forbes [Internet]. 2018 Feb 23. Available from: https://www.forbes.com/sites/petercohan/2018/02/23/has-mcafees-value-grown-since-intel-sold-51-to-tpg/#442958115af3

9. Solomon B. Yahoo sells to Verizon in saddest $5 billion deal in tech history. Forbes [Internet]. 2016 Jul 25. Available from: https://www.forbes.com/sites/briansolomon/2016/07/25/yahoo-sells-to-verizon-for-5-billion-marissa-mayer/#5f9609d450f3

10. The Guardian. Publicis/Omnicom deal collapsed after merger turned into power struggle. The Guardian [Internet]. 2014 May 9. Available from: https://www.theguardian.com/media/2014/may/09/publicis-omnicom-merger-collapsed-power-struggle

11. Inagaki K. Beam Suntory: A volatile Japanese–US blend. Financial Times [Internet]. 2016 Jun 15. Available from: https://www.ft.com/content/a9878bea-2eec-11e6-bf8d-26294ad519fc

12. De la Merced MJ, Abrams R. Office Depot and Staples call off merger after judge blocks it. The New York Times [Internet]. 2016 May 10. Available from: https://www.nytimes.com/2016/05/11/business/dealbook/staples-office-depot-merger.html

13. Humer C, Banerjee A. Pfizer, Allergan scrap $160 billion deal after U.S. tax rule change. Reuters [Internet]. 2016 Apr 6. Available from: https://www.reuters.com/article/us-allergan-m-a-pfizer-idUSKCN0X3188

14. Dalesio EP. Shareholders weigh British American, Reynolds tobacco merger. Business Insider [Internet]. 2017 Jul 19. Available from: https://www.businessinsider.com/ap-shareholders-weigh-british-american-reynolds-tobacco-merger-2017-7?IR=T

15. Christensen J. We know it can kill us: Why people still smoke. CNN [Internet]. 2015 Nov 19. Available from: https://edition.cnn.com/2014/01/11/health/still-smoking/index.html

16. S&P Global. Mergers and acquisitions: The good, the bad, and the ugly (and how to tell them apart). S&P Global [Internet]. 2016 Aug 26. Available from: https://www.spglobal.com/en/research-insights/articles/mergers-acquisitions-the-good-the-bad-and-the-ugly-and-how-to-tell-them-apart

17. United States Environmental Protection Agency. Case summary: Court decision in Tronox Bankruptcy Fraudulent Conveyance Case results in largest environmental bankruptcy award ever. United States Environmental Protection Agency [Internet]. Available from: https://www.epa.gov/enforcement/case-summary-court-decision-tronox-bankruptcy-fraudulent-conveyance-case-results-largest

18. Elliott M. The anatomy of the GE–Honeywell disaster. The Time [Internet]. 2001 Jul 8. Available from: http://content.time.com/time/business/article/0,8599,166732-1,00.html

19. BHP Billiton chief Marius Kloppers to retire, profits plunge. The Telegraph [Internet]. 2013 Feb 19. Available from: https://www.telegraph.co.uk/finance/newsbysector/industry/mining/9881871/BHP-Billiton-chief-Marius-Kloppers-to-retire-profits-plunge.html

20. Financial Times. Pfizer and AstraZeneca: One year after deal that never was. Financial Times [Internet]. 2015 May 27. Available from: https://www.ft.com/content/e8320ccc-0327-11e5-8333-00144feabdc0

21. Financial Times. New drugs help AstraZeneca sales rebound. Financial Times [Internet]. 2019 Feb 14. Available from: https://www.ft.com/content/eee7f494-3020-11e9-8744-e7016697f225

22. Independent. Was ABN the worst takeover deal ever? Independent [Internet]. 2009 Jan 20. Available from: https://www.independent.co.uk/news/business/analysis-and-features/was-abn-the-worst-takeover-deal-ever-1451520.html

23. The deals that have made Disney so powerful. The Los Angeles Times [Internet]. 2017 Dec 14. Available from: https://www.latimes.com/business/hollywood/la-fi-disney-deals-20171214-htmlstory.html

24. Grimond M. Ciba-Geigy and Sandoz to merge into pounds 40 bn giant. Independent [Internet]. 1996 Mar 8. Available from: https://

www.independent.co.uk/news/business/ciba-geigy-and-sandoz-to-merge-into-pounds-40bn-giant-1340926.html

25. Gurman M. How Apple built a chip powerhouse to threaten Qualcomm and Intel. Bloomberg [Internet]. 2018 Jan 29. Available from: https://www.bloomberg.com/graphics/2018-apple-custom-chips/

26. India Today. 2000-Tata Tea-Tetley merger: The cup that cheered. India Today [Internet]. 2009 Dec 28. Available from: https://www.india-today.in/magazine/cover-story/story/20091228-2000-tata-tea-tetley-merger-the-cup-that-cheered-741660-2009-12-25

PUBLIC RELATIONS FAUX PAS

'Das Auto' and **Volkswagen** were inseparable in their advertisements for decades, proclaiming to the world that it was 'THE CAR' to ride. But the company admitted to illegally equip 11 million of its diesel vehicles with software used for cheating on emission tests through 2006 and 2015. The deceit involved activating its sensing device when the car was being 'emission-tested' so as to show reduced discharges. The software, however, did not function during regular driving, thereby showing the emissions at actual levels which were far above permissible limits.

The auto major, which sells global brands such as Audi, Porsche and Lamborghini, grossly faltered to grapple with the fallout, struggling with its PR messaging since the time the company was caught cheating.

From the time the American regulators found that something was amiss, Volkswagen simply lied that its diesel cars had a technical problem that was causing emissions to surge on the road. By mid-2015, the world got to know that Volkswagen had tampered with its emission system to under report the killer gas, nitrogen oxide, discharge content—deceitfully fitting defeat devices to vehicles. Only in September 2015 did the company admit its fault.

In Volkswagen's case, it is hard to believe that the top management was not aware of a fraud of such magnitude for a decade! Having learnt of the dishonest acts, the company should have depicted remorse, but it did not. Rather than owning responsibility, the company's new CEO, Matthias Müller (since replaced in April 2018), brazenly said in January 2016, 'It was a technical problem. We had not the right interpretation of the American law ... we did not lie. We didn't understand the question first.'

Once Volkswagen admitted to its blunder, the company kept getting thousands of calls and e-mails at the same time—it was something like a tsunami, acknowledged Hans-Gerd Bode, Volkswagen's communications chief. He admitted, 'a crisis like this the company was not prepared for; we don't know the right way out.'[1]

It was a huge fall from grace for a company which for generations had maintained a friendly market image and manicured scripts for press interactions. The problem was of gigantic proportions straddling across the globe, unlike the single-market PR disasters of **British Petroleum's (BP)** Gulf of Mexico oil spill or **Google's** fight with European regulators over data privacy.

Rather than facing the problem head on when the glitches came to light, Volkswagen tried to keep the concerns under wraps, hoping things would die down automatically. Even its the then chief executive Martin Winterkorn blamed it as 'mistakes of a few people'.[1] How can anyone believe that only a 'few' can commit a scandal concerning millions of vehicles, that too over several years? (Winterkorn has since been charged in May 2018 with conspiring to defraud the United States.[2])

While there have been several auto sector recalls and scandals, the Volkswagen episode is particularly different. The customers seem to have been more tolerant of mechanical and human failures like the **GM's** defective ignition switches, **Toyota's** sudden vehicle acceleration or **Honda's** not reporting its safety problems. But Volkswagen's emission scandal involved hiding and lying over a long period of time.

'Das Auto' has since been replaced by a simple tag line 'Volkswagen'— what a humbling fall from grace for a company priding itself for manufacturing the finest cars in the world! The reasons are not far to be fetched. Deceptive moves to by-pass emission regulations, lying when problems came to light and disregarding proper public messaging, created a perfect recipe for a corporate catastrophe. (Volkswagen pleaded guilty in January 2017 for using false statements and ended up paying $4.3 billion in penalties.[3])

Volkswagen definitely made things worse for themselves—not acknowledging there was a problem—which was that their diesel car emissions did not meet the tough US guidelines. While PR managers are supposed to be damage-control specialists, in the German automaker's case, this was a PR nightmare.

Controlling damage is perhaps the most important ask from the PR team. However, events sometimes take their own turns and twists, and no amount of spin can straighten things up.

Businesses commit grave errors trying to figure out ways to handle a crisis only after it has occurred. This catch-up game makes things worse.

Hence, it was a mistake not to plan in advance for an eventuality. Not putting a crisis-management strategy into place to handle adverse business consequences is poor management.

PR is only as good as the product or service. It is as good as the narrative that can be created around it. The story has to be real and cannot stand on falsehoods or hoodwinks. As long as the narrative can be supported, the PR exercise will remain meaningful and relevant. Not adhering to these basics will be a grave error.

Shove It under the Carpet

If a catastrophe has struck or a major problem observed, should the company let the sleeping dogs lie? The typical response is—'public memory is short', or 'it will pass'. This is the dilemma the PR team often faces—to say or not to say!

Not acknowledging that there is a problem is the genesis of a PR disaster.

People were dying, cars were skidding, accidents occurring and the treads of *Firestone tyres* were separating since 1998. But the company turned a blind eye until 2000 when the National Highway Safety Association launched a massive investigation. After much wavering, tens of deaths and hundreds of injuries, **Bridgestone** finally accepted the blame, announcing one of the largest recalls in US history of 6.5 million tyres.[4] Bridgestone managers made a mistake to keep mum and not take the bull by its horn to resolve reported accidents.

In some companies, fraudulent schemes go on for years, until these come to light somehow. Keeping things under wraps helps con artists to milk the system to their advantage. The American international banking giant **Wells Fargo**, like Volkswagen, practised fraudulent acts involving creation of fake accounts for years, and when the schemes came to light, it suffered unmitigated PR debacles.

A waiting game is a PR fiasco. **British Airways** delayed too long to address bad headlines when it was damned for the cancellation of hundreds of flights in May 2017 after an IT failure.[5] Similarly, **G4S**, the world's biggest security company, was denounced during the 2012 London Olympics for not hiring enough security guards and organizers had to bring in the army. They gave just two weeks' notice before the opening ceremony that they would not be able to provide all 10,000 guards they had agreed to, without much remorse. G4S's then head, Nick Buckles, later described the situation as 'humiliating shambles'.[6] The whole affair cost the company more than £70 million ($110 million) and significant loss of image.

Tailpiece

Sadly, even companies of international repute do not follow the basic rules of PR—humility, transparency and regret.

When a big fire spreads, it is difficult to control the damage. It is common sense to douse it when it just starts simmering. Thrusting the truth under the rugs, hoping divine intervention will work, is a lousy strategy.

Negative Is Not Positive

Can negative consequences be turned on their head to create a positive impact?

That is what **Philip Morris** thought would do on smoking-related deaths. Cheekily, they released results in 2001 of a study conducted in the Czech Republic audaciously proving that smokers' deaths had 'positive effects' financially for the Czech government! They said smoking helped to save around $150 million, including saving 'between 940 million and 1.2 billion korunas ($25–$30 million) in healthcare, pension and public-housing costs due to the early deaths of smokers'. It was a PR calamity.[7] The company was said to have cancelled similar further studies.

While there is a popular saying that 'there are three types of lies—lies, damned lies and statistics', but to take it to the extent Philip Morris did to justify smoking is ridiculous. It is a massive error to assume members of the public are as malleable as statistics is.

Tailpiece

Good product or service speaks for itself. No amount of storytelling, PR or marketing gimmickry can make a suboptimal or incomplete product or service a great one. Imagining that the public can be tricked through hocus-pocus is a grave error.

Don't Be Silly

Acting foolishly is an irresponsible act, but to boast about it is simply ridiculous.

Martin Shkreli, the CEO of **Turing Pharmaceuticals**, became the subject of significant criticism in September 2015 after the company boosted the price of the lifesaving drug *Daraprim* by over 5,000 per cent after acquiring the drug in August. Not only did Shkreli defend the move, but he actually boasted of his business prowess and kept making comments about how women find him very appealing.[8] These terrible mistakes made him pay heavily, as he was arrested a few months later on fraud charges and was fired.[9]

In another shocking event, the 9/11 episode to any New Yorker reflects the worst of fears. To add fuel to the miserable thought, in 2009 the US Department of Defence organized an Air Force One photo-op when all of a sudden the New Yorkers saw a plane flying oddly low over the city, pursued by a fighter jet. This was done without notifying the New Yorkers, which created widespread panic throughout lower Manhattan, with many people evacuating their offices. President Obama was enraged over the irresponsible act. The official responsible resigned.

How can anyone do acts which are apparently foolish? Sentiments of consumers or members of the public should be considered before any action or promotion is planned. Images can be sullied through idiotic acts.

Tailpiece

Public memory is usually short. Businesses tend to assume customers will be quick to look over the past based on previous experiences. The good news is that corporate disrepute is typically fleeting. The bad news is: This cannot be assumed for all time. A competitor may just get in, put a superior product and usurp you. Hence, tell a good story, and not a silly one. To assume customers are stupid is utterly bizarre.

Crisis of Confidence or Character

High-profile PR howlers have proved costly to a wide range of enterprises.

Rupert Murdoch's **News International** (now **News UK**) denied for years that phone hacking was widespread at the *News of the World* and asserted it was the work of one crook reporter. But only when in 2011 several civil claims threatened to expose the lousy practice, did the company switch ploys. It opened up to the police, setting up a compensation system for victims and issuing a public apology.[10]

Likewise, **FIFA**, world football's governing body, spent more than a decade repudiating that its executive committee members were accepting pay-offs for allotting attractive rights deals and awarding World Cup play locations. The veil got lifted in 2015 when criminal investigations were opened in the United States and Switzerland.[11,12]

In situations of such high-profile PR gaffes and before working out the right strategy for handling these disasters, you must first identify whether it is a crisis of 'competence' or 'character'.

'Competence-crisis' examples would be the lithium-ion battery defects in Boeing's *787-Dreamliner* aircraft or *Ford Kuga* catching fire, killing a man. While product incompetence can immediately affect sales, 'character-crisis' may have long-term implications. Instances of character failures are living legends Martha Stewart or Rajat Gupta denying their involvement in 'white-collar' crimes, but ultimately getting convicted. Not distinguishing the PR disasters of 'character' from 'competence' would lead to an inappropriate approach to heal the bruise in consumer and public memories.

Whether it is a crisis of confidence or character, an organization's reputation needs to be protected and salvaged if it is ever on the block. Emphasize business' positive track record so far, take responsibility, talk to affected customers or people directly, avoid being vague, have a fall-back crisis management plan and decide on the spokesperson.

Tailpiece

On the lighter side, it is said that it takes four PR persons to change a bulb: one to assess, one to replace, one to write the holding statement and one to be the spokesperson!

Allegations Are Killers

Most in India would have some relationship with one of the most noticeable Indian brands, the ICICI Bank. Be it an account holder, borrower or just an ATM user, the omnipresent bank touches almost everyone.

In March 2018, however, most of the citizens were in for a shock! The media carried headline stories of possible ill-governance while sanctioning loans by ICICI bank's CEO herself, Ms Chanda Kochhar. It took the bank's board three months to institute a probe into the allegations, while denying anything was wrong during the interim period. A PR debacle came into its making.

Two top-notch celebrities were accused of sexual misconduct. Cristiano Ronaldo, the star footballer and Nike brand ambassador, and US President Donald Trump, Trump-Tower endorser. Brands represented by these personalities came under fire. The accusations therefore needed to be handled aptly and promptly.

Have you ever been 'framed' by a malicious lie? Or has this happened to someone you know? If so, then you are a victim of one of the growing social injustices of our times.

Hundreds and thousands of accusations are made in a year, and some of these, unfortunately, include intent of extracting some compensation.

A company's morale can get shattered when employees see media reports of their bosses embroiled in ethical, sexual or financial scandals; it slays goodwill created over the years.

Right or wrong, accusations have the potential to inflict great pain on both, the alleged person and the business. It is important to take immediate action to appoint credible people to investigate the suspected misconduct, to file police complaint when required and to make public actions taken. If the allegations have been made in the public domain, then media response is helpful. Silence is not golden when a carnal transgression is alleged.

In early 2017, allegations were made about sexual harassment for over two years on the Indian news portal **ScoopWhoop** co-founder Suparn Pandey. During the same period, the founder of the Indian web-series producer **The Viral Fever** (TVF), Arunabh Kumar, was accused by multiple women of sexual infringements.

When TVF's founder CEO was accused of sexual harassment under the pseudonym 'Indian Fowler', the company handled it clumsily. It denied categorically the existence of any employee fitting the description of the anonymous whistle-blower. What was pathetic was the human-chain-like defensive and threatening stance taken by TVF without even exploring the need of an investigation. Lack of sensitivity and grace in handling allegations is a huge mistake that adds to the damage already inflicted.[13]

Sometimes the handling of allegations gets very silly. When ScoopWhoop's co-founder was dumped with a harassment case, the company had the cheek to say—'will take action if found guilty', and that they were 'following the rule book on workplace harassment'. Unfortunately, the comments did not provide much comfort to the 40 per cent women workforce in the company.

The business world is full of stories about the misuse of power and harassment. Many are adept at cover-up and denials. Some victims get justice, while most go down unheard and unresolved. However, anonymous complaints are not without controversies. But the possibility of closing allegations without even a probability of investigations is poor governance. Such behaviour irks more than it satisfies any—a slip-up that is best avoided.

Allegations could be on many fronts—corruption, fraud, tax evasion, money laundering, sexism and racism, to name a few.

When companies cannot handle allegations quickly, advertisers and customers often chastise. Bill O'Reilly, perhaps the biggest star in cable news, faced multiple allegations of sexual harassment, but his employer, **Fox News**, sat on the allegations. When dozens of advertisers deserted his show, the news channel had to buckle in April 2017 and fired the famed anchor. The company, which promotes public opinion, failed miserably to address its own public image. It had to eat a humble pie to avoid public shame.

Tailpiece

Whether the allegations made are true or not, only time can reveal. But the lack of an immediate PR action can create insurmountable harm with adverse consequences!

I Am Sorry

The three simple words can calm down many a frayed mind, but, unfortunately, not often said.

When a passenger sitting inside an aircraft holding a valid ticket was dragged down by the security of **United Airlines** in April 2017 to make space for an airlines staff, social media were shocked. Cellphone video of the violent eviction became viral within hours.

Oscar Munoz, United Airlines' boss, recalled his 'shame' on watching the clippings, but the contrition came almost 48 hours after the incident—by the time millions had seen the awful airlines behaviour—and grave damage was done to United's image.[14] The company's share prices fell by 4 per cent. United Airlines' chief, reacting to the episode of dragging out a passenger from his seat, made three attempts to explain the situation and fell on his face every time. In his first attempt, he callously used the now infamous words that the passenger had to be 're-accommodated'. It just lacked any repentance. In his second attempt, he blamed the passenger, saying he was 'belligerent'. And only in his third statement after two days did he offer 'deepest apologies'. He obviously missed his moment.

In early 2018, India's **IndiGo** airlines removed a Bengaluru-based passenger when he allegedly complained about mosquitoes. The airlines took time to express repentance and the government had to institute an enquiry to soothe frayed passenger tempers. It is not the right way to protect public image for an airline which has been battling alleged passenger complaints for 'discourteous and rude' behaviour.

It is common sense that sincerity, transparency and humility should prevail in communication expressing contrition. But it needs to be done quickly in this age of superfast social media.

One of the most popular consumer magazines *Cosmopolitan*, which generally focuses on physical attractiveness, in April 2017, tweeted: 'How This Woman Lost 44 Pounds Without *ANY* Exercise'. It featured a photo of a fit woman in a pink lace-up crop top. Readers who clicked on the link to find out more about the astonishing weight loss secret were taken aback to find that the woman has been diagnosed with a rare cancer.[15] It was an exasperating story on slimming down. *Cosmo* simply later changed the headline to 'A Serious Health Scare Helped Me Love My Body

More than Ever'. Readers waited for days for an apology but it never came. *Cosmo* did not own up to this insensitive mistake, a terrible PR gaffe to say the least.

Tailpiece

'Sorry' is the fastest way to solve the toughest situation, yet the hardest word to utter. In the commercial world, it is good to say so and, that too, well on time! It soothes many a bludgeoning sentiment.

PR Rep: A Scapegoat

When calamitous conditions ensnare organizations due to either misdemeanours or poor judgement on the part of powers that be, public image takes a beating. PR managers are supposed to create a positive impression of the company they represent or douse fires in case of poor publicity. The situation sometime gets so tricky that the PR manager becomes the scapegoat.

The ride-hailing company **Uber's** communications head left in a huff in April 2017, when CEO Travis Kalanick faced accusations of sexism and sexual harassment in the workplace and after a video surfaced showing him haranguing a driver. It is understood that things became too hard for the PR lady to handle when the boss himself was getting beyond reproach.

Tailpiece

Passing the buck is a fairly common approach in the corporate world. By definition, PR handles reputation and information—rather pliable subjects. Hence, it becomes sometimes easy to make PR managers hold-the-can during the ignominy. It is a mistake which organizations make, but is often practised to save the skin of powers that be.

Retrieve PR Rupture

Profits significantly below market expectations, harsh consumer complaints about a product, serious staff allegations against the

CEO and so on can make the best of PR specialists freeze in their seat.

Bad news or negative developments can mortgage a company's reputation, creating serious reputational debt. Not handling it properly or not communicating enough can result in colossal damage to a corporate's repute. Salvaging the situation is important. Here are some tips that may help avoid often-committed PR slip-ups:

- *Take charge:* If the company is in trouble or negative news emanates, the leadership should take charge and not flee. Addressing key concerns and highlighting achievements helps to cool the situation. Airlines companies often get exposed to emergency situations where no one seems to be in charge—delayed or cancelled flights with passengers left to fend for themselves. An infamous episode took place on Valentine's Day in 2007 when nine **JetBlue** flights at JFK airport were delayed for up to 11 hours because of harsh weather, and keeping 1,000 passengers trapped in the runway-bound planes for the entire period. It was horrific with drinking water depleting, toilets clogging, and passengers not allowed to deplane and just walk to the terminal, which was within sight. The worse, there was no one to take charge, give a decision and calm the scared customers. The service-oriented brand took a beating.[16]

- *Empathetic, positive response:* Mistakes can happen; everyone can falter. A business could have made a one-time error, ending even in loss of lives but that does not mean everything has collapsed. That the organization produces goods and services safely for years should be brought out into the open. For example, railway companies run a public service but with great risk of accidents—and they do occur, which may entail loss of lives. Communicating the positive side of the business that safely carries thousands of people daily is important. This is what happened when a **Virgin** Train crashed in Cumbria in 2007. Virgin's boss Sir Richard Branson promptly responded: 'I have been in the transportation business for nearly 25 years. We have transported half a million passengers and fortunately have never had to be in this situation before. One can only imagine what it was like for the passengers.' The message of empathy cooled the sentiments of the public.

- *Definitive response:* Avoid vague and impersonal reactions. An ambiguous and elusive response creates more trouble than healing the wounds. The 1984 leak of toxic methyl isocyanate gas at a **Union Carbide** plant in Bhopal produced history's worst industrial disaster, killing over 15,000–20,000 people, which stunned the world. The plant manager declined to discuss the irregularities. The managing director of the company refused to talk about details of the accident or the conditions that produced it, but said, 'There is no way with 14 factories and 28 sales branches all over the country and 9,000 employees that I could personally supervise any plant on a week-to-week basis.' How vague and irresponsible a statement it could be when such a catastrophe strikes an organization.

- *Talk to customers directly:* If there is a problem, let your customers know the status. Tell them what you are doing and how the customer interest is utmost in the company's mind. Avoiding communication adds to the grief. When **Nestle India** was sent a notice in 2015 by the FDA authorities saying that they had found high levels of lead and MSG in Maggi noodles, the company blocked all lines of communication with consumers. For more than a fortnight, barring a computer-generated statement, there was no word from Nestle, not even a two-minute reply. Not speaking to the consumers only adds fire to fuel.[17]

- *Have plan B in place:* With Facebook, Twitter and WhatsApp exploding like no one had ever predicted, these new media not only are the bearer of your achievements but also could kill the business ambitions overnight through bad publicity. A proactive and clear approach should be followed while handling complaints, especially for social media.

Acknowledge that something has happened, even when a solution is yet unavailable. For example, **Coca-Cola**, in its enthusiasm to greet Russians in its New Year, tweeted in 2016 on VK, the most popular Russian social media network, showing a cartoon with a snow-covered map of the country. It seemed perfectly all right, except that the map of Russia did not include Crimea. Russians went ballistic as they posted pictures pouring the soft drink into toilets with the hashtag #BanCocaCola. Coke quickly published the map again after a few days, this time including Crimea, and apologized. But by including Crimea, Coca-Cola unleashed a backlash in Ukraine, where demands for a boycott of the soft drink got under way. Coca-Cola should have had a contingency plan but failed—a marketing plot going terribly wrong.

- *No comments is a strict 'no-no':* A sticky situation or an uncomfortable development is the time when people would want to know more. But the most common deliverance from the PR team is: 'No comments'. That is a PR gaffe. 'No comments' is generally presumed to be an admission of guilt—best avoided therefore.

- *Single spokesperson:* Decide who will represent the company in communicating its standpoint. It need not be the CEO. In fact, it should not be. The first point of contact in communicating with the media, analysts and investors should be the designated spokesperson, and CFO is a good option. CEO or members of the board should speak only when there is a strategic need to do so.

Tailpiece

Goodwill is any organization's greatest asset. It needs to be protected as if you are protecting your own life. PR is about making the public understand and appreciate the company's viewpoint. It is as good as the extent it can be backed up through the narrative being created and shared. Unless the story is real and can be supported, PR efforts will have egg on its face. Not recognizing it is hara-kiri.

In Closing

Days after a successful marketing launch in the summer of 2010 of iPhone 4, Apple was hit by reports that if you gripped the phone in a seemingly natural way, signal strength would drop off. This was catastrophic news as consumers were already suffering from dropped calls in poor AT&T coverage areas. For weeks, people made fun of Apple. But by mid-July, the issue was gone and pretty much forgotten—a seemingly unachievable PR feat. During the same period, however, BP made a mess of its oil spill disaster in the Gulf of Mexico and created a PR nightmare.[18]

What did the PR teams do in the above two seemingly difficult scenarios? Apple accepted the problem and worked on it. BP went weirdly arrogant and depicted disconnection from the seriousness of the event. The outcome is for everyone to see—Apple survived and BP agonized.

Public relation is a soft issue; and softer is corporate, product and brand image in the minds of people. It is all about perceptions. A PR disaster can significantly alter the equation against any corporation. While the basis, severity, type, effect and extent of incidents are often difficult to assess, swift professional handling helps to cool any possible wounds inflicted.

The job of PR is to build, preserve and safeguard reputation. Thus, the PR manager needs to be aware and informed of all developments that may impact business repute. But the bad news is PR managers do not often have access to all strategic information within an establishment nor do they usually have the clout to ensure an ideal organizational behaviour. How do you manage image when there is little management over events?—Mistakes many organizations make.

References

1. Hakim D. VW's crisis strategy: Forward, reverse, U-turn. The New York Times [Internet]. 2016 Feb 26. Available from: https://www.nytimes.com/2016/02/28/business/international/vws-crisis-strategy-forward-reverse-u-turn.html

2. Ewing J. Ex-Volkswagen C.E.O. charged with fraud over diesel emissions. The New York Times [Internet]. 2018 May 3. Available from: https://www.nytimes.com/2018/05/03/business/volkswagen-ceo-diesel-fraud.html

3. Carey N, Shepardson D. Volkswagen pleads guilty in U.S. court in diesel emissions scandal. Reuters [Internet]. 2017 Mar 10. Available from: https://www.reuters.com/article/us-volkswagen-emissions-idUSKBN16H1W4

4. History. Bridgestone/Firestone announces massive tire recall. History [Internet]. Available from: https://www.history.com/this-day-in-history/bridgestonefirestone-announces-massive-tire-recall

5. The Guardian. BA cancels more than 100 Heathrow flights after snow and ice. The Guardian [Internet]. 2017 Dec 11. Available from: https://www.theguardian.com/uk-news/2017/dec/11/british-airways-cancels-100-flights-snow-ice-delayed

6. Lindlar C. G4S Olympic security blunder: It's not the first time the firm have come under fire. HuffPost [Internet]. 2012 Jul 7. Available from https://www.huffingtonpost.co.uk/2012/07/12/g4s-security-olympics_n_1667268.html?guccounter=1&guce_referrer_us=aHR0cHM6Ly93d3cuZ29vZ2xlLmNvbS8&guce_referrer_cs=THKvYdjrg32k1uEFKolHfg

7. Public finance balance of smoking in the Czech Republic: Arthur D Little Report. Tobaccofreekids [Internet]. 2000 Nov 28. Available from: https://www.tobaccofreekids.org/assets/content/what_we_do/industry_watch/philip_morris_czech/pmczechstudy.pdf

8. Pollack A. Drug goes from $13.50 a tablet to $750, overnight. The New York Times [Internet]. 2015 Sep 20. Available from: https://www.nytimes.com/2015/09/21/business/a-huge-overnight-increase-in-a-drugs-price-raises-protests.html

9. Smith A. Martin Shkreli sentenced to 7 years in prison for fraud. CNN Money [Internet]. 2018 Apr 18. Available from: https://money.cnn.com/2018/03/09/news/martin-shkreli-sentencing/index.html

10. BBC. Phone-hacking trial explained. BBC News [Internet]. 2014 Jun 25. Available from: https://www.bbc.com/news/uk-24894403

11. Ruiz RR. Justice Dept. escalates inquiry on global sports corruption. The New York Times [Internet]. 2018 Jan 31. Available from: https://www.nytimes.com/2018/01/31/sports/fifa-ioc-usoc-iaaf.html

12. Conn D. How the FBI won 'the World Cup of fraud' as Fifa scandal arrives in court. The Guardian [Internet]. 2017 Nov 6. Available from:

https://www.theguardian.com/football/2017/nov/06/fifa-scandal-fbi-new-york-trial-chuck-blazer-sepp-blatter

13. India Today. Are there over 50 sexual harassment accusations against TVF CEO Arunabh Kumar now? India Today [Internet]. 2017 Mar 15. Available from: https://www.indiatoday.in/fyi/story/arunabh-kumar-sexual-harassment-50-complaints-against-tvf-ceo-965641-2017-03-15

14. Czarnecki S. Timeline of a crisis. PRWeek [Internet]. 2017 Jun 6. Available from: https://www.prweek.com/article/1435619/timeline-crisis-united-airlines

15. Amatulli J. Cosmo's headline about cancer survivor's weight loss is a doozy. The HuffPost [Internet]. 2017 Apr 11. Available from: https://www.huffingtonpost.in/entry/cosmos-headline-about-cancer-survivors-weight-loss-is-a-doozy_us_58eced9ae4b0df7e204585a0?ec_carp=2566713079084490522

16. Hanna J. JetBlue's Valentine's Day crisis. Harvard Business School Working Knowledge [Internet]. 2008 Mar 31. Available from: https://hbswk.hbs.edu/item/jetblues-valentines-day-crisis

17. Comcowich W. PR crisis management lessons from the Nestlé Maggi noodle controversy. Glean.info [Internet]. 2018 Oct 4. Available from:https://glean.info/pr-crisis-management-lessons-from-the-nestle-maggi-noodle-controversy/

18. Kimberly JR. How BP blew crisis management 101. CNN [Internet]. 2010 Jun 21. Available from: http://edition.cnn.com/2010/OPINION/06/21/kimberly.bp.management.crisis/index.html

WHEN THE BOSS BUNGLES

'Uneasy lies the head that wears a crown' is, perhaps, one of the most popular phrases. Yet most of us would keep dreaming of sitting in the corner room of a corporation's office. CEOs often enjoy, or at least expect to savour unbridled power and mouth-watering benefits, but their seats are generally hot and turbid.

Numerous are the reasons for which CEOs are shown the door, especially scapegoating, which is as old as human nature. Bizarrely, an Austrian aerospace parts-maker, **FACC**, fired its CEO after his apparent mistakes led to the firm being defrauded by €42 million ($47 million) in a whaling attack.[1] What transpired was a fraudster impersonating as the CEO or senior board member e-mailing a member of the finance department to request money transfer out of the company. The CEO got the sack and this was found to be a nice escape route for the board.

In another bizarre instance, **Hong Kong Express** sacked its CEO after the budget airline came in for harsh criticism for causing travel pandemonium during the first week of the 2017 busy October holiday season with a series of unexpected flight cancellations.

CEOs are supposed to have their hands in every pot—juggling everything that whizzes past the chief's table while keeping sharp eyes on all departments and major tasks. The boss can only hope that nothing falls through the cracks.

Many factors influence business performance. When any team or business goes south, it is normal to blame the captain. The boss may or may not be responsible, as things may or may not be controllable. But the chief is the one to take the heat when things are under fire. To learn from the situation is the best outcome for the CEO to engage in. Inexperience is often a great experience to have.

Bossy Bloopers

To err is human, and bosses are no exception. Even the best of the very best sometimes gets it wrong. And, surely, the lesser mortals do get it wrong many a time.

Underestimating competition is a major mistake many make. The incomparable Bill Gates of **Microsoft** underestimated the search engine market. When he realized that he should focus on it and launched *Bing*, it was too late to compete with *Google*, which was way ahead of the rest. So did health tracker **Fitbit** CEO James Park, ignoring Apple's long announced entry into *Apple Watch* and *HealthKit*, which led to Fitbit sliding. The delayed response was similar to smartphone company **BlackBerry** founder Mike Lazaridis's denial, post-iPhone launch.

Wrong judgement is often committed by the tried and tested CEOs. When the former head of Apple retail, Ronald Johnson, took the helm of the struggling retail chain **JCPenney** in 2011, the failing corporation seemed to have got a saviour. Unfortunately, Johnson committed a series of bad errors. He fired the company's long-time ad agency, laid-off thousands of middle managers and stopped discount sales. The company saw its revenue sinking by 25 per cent in 2012, and Johnson was sacked in 2013.[2]

Distinguishing yourself from the crowd is any marketer's success slogan. But even the chiefs of the largest corporates often ignore this simple mantra. Steve Ballmer, while being at the helm of **Microsoft** until February 2014, constantly fell short of Apple's launches. Ballmer launched the *Zune* to compete with *iTunes*, only to be five years too late. He launched the *Surface RT tablet*, but it did not sell, resulting in a loss of nearly a billion dollars. He failed to separate his products from those available in the market.

Inadequate preparation while launching a product is a major CEO faux pas. Trying to be an early mover or to be the first in the market is a good strategy, but one should do thorough preparation and testing before any launch. Even Tim Cook of **Apple** made the cardinal error of launching in 2012 its *iOS 6 Maps*, which was peppered with bugs. This gave *Google Maps* an edge and Apple thereafter continued to play second fiddle to its competitor.[3]

Frauds are business killers. Cheating, lying and deceiving are all grave mistakes any CEO can indulge in. There are numerous examples of how shortcuts to making a fast buck have led to destruction of businesses. Ken Lay's corruption killed **Enron Corporation**. He then dumped his own stocks, but encouraged his employees to buy them saying that Enron will bounce back—utter lies throughout. **Merrill Lynch** CEO, John Thain spent $1.2 million hard-earned corporate fund on antique furniture, carpeting and curtains for the troubled bank's executive offices, and lost his job in 2009.[4] Vijay Mallya of **Kingfisher Airlines** threw multi-million dollar parties when ₹9,000 crore ($1.3 billion) worth debts were lying unpaid to his bankers. The money could have been spent for better cause and purpose.

Tailpiece

Everyone makes mistakes, and CEOs are no exceptions. Mistakes often flutter by in our daily lives, leaving little space to ponder over the gaffes. However, when howlers get noticed, learning from it is the key to avoid recurrence.

Autocratic Boss

Many of you may not have heard the name **Borgward**. In the mid-1950s, for a brief period, the second-biggest German automaker after Volkswagen was neither Mercedes nor BMW. It was Borgward, bootstrapped by the impulsive entrepreneur-engineer Carl Borgward, producing stylish cars for the middle-class Germans. Unable to pay its creditors, the company wound up in 1961 despite having a technically superior car. The last of the piece-de-resistance the company made was the *Isabella*, a midmarket car introduced in 1954, which outperformed the competition.[5]

But why did Borgward fail? The main problem was the founder, who was an autocrat. He ran the company as his own fiefdom. When the cash flow crisis hit in 1961, Borgward found few friends. He clashed with the Bremen government which had made a bailout loan to the company as it was a big employer. Fed up with Borgward's attitude, government officials stopped disbursing the loan. He became his own worst enemy. Borgward lost control over the company. (The storied German carmaker's grandson is now trying to make a comeback in China under the *Borgward* brand name.)

Autocratic behaviours are rationalized by its executioners as being nimble footed and quick decision-makers. This is an awful justification! Arrogance is hated and despotism is looked down upon. If the leader cannot instil confidence and motivate performance, and if it is all about self-esteem and ego, what good it is to be the boss?

Reputation was shredded when the former chief executive of the **Royal Bank of Scotland**, Fred Goodwin, was stripped of his knighthood by the Queen of England for his role in the creation of the biggest recession since the Second World War. Goodwin was famous for his autocratic style. He was known to be a control freak. It is reported that he even designed his Christmas cards and micromanaged the construction of his new head office, costing over $600 million, but apparently was blissfully ignorant of the vast toxic loans his bank extended. RBS collapsed, and the British government had to rescue it through the citizens' hard-earned money.[6]

The French multimedia giant **Vivendi's** Jean-Marie Messier was also an autocrat. It is reported that he misused corporate funds and spent $17 million on a flat in New York for his personal use whenever he visited the city. The flamboyant businessman, who took the global group to the brink of bankruptcy after a spending spree that crippled the company with debt, admitted in 2010 that he had 'made mistakes'.[7]

However, could there be 'enlightened' dictators in the corporate world? The brilliant but egoistic Steve Jobs ruled his company, Apple, with an iron fist and demanded absolute secrecy and loyalty from his employees. The famous Henry Ford was known as a tough leader who monitored and controlled every major decision of his auto company and monitored his employees even outside of work. Tesla's Elon Musk, the great innovator of today, makes extreme demands and sets unrealistic deadlines for his employees.

These are all successful CEOs creating immense value to their companies and to humankind, though with dictatorial streaks.

If you are an employee of an organization, you are normally not expected to visualize strategies nor write the vision statements. You are supposed to follow your leader in doing what you are supposed to do, with passion and earnestness. Following your leader is a cool act.

If the leader is a visionary, motivating and communicative, dictatorial strains may not entail value destruction.

But when autocratic leaders are blind to their mistakes, they often discourage others from bringing the 'bad news' or sharing harsh realities by their colleagues and employees. Lack of encouragement to opinions and consensus building within a team may lead to catastrophic consequences. Unless benevolent and well meaning, dictatorial leadership styles are often mistaken steps to lead.

Tailpiece

Leadership is not about a popularity contest, but allure and appeal help to lead. Charismatic leadership is a style which involves influencing, inspiring and magnetically drawing people, juxtaposing autocratic style.

It is pertinent to note that managing people is a lot more than sheer personality and disposition; continued success needs many other attributes in a leader—dictatorship or charisma are not the only traits that are relevant.

Unspeakable CEO Speaks

Intelligent as they are—the CEOs guide others and run businesses. But their tongues often let them down—making statements which are damaging and unforgivable. They are supposed to be futurists.

However, they may make the cardinal mistake of opening their gab and make statements that may have damaging implications for their organizations.

Would you believe that a CEO's comment can bring his business empire down? Perhaps the most infamous four-letter word ever uttered was by Gerald Ratner, chairman of the world's largest chain of jewellers in 1991. He described some of his store's products as 'crap'. Though meant to be a joke cracked during the course of a conference speech, the **Ratners Group** slid into a mess. All of a sudden, the worldwide 2,500 high-street jewellery shops became a no-go for customers. Ratner had to leave his company, unable to recover from his 'terrible mistake'.[8] (Ratner now runs the web-based jewellery retail business *geraldonline.com* set up in 2002; his Ratners Group has since been renamed the Signet Group.)[9]

An ill-conceived statement of a chief executive can cost him or her the job. Chairman of one of the world's biggest advertising company **Saatchi & Saatchi**, belonging to the *Publicis Groupe*, Kevin Roberts was fired in August 2016 when he made dismissive comments about gender diversity in the ad industry. He said that the debate about gender diversity on Madison Avenue 'is all over' and that he did not spend 'any time' on gender issues at his agencies. He also said that the problem was 'way worse' in other industries and suggested that women were happier in non-management roles.[10] These statements were good enough for him to be shown the door.

One of the worst manmade disasters has been an explosion on an oil platform, killing 11 workers, sending over 3 million gallons of oil gushing into the Gulf of Mexico and fouling hundreds of miles of shoreline. **BP**, one of the largest companies in the world, was held responsible for the oil blowout from the Deepwater Horizon drilling rig in the Gulf of Mexico in 2010.

But its former CEO, Tony Hayward, was unrepentant. 'I think the environmental impact of this disaster is likely to have been very, very modest,' whined Hayward. He made the matter worse by complaining 'what the hell did we do to deserve this' and demanded, 'I would like my life back.'[11] Hayward was replaced six months after the incident. The CEO's remark was not only a PR disaster, but ultimately it did not help the cause of BP from paying almost $62 billion in clean-up costs, fines and compensation. CEOs cannot lack sensitivity.

A CEO known for his often loose remarks and antagonizing people is **Ryanair** chief Michael O'Leary. He once called his own airline customers 'stupid' when some of them forgot to print out boarding passes. But when he took on the environmentalists, it was sheer contempt. He remarked: 'The best thing you can do with the environmentalists is shoot them. These head-bangers want to make air travel the preserve of the rich. They are luddites marching us back to the 18th century. If preserving the environment means stopping poor people flying so the rich can fly, then screw it.'[12] When a CEO of any company makes such comments, you would agree that it does not augur well for any one, let alone the organization's goodwill.

You do not often hear a CEO threatening to kill someone, that too a future president. And that is exactly what happened at **PacketSled**, a US-based cyber security start-up. After the US presidential election, an inebriated Matt Harrigan said on Facebook that he was going to kill Donald Trump.[13]

CEOs are not only judged by how they guide and treat people, but also how they talk to and about them.

Tailpiece

The business lesson is clear—for better or worse, the CEO is often the face of the corporation. When the CEO's mouth misfires, a blunder gets committed as the corporate reputation, culture and its long-term performance suffers. CEOs are supposed to be a cut above the rest—but they often have such slips of tongue that even earthly mortals would feel sorry for the bungles.

Sack the Boss

They say it is lonely at the top. The corner office occupant's career has as much swivel as his chair—has a potential upside for huge pay-offs or probable downsides in times of failure. CEOs are often changed or fired when one wants to signal a new start—the boss thus remains vulnerable.

CEOs are now getting sacked more often than they were in the past. A study appearing in the November 2016 issue of *The New Yorker* found that the percentage of forced CEO exits tripled between 1970 and 2006. Another study depicted that boards now 'aggressively fire CEOs for poor industry-adjusted performance'. In addition, the average duration of a boss's tenure has fallen. In 1984, 35 per cent of CEOs had been in the job for 10 years or more; in 2000, only 15 per cent had. By 2009, according to one study, the average tenure at the world's biggest companies had fallen to around six years. (It has rebounded somewhat since, because CEOs are naturally less likely to be fired when businesses are turning healthy profits.)

The chief executive's chair is a tough one to fill and retain. According to the Conference Board quoted in the *Harvard Business Review* magazine, from 2000 to 2013, about a quarter of the CEO departures in the Fortune 500 companies were involuntary. This is terrible news as top-boss turnover costs a staggering over $100 billion in lost market value annually, a global 2014 PwC study of 2,500 largest companies revealed.

Business heads are sometimes forced to resign when they seemingly act against some popular public opinion. CEOs often commit errors of judgement when they take positions on public opinions, which need not necessarily be related to the business they are running. **Mozilla Firefox** chief executive and inventor of programming language Javascript, Brendan Eich, had to step down in April 2014 after an online dating service urged a boycott of the company's web browser because of a donation Eich made to opponents of gay marriage. The software company came under fire almost immediately after appointing Eich as the CEO.[14]

In fact, way back in 2008, Eich gave money to oppose the legalization of gay marriage in California, a very controversial issue especially for a company that vaunts its policy of inclusiveness and diversity. The company knew about it, yet did not act. 'We didn't act like you'd expect Mozilla to act', wrote Mozilla Executive Chairwoman Mitchell Baker in a blog post. 'We didn't move fast enough to engage with people once the controversy started. We're sorry.'[15]

Some CEOs resign, taking responsibility for their deeds. Tadashi Ishii, chief of Japanese ad agency **Dentsu**, resigned in December 2016 taking moral responsibility after a 24-year female employee jumped to her death from the company dormitory on the Christmas of 2015. She tweeted to her friends of enduring harassment by her bosses and gruelling long hours of work.[16] Not caring about employee welfare is indeed a mistake which CEOs can ill afford to commit.

Discretion is the better part of valour. CEOs owing to their position of power get undue attention from employees of the opposite sex, especially the subordinates. Ease of access and undue hero worship lead to CEOs sometimes committing the cardinal mistake of entering into relationships with colleagues, which could be scandalous and fraught with risks.

In 2013, the IT outsourcing company **iGate Corp** sacked chief executive, Phaneesh Murthy, after a sexual harassment investigation by the company revealed that he had not disclosed a relationship with a subordinate.

Unfortunately, this was not his only instance of transgression. One of the industry's best-known executives, Phaneesh was earlier forced to quit India's second-biggest software services exporter Infosys Ltd in 2002, following a sexual harassment lawsuit, which was settled out of court.[17]

Phaneesh, of course, did not learn from his past behavioural lapse and repeated his faux pas only to be caught and thrown out.

Inappropriate styles of management lead to CEOs getting sacked. **Sanofi's** board in October 2014 ousted its chief executive of six years Chris Viehbacher, criticizing him for an authoritarian management style and lack of communication with the board.

Its CEO, who was known for straight talk and brusque management style, transformed the French pharma company, Sanofi, from a national champion into a global business. Serge Weinberg, the chairman, told that the board members did not disagree with the CEO's strategy, but were unhappy with his execution and failure to communicate with them.[18,19] Success in business is not everything. Chief executives need to remember that they do not operate in a vacuum. They need to be communicative and conduct themselves such that they are in the good books of the board and the principal shareholder groups.

Several CEOs lose their jobs owing to frauds committed on their employer. Position of power and greed overtaking discretion, chief executives often make roost from situational advantage.

Reebok India's CEO, Subhinder Singh Prem, was sacked in 2012 when he was found stealing products and fudging accounts by setting up secret warehouses. Similarly, Philip Clarke was sacked in July 2014 as CEO at **Tesco**, a British retailer, when a massive fraud and false accounting came to light.[20] Yet, in another instance, in a high-profile departure, Bob Diamond quit as **Barclays** CEO in 2012 after the bank was fined for trying to manipulate interbank lending rates.[21] These are instances of CEO blunders committed due to poor oversight, mismanagement or greed.

More often than not, CEOs are fired when they are unable to make their organizations perform financially according to expectations.

The year 2015 saw a bloodbath of European chiefs of banks. Peter Sands of **Standard Chartered** was sacked. Brady Dougan of **Credit Suisse** was shown the door. So were the joint chiefs of **Deutsche Bank**, Anshu Jain and Jürgen Fitschen. **Barclays** had enough of Antony Jenkins in 2015 after a three-year wobbly stint.

CXO departures create turmoil and uncertainties.

During 2010–2016, the one-time Indian pharmaceutical doyen, **Cipla**, had seen two different CEOs, as many chief operating officers and four CFOs. The company is experiencing challenging times in business. The Indian auto sector has a similar track record in recent times. Since 2010, **Honda** had five different CEOs, **Nissan Motor** and **GM** four, while **Volkswagen**, **Ford**, **Fiat** and **Tata Motors** had three CEOs, reports the *Economic Times*. Except Honda, all others have encountered dropped sales. However, **Maruti Suzuki** and **Hyundai** did not fire their top deck and yet posted good growth during the same period. It is a grave error to make the boss an easy scapegoat during troubled times!

When business bottom lines look shaky and slow, CEO positions become unsafe and uncertain.

Tailpiece

When the key person departs, it can create from ripples to storms in an organization. Boards need to take boundless care to handle the awfully sensitive situation, which could arise when the boss goes away—either being asked to go or on own volition.

Departing CEO Deeds

Leading a company is not rocket science—neither is it a stroll in the park. Even though the CEOs are on a leisurely stroll or running helter-skelter, they react differently when they are shown the door. Some protest, many resign nonchalantly, while several cry foul.

Some CEOs, when asked to go, make a lot of noise, protesting their removal. As did pizza-chain **Papa John's** founder John Schnatter when he was forced out in July 2018 after he made racist comments. He shot back saying he has 'no confidence' in the management team and his attorney remarked he wasn't 'going quietly'.[22]

Some go without a whimper, accepting the inevitable. When the Singaporean charity, the **National Kidney Foundation** terminated in November 2016 its CEO Edmund Kwok over a 'personal indiscretion' with a male staff member, Kwok went away quietly.

Sometimes CEO departures are made to look a tame affair. The outgoing CEO is given the fig leaf of a handing-over period and pay-offs, whereas in essence it is a case of sacking the business head. Chitra Ramakrishnan, the CEO of India's **National Stock Exchange (NSE)**, resigned in December 2016 citing 'personal reasons'. However, in all probability, Chitra had to resign when a forensic audit of NSE's algo-trading system found that there were manipulations and unfair preferential access to some stock brokers in algorithmic trading. Fraudulent intent or sheer oversight both can lead to undesirous consequences.

Many take the trouble of retiring gracefully by handing over tasks to the nominated successor. When **Intel** CEO, Paul Otellini, retired in 2012 after 40 years in service, there was prior planning and handing over to the successor. An orderly behaviour resulted in the continuity of purpose. Exit planning is important for any organization's sustained success.

The worse, however, perhaps is when the boss goes to town complaining bitterly of being fired and, then, squeaking that products sold are suboptimal. This is what happened when Lucinda Chambers, the fashion director of *British Vogue*, where she worked for 36 years, knocked the magazine off and trashed the entire fashion industry, after being sacked in 2017. According to her, glossy magazines do not empower women but encourage them to buy terribly overpriced stuffs that they do not need. She criticized some of the 'crap' magazine cover shoots she had produced, blaming in part Vogue's allegiances to major advertisers. She also suggested that Vogue had become an increasingly uninspiring read.[23,24] The question, however, is why did she continue to work for her employer her entire adult life, when she knew what she was delivering was just utter nonsense?

When CEOs, or for that matter almost anyone who leaves under a cloud, or even if not so, usually keep their mouth shut, the silence is partly due to a feeling of disgrace or of self-interest thinking a fight with an ex-employer does not help, or due to non-disparagement clauses signed while joining the organization. Be as it may be, when the leaving CEO speaks badly, it brings great harm to the business image. It would be a mistake not to consider the negative fallouts of such eventualities if any.

Tailpiece

The game of thrones is not without its share of thorns. We all know that the most coveted seat in 'Westeros' (the kingdom of premier fantasy) is the Iron Throne; similarly, in any office it is the so-called corner room. The high-profile chair can also become the cornerstone of rationalization for corporate mistakes, poor performance, bad business environment, fraud, greed, lack of confidence, or simply be made the scapegoat.

CEO vs Founders

Disaster often strikes when the trust between the founders of the business and those chosen to run the organization breaks down. The passing of the baton from the old entrepreneur to the new professional may fumble; professionalization efforts of entrepreneurial enterprise may get botched. In the quest for professionalization, the founder–CEO relationship is often found to be fragile and delicate.

Tatas and **Infosys** have been known benchmarks of good governance in the Indian business world. But when its founders fight with their anointed successors, the brittle bond between the owners and the managers snaps.

India's second-largest software services company **Infosys** co-founder and ex-chairman Narayana Murthy complained that there has been serious violation of the company's 'core values'— lapses in corporate governance; a seemingly high severance package for the former CFO; a revised compensation of $11 million to its CEO. In fact, he publicly regretted having handed over the reins in 2014 to a professional manager Vishal Sikka, who eventually resigned in a huff in 2017.

A similar story unfolded in the **Tata** Group, where its chairman, Ratan Tata, with much fanfare, handed over the keys of his family empire to Cyrus Mistry in 2012. Unfortunately, it ended in the biggest corporate spat in 2016, with Mistry being summarily sacked. Since his dismissal, Mistry disclosed, rightly or otherwise, various sleaze stories of the group taking place inside its much-vaunted walls.

These face-offs—between the highfliers of the past and the combatants of the present—negate a lot of value to any organization. Such squabbles consume enormous quantum of time and energy, diverting the management's attention to valueless endeavours.

How do things come to such a pass? Why do relationships go so sour between the entrepreneur and the new leadership? What should one do?

Very often the founder finds it difficult to stay out of management and give a free hand to the professional team appointed. Moving out of the corner office can be very gut-wrenching for the entrepreneur, yet important and necessary for the founder to take a call.

More often, than not, it is very important to delineate the powers of the CEO and distinguish these clearly from those of the founder. Sometimes the entrepreneur stays on as the chairperson, while others retire. But most of the times the founder expects to be kept informed and consulted for major decisions. And when this does not happen, trust breaks, relationship snaps and hell breaks loose.

Tailpiece

Every CEO having a founder lurking round the corner needs to take care of the tricky and yet possible frail relationships. Or else, it will be a potential death knell for the organization. It is about relationships and two-way ongoing communications. At the end, for success, it would involve the two people getting along and trusting each other in their endeavours.

Fire the Founder

The number of regal founders is limited; there are more working founders nowadays. Founder-entrepreneurs take risk and run around for money, men and material. Then they put them together after great effort and commence pursuing their business dreams. Some succeed. Many fail. Several grow, while others keep struggling for survival.

Should the founder remain forever? Is it a mistake to keep the founder as the beacon of hope for all times, just because the businessperson is the venture creator? Or should the founder be replaced as the business grows through tide and time?

Some insights have been thrown by Noam Wasserman, in his book titled *The Founder's Dilemmas*. The author has done research in the US environment, and the findings may not be applicable to all geographies—but these do provide some clues.

He analysed 212 American start-ups that sprang up in the late 1990s and early 2000s. He observed that most founders surrendered management control long before their companies went public. By the time the ventures were three years old, 50 per cent of founders were no longer the CEO; in year four, only 40 per cent were still in charge; and fewer than 25 per cent led their companies' initial public offerings. Several other researchers have also found similar trends in various industries and in other timelines.

Wasserman also said that almost three-quarters of founder CEOs are sacked rather than step down voluntarily. The major reason for these dismissals is that most founders do not make the best long-term chief executives, but they find the handover of control an agonizing loss. As a company grows, its very success often exposes the founder's lack of managerial skills, thus hastening the day a successor is required.

Most entrepreneurs are risk takers and hardworking souls, with a vision to convert an idea into reality. They can often be described as maverick, dogged, enthusiastic and obsessive. A sense of inherent optimism makes them tread the path of entrepreneurship, unlike many of us who are employees of corporations, howsoever senior we may be, where risk averseness, rationality, reality and a bit of pessimism overtake our thinking and approach. But entrepreneurs more often than not lack 360-degree managerial capabilities to endure a business over time.

An engineer by training could start a manufacturing set-up. But as it grows, the founder may lack financial skills to negotiate additional funding, recruiting and motivating its workforce, plan sales, develop marketing strategies and build a good process to prevent losses. Many of these skills could be foreign to the entrepreneur—and, at this stage, handing over to a professional would be a good bet to take. Not taking cognisance of this reality will be hara-kiri.

Many realize these entrepreneurial weaknesses well on time and decide to fire themselves. James Dyson, the British inventor of the dual-cyclone bag-less vacuum cleaner company **Dyson**, appointed Martin McCourt to run his company in 2001, and instead became 'chief engineer'. Both understood their respective strengths and joined hands to make a success out of their enterprise. (Martin left Dyson in 2012.)[25]

Some founders need to be fired for the larger good of the organization. Dov Charney, founder and CEO of **American Apparels** for 25 years, had to be pushed out of his job in August 2015. The board fired him, accusing misuse of company funds and sexually harassing his employees.[26] Similarly, the Indian real-estate search portal **housing.com** board brought in Jason Kothari in 2015 to ultimately replace mercurial co-founder Rahul Yadav.

Founders are invariably emotionally linked to the business that has been built from the scratch. Decision-making may be hinged more on sentiment rather than on facts and figures. I know of an entrepreneur who refuses to let go his long-time friend who looks after sales. Though he has become old and useless, the entrepreneur will not make any change due to the bond from the past. Such irrational decisions definitely impinge upon the successful running of a business.

Professional managers, venture capitalists and private equity funds, the so-called new-age investors, are guided by business results, preceding emotional bonding and historical experiences. Whoever delivers will be preferred—whether professionals or owners. Sometimes professionals are preferred. For instance, the

Indian e-commerce giant Flipkart, replaced the co-founders, its largest shareholder in 2017, by appointing its own employee as the CEO. However, some investors prefer the old over new—founders over professionals, like Jeff Bezos at Amazon, David Packard at HP, Akio Morita at Sony and Kiran Mazumdar-Shaw at India's Biocon Ltd.

Tailpiece

It will be a blunder for the founders to hang around even when their utility had been extinguished. But many are irreplaceable and some provide organizational continuity. There is no one-size-fits-all solution. Every CEO cannot be Bill Gates of Microsoft, but even he chose to hand over the reign to Steve Ballmer in 2000 after creating an unparalleled business venture.

A younger generation of founder-chief executives are now playing an active role in running their businesses with aplomb, led by Mark Zuckerberg of Facebook, Larry Page of Google's parent company Alphabet Inc and Bhavish Aggarwal of Ola Cabs. Only time will tell whether they will need to be fired one day!

Avoid CEO Traps and Snags

A wrong boss kills an organization—it is like placing a square peg in a round hole—and then suffering till corrected. The pony-tail bearing, hip CEO Jonathan Schwartz, killed **Sun Microsystems**[27]; Ken Lay of **Enron**,[28] Chuck Conway of **Kmart**[29] and Subrata Roy of **Sahara Group** took their companies to the cleaners through fraud and manipulations[30]; Jürgen Schrempp messed up the merger of **Daimler** and **Chrysler**[31]; Eckhard Pfeiffer ruined one of the original PC companies, **Compaq**[32]; **Kingfisher Airlines** was destroyed by the extravagant Vijay Mallya; and the instances of CEO failures are unending.

On the other side of the spectrum, there are very successful chiefs like Indra Nooyi at *Pepsi*, Tim Cook at *Apple*, Sundar Pichai at *Google* and Satya Nadela at *Microsoft*.

Why do some seemingly infallible CEOs fail? What should one do to avoid the pitfalls?

There is no such thing as a perfect person. Getting into the boots of a CEO is the greatest leap a person can take in his career—and yet the person will not be flawless and unerring.

Some quick to-do lists will help avoid common CEO faux pas. Needless to mention, there are many more attributes which help to make a successful boss.

- *Imaginative with ability to differentiate from the crowd:* It is common knowledge that Steve Jobs got kicked out from his own company—the famous Apple. The company was nearing bankruptcy. Twelve years post his departure, the company could only think of getting him back, relying on his singular ability to think imaginatively and laterally. The rest is history. His innovations led to iPhone and iPad becoming blockbusters, and Apple became the most valuable company in the world. Differentiation is the way you can make your business distinctive.

- *Ability to be a team player:* The CEO's roles are often exaggerated when their company performance gets under the scanner. We should remember no one can work in isolation—even if the person has an extraordinary calibre. The Danish healthcare company *Novo Nordisk's* CEO Lars Rebien Sørensen, who was ranked the world's best-performing CEO for 2016 by the *Harvard Business Review*, said in an interview: 'To be honest, I think we're highly overrated. At least in my business, success is far more of a team effort than the public would like to believe',—a cardinal characteristic and ethos which set Sørensen apart from the rest.[33]

- *Motivating people and generating a sense of purpose:* Management is a science and the art of managing people. People are any organization's greatest asset—and if this critical resource cannot be galvanized properly, no amount of management mumbo-jumbo will help performance. The CEO of *Inditex*, the Spanish fashion retail giant, Pablo Isla once commented: 'Motivating people and generating a sense of spirit inside a company are essential parts of the CEO's role. We need to appeal to our employees' emotions to help create an environment where they can innovate.'[34] No wonder Isla was selected one of the best CEOs for 2016 by *Harvard Business Review*.

- *Russell Reynolds' top attributes:* For making it to the top, certain attributes differentiate CEOs, says a study by Russell Reynolds, an executive search and assessment firm. Out of the 60 common attributes used to assess leaders, CEOs differ from other executives in three key attributes: (a) willingness to take calculated risks; (b) bias towards action; and (c) ability to efficiently 'read' people.[35] These varied attributes suggest that CEOs should possess a wide range of capabilities and, most importantly, should know when to deploy one opposing capability over another to achieve the right upshot.

- *Chairman's 3 Cs:* Long time back, when I joined my alma mater, Hindustan Unilever, as a young management trainee, I remember our chairman Dr Ashok Ganguly saying that he believes each trainee is a potential CXO. But each one should possess the three Cs—capability, credibility and compassion—to occupy someday the corner office chair. This sane advice still rings an alarm bell in my mind. No boss can give orders to anyone, unless he is competent enough to do so. Reliability and trustworthiness lets people listen to when he speaks. Think of the boss you may have had—having little empathy would have made you hate the leader. Look around, and you will see successful leaders having the basics of the three Cs—to make them the captain who conducts.

Tailpiece

CEOs are like diamonds—rough and yet valuable. They are all flawed in some way, but formed and hardened under intense pressure. If not discovered and polished, the rough edges will turn the person into a common stone—unused, unfit and unfruitful.

In Closing

Everyone commits mistakes, so do the unerring CEOs. The boss may be the perfect fit for the job or a misfit, an organization's success or failure always hinges around this C-suite occupant.

Uncertainty and change are part and parcel of businesses today. Many leaders see any interruption as an opportunity, challenging themselves to disrupt and grow their organization, while some succumb, unable to keep pace with change.

The bad news is some studies show declining CEO tenure and level of public trust. Hence, bosses should quickly develop competence to lead in this demanding and changing world.

Business heads can commit many mistakes, and the list is endless—not keeping a keen eye on the cash tiller, tendency to micromanage, hiring wrong people, not focusing enough on sales, overlooking customer feedback and not heeding bad news. It takes decades to build a reputation, but minutes to wreck it.

References

1. Reuters. Austria's FACC, hit by cyber fraud, fires CEO. Reuters [Internet]. 2016 May 25. Available from: https://www.reuters.com/article/us-facc-ceo-idUSKCN0YG0ZF

2. Tuttle B. The 5 big mistakes that led to Ron Johnson's ouster at JC Penney. Time [Internet]. 2013 Apr 9. Available from: http://business.time.com/2013/04/09/the-5-big-mistakes-that-led-to-ron-johnsons-ouster-at-jc-penney/

3. The Guardian. Apple Maps: Tim Cook says he is 'extremely sorry'. The Guardian [Internet]. 2012 Sep 28. Available from: https://www.theguardian.com/technology/2012/sep/28/apple-maps-tim-cook-apology

4. Financial Times. The shaming of John Thain. Financial Times [Internet]. 2009 Mar 13. Available from: https://www.ft.com/content/c1b3ac7e-0ec1-11de-ba10-0000779fd2ac

5. Kershner K. The crazy story of Borgward, the German carmaker you've never heard of. Auto-How Stuff Works [Internet]. 2017 Apr 21. Available from: https://auto.howstuffworks.com/story-borgward-german-carmaker-never-heard.htm

6. Wikipedia. Fred Goodwin. Available from: https://en.wikipedia.org/wiki/Fred_Goodwin

7. Davies L. Former Vivendi boss Messier admits making 'mistakes' as he faces fraud trial. The Guardian [Internet]. 2010 Jun 2. Available from: https://www.theguardian.com/business/2010/jun/02/messier-fraud-trial-begins

8. Buckingham L, Kane F. Gerald Ratner's 'crap' comment haunts jewellery chain. The Guardian: From the archive [Internet]. 2014 Aug 24. Available from: https://www.theguardian.com/business/2014/aug/22/gerald-ratner-jewellery-total-crap-1992-archive

9. Signet Jewellers. Wikipedia [Internet]. Available from: https://en.wikipedia.org/wiki/Signet_Jewelers

10. Davies R, Jackson J. Saatchi and Saatchi boss resigns amid sexism row. The Guardian [Internet]. 2016 Aug 3. Available from: https://www.theguardian.com/media/2016/aug/03/saatchi-saatchi-boss-kevin-roberts-resigns-amid-sexism-row

11. Wray R. Deepwater Horizon oil spill: BP gaffes in full. The Guardian [Internet]. 2010 Jul 27. Available from: https://www.theguardian.com/business/2010/jul/27/deepwater-horizon-oil-spill-bp-gaffes

12. Hogan M. Michael O'Leary's 33 daftest quotes. The Guardian [Internet]. 2013 Nov 8. Available from: https://www.theguardian.com/business/shortcuts/2013/nov/08/michael-o-leary-33-daftest-quotes

13. Addady M. This tech CEO was fired for death threats against Donald Trump. Fortune [Internet]. 2016 Nov 15 http://fortune.com/2016/11/15/tech-ceo-death-threats-donald-trump/

14. McBride S. Mozilla CEO resigns, opposition to gay marriage drew fire. Reuters [Internet]. 2014 Apr 4. Available from: https://www.reuters.com/article/us-mozilla-ceo-resignation/mozilla-ceo-resigns-opposition-to-gay-marriage-drew-fire-idUSBREA321Y320140403

15. Lee D. Mozilla boss Brendan Eich resigns after gay marriage storm. BBC News [Internet]. 2014 Apr 4. Available from: https://www.bbc.com/news/technology-26868536

16. O'reilly L. The boss of Japan's biggest ad company Dentsu is stepping down after an overworked employee committed suicide. Business

Insider [Internet]. 2016 Dec 28. Available from: https://www.business insider.in/The-boss-of-Japans-biggest-ad-company-Dentsu-is-stepping-down-after-an-overworked-employee-committed-suicide/articleshow/56223883.cms

17. Jayashankar M, Ramnath NS. The Phaneesh Murthy saga: How the cookie crumbled. Forbes India [Internet]. 2013 May 24. Available from: http://www.forbesindia.com/article/boardroom/the-phaneesh-murthy-saga-how-the-cookie-crumbled/35313/1

18. Jolly D, Pollack A. Sanofi fires its chief executive but retains his global strategy. The New York Times [Internet]. 2014 Oct 29. Available from: https://www.nytimes.com/2014/10/30/business/international/christopher-viehbacher-sanofi-chief-ousted-by-board.html

19. Bloxham E. Why Sanofi CEO Chris Viehbacher had to go. Fortune [Internet]. 2014 Dec 5. Available from: http://fortune.com/2014/12/05/sanofi-ceo-ouster-succession/

20. Hipwell D. Former Tesco chief Philip Clarke was bully and corporate vandal, says colleague. The Times [Internet]. 2018 May 4. Available from:https://www.thetimes.co.uk/article/former-tesco-chief-was-bully-and-corporate-vandal-says-colleague-vb7qk6mv8

21. BBC. Barclays boss Bob Diamond resigns amid Libor scandal. BBC News [Internet]. 2012 Jul 3. Available from: https://www.bbc.com/news/business-18685040

22. Whitten S. Papa John's founder 'isn't going quietly,' lawyer says—Schnatter just dragged Kanye West into fight with the board. CNBC [Internet]. 2018 Jul 17. Available from: https://www.cnbc.com/2018/07/17/papa-johns-founder-speaks-out-on-resignation-the-board-and-kanye-west.html

23. Paton E. Lucinda Chambers, fired Vogue director, gives fashion industry a kicking. The New York Times [Internet]. 2017 Jul 4. Available from: https://www.nytimes.com/2017/07/04/fashion/vestoj-lucinda-chambers-british-vogue.html

24. Cartner-Morley J. At home with Lucinda Chambers: 'The way I left Vogue could have been more elegant'. The Guardian [Internet]. 2018 Oct 5. Available from: https://www.theguardian.com/fashion/2018/oct/05/home-lucinda-chambers-leaving-vogue-eclectic-style

25. Bloomberg. Executive Profile: Martin McCourt. Available from: https://www.bloomberg.com/research/stocks/private/person.asp?personId=170912721&privcapId=46503587

26. Freeman H. American Apparel founder Dov Charney: 'Sleeping with people you work with is unavoidable'. The Guardian [Internet]. 2017 Sep 10. Available from: https://www.theguardian.com/lifeandstyle/2017/sep/10/american-apparel-dov-charney-sexual-harassment

27. Arthur C. Jonathan Schwartz tweets his last goodbye to Sun Microsystems. The Guardian [Internet]. 2010 Feb 4. Available from: https://www.theguardian.com/technology/blog/2010/feb/04/jonathan-schwartz-sun-microsystems-tweet-ceo-resignation

28. Barrionuevo A. Enron chiefs guilty of fraud and conspiracy. The New York Times [Internet]. 2006 May 25. Available from: https://www.nytimes.com/2006/05/25/business/25cnd-enron.html

29. Wachtel K. Former Kmart CEO is ordered to pay $5.5 million by SEC for lying to investors. Business Insider [Internet]. 2010 Nov 17. Available from: https://www.businessinsider.com/former-kmart-ceo-ordered-to-pay-55-million-by-sec-for-misleading-investors-2010-11?IR=T

30. Rautray S. Supreme Court directs Sahara chief Subrata Roy to appear before it on February 28. The Economic Times [Internet]. 2019 Jan 31. Available from: https://economictimes.indiatimes.com/news/politics-and-nation/supreme-court-directs-sahara-chief-subrata-roy-to-appear-before-it-on-february-28/articleshow/67773422.cms?from=mdr

31. Hawranek D. The story behind the departure of DaimlerChrysler's CEO. Speigel Online [Internet]. 2005 Aug 1. Available from: https://www.spiegel.de/international/spiegel/a-failed-masterpiece-the-story-behind-the-departure-of-daimlerchrysler-s-ceo-a-367717.html

32. Darwin J. Compaq forces Pfeiffer to resign. Houston Business Journal [Internet]. 1999 Apr 25. Available from: https://www.bizjournals.com/houston/stories/1999/04/26/story1.html

33. The best-performing CEOs in the world. Harvard Business Review [Internet]. 2016 Nov. Available from: https://hbr.org/2016/11/the-best-performing-ceos-in-the-world

34. Spark of the corporate: Pablo Isla. WisdomJobs.com [Internet]. Available from: https://www.wisdomjobs.com/spark-of-corporate/338-pablo-isla-08-01-2018.html

35. Stamoulis DT. How the best CEOs differ from average ones. Russell Raynolds Assoc [Internet]. 2016 Nov. Available from: https://www.russellreynolds.com/newsroom/how-the-best-ceos-differ-from-average-ones

CORPORATE GOVERNANCE ILLS

The company which I run uses IT systems supported by the Indian multinational **Infosys**, and so do hundreds others such as HP, HSBC and Deutsche Bank. Was any customer concerned about the serious corporate governance questions raised sometime back by its co-founder ex-chairman Narayana Murthy? My family watches the daily dose of soap operas through **Tata** Sky. Several of my friends drive to work in Tata Indica, and many love their daily dose of Tata Tetley tea. Are they concerned about the fight it had at the very top of the organization where its ex-chairman Cyrus Mistry raised grave governance allegations against Ratan Tata, Chairman Emeritus of Tata Sons?

The question is why sometimes there is so much raucous about corporate governance?

'Customer is the king' is the oft-repeated slogan in corporate corridors. Organizational governance is all about running a business well. The major objective is to ensure that the products produced or services rendered are in accordance with the customers' expectations, delivered promises, have consistent quality and are being priced fairly. If these deliverables are provided, does it really matter if the company bosses are bickering or not?

Yes, it does. If an organization is not run well and there is management infighting and malpractice, it is impossible to render customer satisfaction. Quality goods and services can only emanate from an organization if it has a defined chain of control, appropriate systems and processes, and an ethical value system.

Corporate governance is all about delivering value to the customers—for whom a business in reality exists.

Poor Governance

If you would have invested in the 'king of good times'—**Kingfisher Airlines**—you would have committed a grave error of judgement, your money would have gone, oblivious to the fact that poor corporate governance was eating into your investment. At a time when the airline was grounded in October 2012 and the staff salaries remained unpaid for long, would you believe that the airlines chairman, Vijay Mallya, gifted (or was it bribed) 3 kg of gold to Lord Tirupati on his 57th birthday in December 2012?[1] Can you imagine over ₹9,000 crores ($1.3 billion) of debts to bankers were overdue when he partied hard on his 60th birthday in 2015, spending millions in his sprawling beach bungalow? These were acts of poor governance and unseemly behaviour by the company founder knowing well that his business was crumbling.

Think of the governance model for the sprawling **Sahara** conglomerate, ranging from hotels to Formula One racing cars. The Indian company has failed to return billions of dollars raised under several bond programmes which the Supreme Court has declared illegal. Numerous attempts by Sahara's founder, Subrata Roy, who has been languishing in jail for long, to prove that the money has already been returned, have been declared to be falsehoods—poor governance all the way by Sahara.

The good news is that shareholders' activism is on the rise all over the world, with even established companies such as **Royal Dutch Shell**[2] and **Deutsche Bank**[3] recently having faced opposition from their investors. Boards of large Asian companies have been successfully opposed by minority investors, wielding their power in some of the most conservative business environments. In early 2018, investors in **Fortis Healthcare**, India's second-biggest hospital chain, teamed up to oust one of the company's board members when poor governance was observed. Around the same time, **Hyundai Motor** was forced to cancel a controversial $9 billion restructuring plan, which would have strengthened the control of the company's founding family. In the United Kingdom, in an unprecedented move, the investors rejected **Deloitte's**

Corporate Governance IIIs

reappointment as auditors at building materials group **SIG**,[4] which admitted overstating its profits in previous years. Behind the scenes, clearly a new trend is emerging: investors are gently punishing directors over governance failures and concerns about their dedication to their jobs.

While sometimes shareholder's activism helps in highlighting probable wrongdoings, mostly corporates go scot-free. When the board and the management acting as trustees practise asymmetrical treatment and benefit particular stakeholders, especially the owners or owner managers, it is poor corporate governance. It will be a grave error not to take cognisance of such corporate parasites.

The concept of corporate democracy leads to a few elected representatives to run a corporation. But who chooses the representatives? Many a time it is the motley group of concentrated shareholders having quid pro quo relationships, helping each other to augment their respective cause. Keep a watch for these structures, and reposing faith in such companies is a bungle.

However, I am somewhat optimistic in noting that the recent reforms in the various portals on the corporate legislations, including the revamping of the company law in India through the Companies Act 2013, should be in a better position to address some of the challenges of good governance.

The corporate legislations are now having more teeth, attempting to extract more information in a structured fashion, making the board members more responsible for their behaviours. Added to this, shareholder activism is on the rise.

Tailpiece

Legislations are forcing more boards to be made up of outside directors whose independence is not compromised by family ties to the chief executive or business ties to the company. Directors, meanwhile, are now required to take their fiduciary duties more seriously to regularly evaluate the chief executive's and other board members' performances. Historical evidence shows that companies practising poor governance have ultimately negated shareholder value.

Boot Out Non-performers

Profit is to good governance what waves are to swimming trunks; when the former is high, absence of the latter goes unnoticed. The dipping of business performance tends to shift focus on governance and related matters.

It would be a mistake if sharp knives do not come out to treat the ills of governance. Do they? Is the big question.

Deutsche Bank sacked its British boss, John Cryan, in April 2018 following a boardroom battle over the firm's declining turnaround effort and a cost-cutting plan that went amiss.[5] This incidentally was Deutsche Bank's third change in the leadership position over the previous six years. Similarly, CEO Richard Umbers was shown the exit door in February 2018 at the 120-year-old Australian retail giant **Myer** after the company received its third profit warning in three months. The sacking was prompted by Myer's largest shareholder Solomon Lew, when he lamented that 'the retailer is at peril'.[6]

These steps showed that a new era of corporate performance and behaviour is emanating with boards taking sterner views on poor performance, at least in some parts of the world. The directors seem to be acting more in the interest of the shareholders.

In spite of some good developments, many boards still seem to be closing their eyes to non-performance. A gentleman's agreement 'you scratch my back and I scratch yours' seems to be prevailing in more corporates than ever before. These good and bad practices still coexist, and that is awful news.

Who has not heard of the great Japanese brands—**Sony**, **Panasonic** and **Sharp**? These names have been iconic in their own rights, developing new products and technologies for long. But, of late, all the three companies are distant shadows of their past. These companies ultimately faltered when their top managements failed to keep pace with changes around.

Sony's decay commenced when there was mismatch between the desired company strategy and its management capability, together with lack of clarity about who should do what. I used to love my Sony Vaio laptop, until it malfunctioned around the time Sony discontinued its sale in 2014—shifting to Dell, on which this book is written. When last year I thought of upgrading my Sony smartphone, I could only think of Samsung and not the once invincible Sony. Such was the experience with countless potential customers. Many blame Sony's fall to the loss of intellect and good employees during the reign of Nobuyuki Idei, from 1999 to 2005. Rather than chastising Idei for the stumbling Sony performance, he was anointed to head the advisory board. In fact, his successor Howard Stringer, whose performance was worse, got elevated to chair the board in 2012—both handpicking their successors while earning handsome retirement deals— mistakes committed by many Japanese companies in not booting out poor performers, a prime cause for the decline of many Japanese giants.

Governments across the globe have scrambled to pass laws and write regulations detailing which committees of boards must be formed, what credentials their members must possess, what work they must do, how often they should meet and how many independent members to be in boards. And even with the new strictures, disappointed governance experts worry that boards are still depicting complacency in dealing with ill-governance and booting out poor performers.

Tailpiece

Plenty of companies suffer from rotten management. Keep your eyes and ears open. When possible, push out these value destroyers. It is the best thing to do. Institutional investors around the world have long been accused of being asleep at the wheels. However, they are now taking more interest in the way the companies they have invested in, are run. Corporate laws are also becoming more stringent. Corporate managers will do well to stay true to 'doing the right thing' in order to save their jobs and their organizations.

Crafty Corporates

We chat about responsible governance, admire organizations that we believe are ethical, and felicitate the best governed companies; but can we say that none of these companies cut corners in their daily business lives? Many a time, the desire to enhance profits or cut cost supersedes good governance principles.

Think of some advertising campaigns. From time immemorial, we have watched ads showing a certain variety of soaps making every woman look like a film star. Or using a particular shampoo or hair oil helps in having the perfect hair. Or using a particular face cream will retain youthfulness even in our golden years. Did the advertisers believe their ad campaigns were wholly correct? Of course not! Slightly stretching product functionalities is all right in this make-believe world is what many would say. But what happens when white lies are communicated with alacrity and disdain? The cosmetics, beauty, health, fitness and education industries are often built upon this duplicity.

In 2017, the Advertising Standards Council of India held several top Indian corporates for making exaggerated claims. Makers of Complan, **Heinz India's**, misleadingly proclaimed: 'Only Complan gives three times more ... as every glass of Complan has 34 vital nutrients ... because of which children grow/develop the most.' **Gujarat Co-Operative Milk Marketing Federation's** claim that *Amul Memory Milk* 'contains various Ayurvedic herbs that are traditionally known to boost memory' were found to be unsubstantiated. And worse was when **HDFC Standard Life Insurance** professed the scary advert, 'One in eight Indian men are likely to contract cancer at some point in their life'—it cannot get more horrifying, I guess?

If we cannot repose confidence on the claims by big names of the corporate world, whom do we trust? And the list is just a glimpse—you will be appalled to see the catalogues of the recalcitrant.

In Portugal, Espirito Santos, or Holy Spirit in Portuguese, carried a religious aura around the name of this banking dynasty, similar in many ways to the Rothschild family in Europe or Rockefellers in the United States. But the enigmatic family kingdom came crashing down in August 2014 when **Banco Espirito Santo**, Portugal's largest-listed lender and second-biggest bank in which the Espirito Santos family held 20 per cent shareholding, needed to be rescued primarily by the Portuguese government. Espirito Santo's main holding companies filed for bankruptcy. The empire crumbled into ruins.

It all happened due to poor governance leading to improper lending to the parent family-controlled businesses whose interests ranged from cattle ranches to diamond mines. In addition, there are allegations of accounting fraud, non-transparent movement of funds between Espirito Santos entities and the use of insider information by the controlling family, which has run the bank for generations.[7,8]

Banks exist to lend money which you and I save with them. Their decision on letting to use money ought to be based on commercial justifications of the borrower's ability to service the debt. It is but natural if the lending takes place to group companies or related parties who may lack the capability or intent to return the money, the bank's business will become sick. Banco Espirito, which was operationally run by the Espirito Santos family, was no different.

Tailpiece

Businesses are essentially meant to generate profits. But when corporate surpluses are generated by hook or by crook, problems crop up. It is a common saying that cheating is fine until one gets caught. Regrettably, thoroughbred names have fallen foul with unethical business practices; they have disgraced themselves to meet muck on their face.

Corruption and Corporations

Some rather bad news—70 per cent of Indian CXOs are willing to bend rules to justify achieving financial targets against an average of 40 per cent globally. Shockingly, India's business leaders are more inclined to extend the monthly reporting period; backdate a contract and book revenues earlier than they should. These were from the findings of the Ernst & Young (EY) Global Fraud Survey 2016. This is serious substance reflecting the Indian corporates' corrupt mindset at the highest level.

An alarming number of 16 per cent of CFOs and finance team members globally were observed to be willing to make cash payments to win or retain business—higher than 13 per cent for other than finance team members.[9] This willingness of the finance folks to justify unscrupulous behaviour is concerning, given their direct role in providing accurate financial information and controlling business assets. Clearly, the sharp focus of governments and societies on bribery and corruption is not working, and the worse is, respondents to the EY study do not believe things have improved since their last survey in 2014.

Accounting involves some exercise of judgement and subjectivity. But that does not justify playing into grey areas. Given that financial information is the basic document on which everyone relies, the tendency to justify playing with numbers by the corporate finance team is very worrying. The situation should have been reverse—it should have been the finance team driving anti-corrupt practices—but that does not seem to be the inside truth!

Unfortunately, time and again, corporate bigwigs fall into the corruption and bribery trap—either practising or preaching. Corruption and corporates are sometimes closely linked.

The once hugely popular former president Lula da Silva ruling Brazil between 2003 and 2010 had been convicted in 2017 for corruption, as his government was accused of being involved in the biggest corruption racket in Brazil's history—the looting of the state-owned oil company **Petrobras**; a US court convicted a Chinese billionaire Ng Lap Seng, in July 2017, of bribing UN diplomats to help him gain backing for a conference centre in Macau, highlighting the undue influence of cash at the exalted international body; India's investigative agency, the Central Bureau of

Investigation (CBI) arrested **Bhushan Steel's** vice chairman Neeraj Singhal in 2014 for allegedly offering a bribe of ₹50 lakh ($71,000) to **Syndicate Bank** chairman Sudhir Kumar Jain for extending its credit limit; engineering giant **Rolls-Royce** paid £671 million ($870 million) in penalties when it was found to have bribed millions of pounds and a luxury car to middlemen to secure orders in six countries, including Indonesia, Russia and China.[10]

Corporate sleaze and vice are maladies numerous geographies have been afflicted with. This awful governance practice leads to disastrous consequences, such as enhanced transaction costs and lower efficiency, inhibiting growth and development.

Tailpiece

When the finance manager faces an overstated income tax demand or needs to hurry up a permission which his boss is looking for, but is unable to proceed without oiling the palms of the concerned bureaucrat to make the files move, what does the manager do? This conundrum perhaps will not go away in a hurry—when growth in the developed world has stagnated, leading most businessmen to focus on China, India or Brazil. Unfortunately, bribery is the cost of doing business in several countries!

The Trap of Overpromise

CEOs and top management sometimes overpromise to keep the stock market adrenal flowing. This could lead to unsustainable increase in the share price, which in turn would enhance market capitalization, leading to heightened company valuation.

Canadian company **Valeant Pharmaceuticals** and America's solar company **SunEdison**—both darlings of the stock market till its melt down kicked off in mid-2015—followed this seemingly innocuous practice of overcommitting.

Both grew through acquisitions, adding mountains of debt along the way. Both bragged of innovative business models and multiplying profits through acquired assets.

In early 2008, the Canadian drug-maker **Valeant** appointed ex-consultant Michael Pearson as its CEO. He brought in great investor hope for the 1960 incorporated company. Pearson started picking up small undervalued pharmaceutical companies and chopped their R&D costs dramatically. This resulted in immediate increase in profits. Pearson went ahead and increased selling prices of some of its drugs by two to five times, spawning a new narrative of value creation. He said pharma R&D is non-value accretive and its returns do not justify spending. Further, when there were near-monopoly drugs, why not skim the market by price increases? Pearson did not end here. He also doctored Valeant's accounts to pump up revenues.

The price increase backfired. Government actions forced it to roll back prices. The company lost 90 per cent of its market valuation. (Joseph Papa, the head of the drug maker Perrigo, took charge in April 2016, replacing the embattled Pearson, with the company renamed in 2018 as Bausch Health Companies.)[11]

The overvalued equity story based upon hopes, myths and lies got entrapped in its own game sooner than later.

SunEdison reflects a similar story of failed bid to meet tall promises made. Till the summer of 2015, the company was the sizzling stock in the red hot space of renewable energy. With its involvement in solar energy, the company was unstoppable with market capitalization reaching a whopping $10 billion. But in April 2016, the company had to file for bankruptcy protection, one of the largest ever in the green energy space.

SunEdison's novelty consisted in setting up 'yieldco' subsidiaries, which raised financing to buy assets the parent had acquired or built. The 'yieldcos' in theory could then collect regular fees based on long-term contracts with the power companies. The sales brought in funding for the parent's next investment. Objective was 'yieldcos' would attract premium valuations generating steady cash flows.

The company grew from making chemicals and components for solar modules with an ambition to become the world's leading renewable energy development company. It is a classic tale on the dangers of trying to grow too fast in too many directions, including expanding operations in very competitive markets like India, China and Brazil. It was a mess created by going ahead of themselves. (SunEdison, however, has emerged in late 2017 from one of the biggest corporate implosions in the renewable industry's history, as a newly restructured, privately held and much smaller version of its former self.)[12]

The corporate world is chock-full of examples of overambitious businessmen playing on investor sentiments with their make-believe world going awry.

These are examples of heightened investor expectations which are often not possible to meet, ensuing bad and irrational behaviour on the part of the management. Based on promises made and sleek management presentations, capital markets often overvalue these companies, which in turn poses a behavioural trap. When a stock gets overvalued, luck is the best saviour. Or else, the management resorts to tricks.

Historically, certain industries have been perennially practising overvaluation of equities. The pharmaceutical and oil industries are classic examples.

Pharma companies spend heavily on R&D, even when the return on such investments is measly. Any throttling of R&D buzz warning bells of poor health. Investors lap up companies showing high R&D spends.

Similar experiences are with the oil industry. They keep spending billions of dollars on exploration in spite of the ever increasing marginal cost and severe repercussions on the world's carbon footprints. Just imagine what will happen to the investor psyche in case they get to know that oil companies are likely to throttle exploration-related capital expenditure? That will singularly lead to stock prices tumbling. The oil industry can ill afford such outcome, and hence the value of the oil companies remains high based on the hype and hope.

In order to enhance a feeling of well-being among investors, managers often resort to prop up the market value of the company.

Broadly speaking, this involves two basic gimmicks: For listed companies, somehow ensure bumping up of the equity price; for non-listed entities, to project enhanced present value of the future cash flows. The action plan will also need penning credible-looking business plans, buying companies, investing in R&D, adding assets, augmenting advertisement spends or doctoring accounting information.

Tailpiece

Keeping pace with overpromise is like riding a tiger—once you are on its back, it is difficult to jump off. Chicaneries are committed until good luck makes its way to the improved performance or until the manager moves on elsewhere to escape the consequences of his ill acts.

Share prices are dependent upon future prospects, whereas debt pricing is based on the historical performance. Taking advantage of this pricing rationale, managers keep tinkering with past performance, hope and high stock value. Time and again, companies have failed in their endeavour to convert hope into reality. Unfortunately, this misplaced practice is unlikely to fade anytime soon.

Technology Damned Lies

Many a time, too-good-to-be-true stories of businesses need to be examined with a pinch of salt. Hi-fi stories are sometimes strung when entrepreneurs are looking for money from potential investors or from financial institutions. Technology mumbo-jumbo sometimes becomes the Achilles' heel for the investors. Unable to fathom the full story, investors often fall into the potholes of rogues and tricksters—a serious governance lapse indeed.

A 32-year-old Stanford University dropout beauty, Elizabeth Holmes, started **Theranos** with tall promises made in 2013 of using revolutionary 'nanotainer' technology in the $75 billion laboratory testing business. She claimed the ability to produce accurate test results from just a few drops of blood deposited on a tiny glass vial—allowing patients to avoid painful needles and lengthy blood drawing sittings. The company was valued at $9 billion even in early 2016.

Then all hell broke loose. Medical studies raised doubts about the trustworthiness of the tests. US health regulators went even further. They warned that inaccurate test results put out by Theranos's California laboratory had placed patients' lives at great risk.

In April 2017, the Centre for Medicare and Medicaid Services, United States, revoked the clinical laboratory testing certificate of Theranos. Then, one of the most hyped start-ups imploded. (Theranos's Holmes and the now-defunct company's former president Ramesh 'Sunny' Balwani were indicted by the US Department of Justice in June 2018 on charges that they engaged in schemes to defraud investors, doctors and patients.)[13]

Similar stories of technology fraud have been etched by the automotive industry. Ever since **Volkswagen** in 2015 admitted to engineering its diesel vehicles to cheat emission tests, it looks as though the entire auto sector stretching between the United States and Europe is under investigation for trying to deceive on auto-discharge levels. VW has already spent more than $29 billion in settlements with consumers and government agencies.[14] **Mitsubishi Motors** admitted in 2016 to doctoring fuel-economy ratings. **GM**, **Fiat Chrysler**, **Daimler**, **Renault** and **PSA Group** have all been investigated for or have lawsuits filed during 2017 for emission cheating.[15] Mazda, Suzuki and Yamaha improperly tested vehicles for fuel economy and emission.[16] **Robert Bosch**, the world's largest auto-component company, is struggling against accusations for supplying the technology supposedly used by several auto manufacturers to circumvent emission guidelines.[17]

Volkswagen became the poster child of corporate cheating. The much-hallowed VW letters stand tarnished. The company may continue to manufacture cars for long but this colossal hoax may fade their image into an ordinary automaker one day!

You will be surprised that even television manufacturers may be cheating on energy-efficiency claims. **Samsung** and **LG** of South Korea and **Vizio** of America stand accused of misrepresenting energy efficiency of large-screen TV sets. These sets apparently can figure out the 'test-clip' when used to rate energy consumption. It is understood that during these tests, the backlight dims, resulting in substantial energy savings. Tech frauds are clearly here to stay. VW and others may be a mere speckle.

Tailpiece

Warren Buffet, one of the world's most successful investors, has often remarked that he does not invest in companies where he does not understand the nitty-gritties of business. He says that if you are determined to pick stocks, don't buy into a business you do not comprehend. He is fine with investing in Coco Cola but not with Silicon Valley technology brouhahas.

You need to be careful of companies which market themselves on technological platforms. There are likely to be many hovering around us to take advantage of our unguarded moments and lack of technological understanding. Do not make the mistake of jumping into the bandwagon of anything which does not give you the comfort of clarity.

Corporate Espionage

In 2015, a spy thriller-like action took place in India's oil ministry office in New Delhi. A failed late-night break-in aimed at pilfering documents with prowlers caught with bogus identity cards and an escape car camouflaged as an authorized government vehicle.

Stealing drawings and samples from a competitor or documents from government files, a serious governance lapse, are not uncommon in the corridors of any corporate competitive landscape.

Four of the India's most prominent business groups were involved in a bungled corporate espionage where over 12 were arrested. These included **Cairn India**, an oil exploration company, **Essar**, a diversified Indian conglomerate, **Reliance Power** and **Reliance Industries**, the energy and petrochemical colossus.

The employees were to receive confidential documents from officials at the India's oil ministry, which also led to the arrest of a number of low-level government officials and middlemen operating in energy-related consulting firms. It is claimed the consultants paid individuals and government employees to procure official documents, and then sold them on to clients.

Risks of spying enhance when companies operate in heavily regulated sectors such as defence, energy or telecoms. Information garnered from inside government departments help to gain insights into competitors' business plans. This is in addition to the steps taken to carryout well-resourced lobbying to further the cause of the concerned corporations.

Using middlemen and bribing lower-level government officials to acquire information is a relatively common feature in the business world, especially in the Indian corporate sector. This has often disrupted the plans of international companies wanting to invest in India especially in information-sensitive sectors such as defence.

Tailpiece

Corporate espionages are errors of judgement and need to be avoided at all cost. These short-term measures and few pages of information do not change the future of any business—but cast a large shadow of ill image on the corporates caught in the unseemly act.

Chairman and CEO—Hand in Glove

Many corporate governance ills stem from a leader who is all controlling. It could be a family outfit or a professional setup. Evil thoughts in management practices can be all encumbering irrespective of the management structure.

But a major source of ill-governance stems from the chairperson 'and' the CEO's position being under one head. The separation of the leader of the board (differently called the chairman or chairperson or non-executive chairperson or lead director) and the leader of an organization (usually known as the CEO or the managing director) is increasingly being used as a tool to prevent the misuse of good governance—though this step is not a cure-all for every corporate mischief. Separating the two top positions in a way may lead to provide some checks and balances, rather than a unilateral opportunity of mis-governance.

The 2015 Spencer Stuart Board Index reports that almost half of the boards now split chair and CEO roles as opposed to in 70 per cent of the cases in 2010 where the CEO was also the chairman of the company. More important, the trend shows that in 2015, about 30 per cent of the boards had an independent chairman while in 2010, the figure stood at about 10 per cent. The index is a comprehensive summary of issues and actions of the boards of companies in the Standard & Poor's 500-stock index in the United States.

The increasing trend of dividing the chairman's and the CEO's positions is also the outgrowth of a wave of corporate reforms post Enron, Satyam and numerous other dishonourable episodes.

Whether the separation of the chairman's and CEO's role is effective or not is yet a big question. Warren Buffet, the most iconic business figure in modern times, wraps both the chairman's and chief executive's position into one at Berkshire Hathaway and yet the company is a darling to the investors. However, Steve Jobs of Apple, one of the most successful CEOs, functioned wonderfully under the couched guidance and support of his non-executive chairman, Bill Campbell, a one-time Columbia University football coach. However, even after BP separated its top position into two roles, its crisis management capabilities continue to be a suspect.

Sometimes it takes a scandal or a business problem for a good practice to be adopted. Like many banks, Wells Fargo followed for long the practice of having a single person as both chairman of the board and chief executive. After a bizarre corporate scandal: thousands of the bank's employees used customer data to open millions of fake bank accounts, the bank decided in October 2016 to split the top roles. This was a good decision for corporate governance, since both the jobs had weighty and separate duties, especially for a bank of Wells Fargo's size.

The bad news is that chief executives often resist the split, wanting to stamp their complete authority even at the cost of good governance.

However, separation can cause tension between the two leading figures. It is also not a panacea for inadequacies in corporate governance. But it increases the likelihood of clear oversight of the chief executive and other executives, and makes it harder for one majestic head to become the unchallenged lord of the rings.

Tailpiece

Catalysts to improve corporate governance are multi-fold. Increased pressure from shareholders, overseeing excessive executive pay uncorrelated with the corporate performance and presence of capable independent directors are some measures to prevent the ills of corporate misconduct. Splitting the top position just adds to the armoury of improved business practice. It is a blunder not recognizing this trick of the trade for good governance.

De-rating Rating Agencies

When studying, all of us yearned to secure the coveted 100/100 on any examination paper. Who does not want the highest rating? Low scores would obviously mean something is going wrong.

In business, when anyone wants to provide debts, it is good to know the degree of risk in its recovery. There are marking systems designed to inform the interested parties, given by rating companies such as Moody's, S&P, Fitch, CRISIL, ICRA and CARE.

The ratings look like hyperactive school reports—from AAA, top of the class, to lower grades such as CCC, showing substantial risks to D, the lowest category depicting the borrower in default already.

Now, what happens when rating agencies do not behave well? Who is to be blamed when the ratings based on which investors take their actions turn out not to be kosher?

There have been several occasions when the rating guys faltered and wavered.

The international rating agencies played a central role in the 2008 financial crisis. They assigned the highest grades to mortgage securities that quickly collapsed, leaving investors drowned in losses. The rating agencies failed miserably to assess the credit risk in these securities, which were filled with lousy loans. They did not do their job properly. After the crisis, to settle government inquiries, the rating agencies paid massive penalties, like **Moody's** $864 million and **S&P's** $1.4 billion.

Whether the acts on the part of the rating agencies were delibe-rate deceptions or errors of judgement is difficult to surmise. But the fact that they agreed to pay the big fines imposed by the US justice department does lead us to believe possible involvement of the raters in misleading the public and defrauding the investors.

In India, it is reported that the market regulator SEBI is investigating actions of two rating agencies, **CARE** and **CRISIL.** It is alleged that these two failed to monitor ratings of the troubled auto-parts maker **Amtek Auto** and **J.P.Morgan's credit opportunity fund** holding investments in Amtek, who defaulted on bond repay-ments of ₹800 crore ($12 million) in September 2015. The rating agencies downgraded two ratings from the top slabs in 2015, almost overnight, without much prior warnings.

The saga of rating agencies slipping on ringing risk-bells ahead of time continues. In 2018, the agencies failed to identify financial troubles brewing at IL&FS, a major India-headquartered infra-structure lender struggling to service ₹90,000 crore ($12 billion) debt. Till July 2018, credit rating companies such as ICRA, a unit of Moody's, Fitch-owned India Ratings and CARE failed to see any upcoming credit-default danger signals. However, within two months, the company was downgraded to default status, catching all on the wrong foot.[18] (SEBI, the market regulator, is wondering how three credit-rating agencies failed to spot the stress.)[19] How is it possible that the risk-rating agencies could not smell the rat of huge defaults, when they are supposed to probe for crumbs of negative financial danger signals on clients being assessed for credit risks?

This leads to the belief that the agencies may be committing a cardinal error in only relying on information supplied by the businesses being rated and may not be delving deep to understand the financial positions of its client companies to provide the right assessment of risks.

Another area where the trust on rating agencies gets compromised is when they leak classified information.

The European Union's securities regulator fined **Fitch Ratings** €1.4 million ($1.5 million) in 2016. It was found that some senior Fitch analysts, from December 2010 to June 2012, gave information about upcoming sovereign ratings relating to Greece, France, Ireland, Italy, Portugal and Spain to individuals at Fitch's parent company before it was public.

Tailpiece

The business of rating agencies revolves around credibility and trust. If that gets shaken by compromising acts of the agencies, then it is a big fiasco in the making.

Governance Is an Ethos

The corporate regulations of most countries including India have loads of provisions to ensure satisfactory running of companies. However, the truth is that even the most commendable regulatory fixes and policy guidelines are not half as significant as the quality of the people involved.

Most of you would have noticed that ethics and governance is a matter of top-down philosophy. If the chairman, the CEO or the board believes in good governance, it works. Or else, it is empty vessel making loads of noise.

Let us take an instance where the top echelon would have been involved in the continuance of poor governance.

The Singh brothers, Malvinder and Shivinder, promoters of the storied Indian pharmaceutical company, **Ranbaxy Laboratories**, are facing numerous criminal charges and probes on fraud, cheating and fund misappropriation. The company was subjected to serious governance issues when it was sold to Daiichi Sankyo, concealing information about extensive quality problems, with the courts penalizing the Singh brothers ₹3,500 crore ($550 million) in early 2018.[20] A business empire led by two savvy young men has collapsed with several reports of financial wrongdoings emerging from the closet. A substantial part of the $2.4 billion of their portion of proceeds from the Ranbaxy sale has allegedly been transferred to several family-owned companies. This money is at the centre of probes and controversies. The Singh brothers have also been accused of siphoning off ₹500 crore ($70 million) from Fortis, a publicly traded healthcare company. The brothers now face probes by several government agencies, including the Serious Fraud Investigation Office.[21] These are massive promoter hara-kiris compromising sound governance principles.

In the past few years, scandals have hit big names such as **BP, BAE Systems, GSK, HSBC, Tesco, Reebok India, Olympus, Fujifilm, Volkswagen** and **Wells Fargo.** The problem is not a country or industry specific. Boards have failed to spot such shady practices as environmental neglect, money laundering, sanctions busting, bribery and distorted accounting, while executive payouts continued to zoom. Egregious behaviour on the part of the management to prop up short-term business results through improper means will continue to remain a challenge.

Tailpiece

Governance of organizations after all is not only about following legal stipulations. It is all about delivering customer satisfaction and continuing to enjoy their confidence through proper and responsible control of business affairs.

Governance Cannot Short-Change Anyone

If customer is the king, who are the 'ministers' running the show? Society is a conglomerate of many. Satisfying the needs of customers is not the only objective for which businesses exist. Other stakeholders' interests also need to be protected. Good corporate governance ensures employees are fairly treated and looked after. If the workforce is kicked around, no company can ever produce quality goods or provide decent after-sales service.

Last but not the least, the governance principle of an organization needs to pay all its stakeholders their dues on time. This would include taxes and levies, lenders, vendors and of course the employees. To cite an example, India's once second-largest airlines by market share, **Kingfisher Airlines**, was grounded in October 2012 when it did not pay not only the outstanding banking dues, but also taxes, levies and employee dues. Failing to consider the stakeholder interests, the company dissipated. Forgetting that there are many stakeholders in making a business run is a mistake which any business can ill afford to make.

The main objective of a business venture is to maximize 'shareholder' value. This cannot be achieved unless products and services are up to the mark, employees are treated well, and all dues are paid. In short, it implies maximizing 'stakeholder' value.

Who would not want to buy shares of a good company—and then see it grow?

Stocks of companies with good corporate governance command a premium. There is also good deal of evidence to suggest that a 'responsible' business, involving both management and employee goals, more often than not is a successful one. This obviously means companies that are badly run and squander investor money are usually available at a discount.

Popularly, corporate governance is interpreted to mean having the right number of board members, holding meetings on time, maintaining and filing proper minutes, accounts and records. In reality, however, the principle of corporate governance is much larger. It implies running a company well and producing goods and services to the satisfaction of the customers.

Tailpiece

Good governance is a system of checks and balances that an organization designs to ensure that it can serve its business objectives of appropriate capital utilization for customer satisfaction helping to optimize business returns. If this basic principle of business management is not followed, it is a grave error any corporate can commit.

Short Term vs Long Term

Myopic views of management often result in long-term erosion of value in corporations. This issue of short term vs long term sometimes makes things go awry in the business world. Corporate governance is often short changed to fulfil the ever-growing desire to win for the immediate as opposed to a long-term view.

There are numerous examples on how short-term benefits overlook long-term advantage.

Drug companies are known to take recourse to skimming off the top. **Mylan**, the pharmaceutical giant, had driven up the prices of its signature EpiPen, a branded auto-injecting device for patients with life-threatening allergies. A package of two EpiPens was priced at over $600 in early 2016, up from just over $100 in 2009. Heather Bresch, its chief, when questioned, falsely stated that Mylan made only $100 profit on each pack sold. Days later, Mylan said the correct number was much higher at $166, grossly overcharging the sick and the needy. (In 2017, EpiPen maker Mylan agreed to pay $465 million to the government as a settlement.)[22]

Short termism makes many companies engage in practices that undermine their ability to invest for the long term. Rather than conserving cash, they enhance their dividend payouts. Another typical action to sacrifice long-term well-being is through share buyback schemes, which help to suck out cash from a company. These are some instances of serious sin at the cost of long-term good.

Look at the annual shareholder letters or chairman's messages which you receive through the annual reports of companies in which you would have bought shares. They are usually backward-looking and do not do enough justice to future plans and strategies. It is the disclosures on future landscape that beholds transparency to long-term good governance, rather than harping on the past.

Tailpiece

It is observed that the average tenure of a Fortune 500 CEO is only about five years. Hence, it is rather frightening to imagine a pharmaceutical company CEO saying that he is thinking of investing in a drug that might require 10 years to hit the market. It would take incredible guts for the chief to say that he would take all the expenses now, hit his profits, and the company would reap the benefits later, when he may not be in charge. Do you think this can happen? A classic case of short termism will prevail over long-term benefit decision-making—good governing principles are likely to be sacrificed at the altar of personal benefits.

Treads to Thwart Corporate Cheating

Corporate fraud and poor corporate governance both negate business values. When an organization is likely to be involved in inappropriate governance principles containing fraudulent acts, the biggest issue always is: what can be done to control these if not eradicate?

In order to understand the plausible action plans, we need to recognize the types of fraud we are exposed to in the corporate world. They are 'micro' and 'macro' frauds.

Let us first understand what a 'micro'-fraud is. As the name suggests, it is usually committed by a staff member or someone from inside of a company. Theft by an employee, purchase department bribery to procure goods at a higher price, accounts staff siphoning off receipts from customers and then practising teeming and lading to hide the mischief are some examples of 'micro' fraud.

'Macro' frauds, as the name implies, are usually committed by the top management. Doctoring balance sheets (e.g., Ricoh India accounting scam), producing products not in accordance with customer promise (e.g., Volkswagen producing diesel cars with significantly higher emission levels and lying about it), and having a fraudulent business concept like running a Ponzi scheme (e.g., Saradha Ponzi scam).

It is easier to control micro frauds. Putting strong internal controls, carrying out management audits and providing incentives to whistle-blowers would go a long way in making the corporate world micro-fraud ready.

The problem, however, is with the macro frauds.

If the top management is involved in committing mischiefs, it becomes very difficult to control these. It becomes tougher especially for the non-executive or the independent board members to assure themselves that their company is fraud free.

Appointing a professional management team, making internal auditor report to the audit committee of the board, asking intelligent questions to the management team during board presentations, making periodic visits to factories and workplaces, carrying out time-bound investigations when fraud red flags are raised would be good starting points for the non-executive board members to address 'macro' frauds. Needless to mention, these steps will also render 'micro' frauds difficult to execute.

However, it becomes more challenging for investors and other members of the public to identify corporate frauds. They will have to depend upon audit reports and own analysis of the financial statements, and verify the pedigree and quality of the management team. Not understanding the nature of possible frauds and not taking mitigating steps will be a grave mistake by every stakeholder.

Tailpiece

As greed is not going to diminish among mankind, so will remain the inherent tendency to make a fast buck by cutting corners in the business world. Since it is doubtful that far-reaching investigative steps with naming-shaming of the recalcitrant can actually take place, it is important to be aware of the maxim 'knowledge is power'. It will be a big misstep not recognizing this reality.

What Is Going Wrong?

Corporate fraud and poor governance have assumed gigantic proportions. Worldwide, it is estimated that companies lose around 5 per cent of their revenue ($3.5 trillion) to fraud. In order to avoid paying tax, an estimated one-third of the world GDP, or about $25 trillion of global private financial wealth, has been stashed away in the world's tax havens, far from the prying eyes of the taxmen. Globally, an enormous sum of $2 to $3 trillion is laundered every year. Worse still, less than two-thirds of frauds are ever reported.

In essence, massive sums of money are either being siphoned off through cheating or hidden and laundered to unjustly enrich a few—and many corporates are part of the bandwagon.

Though current business and regulatory developments seem to suggest things are improving on the governance front, but events making headlines in the newspapers and televisions certainly prove that good governance has still some way to go.

What is the problem? Several things, so it seems:

Inept audits: The auditors are still not able to identify and control weaknesses and frauds. Numerous instances exist where auditors perhaps acted in connivance with their client or were inefficient to figure out the hidden bad news. The Big Four auditing firms, **PWC**, **EY**, **Deloitte** and **KPMG**, which boast about their global footprint in more than 150 countries, have all paid multi-million dollar fines for auditing failures and other reasons.[23] Unless the signed audit reports generate confidence among users like you and me, good governance cannot be taken for granted.

Enticing ESOPs and egregious employee ethics: The public at large were made to believe that the growing use of stock options as part of executive pay would align the management's interest with theirs; instead, it tempted the executives to push up share prices with inappropriate actions, doctored earnings. As an example, **BP** chief Bob Dudley, whose $7 million performance share payout was the largest component in 2015 remuneration valued at $19 million, in spite of the company paying billions of dollars in penalties by messing around with its environmental safety standards. Deferred shares granted in smaller spurts but without future performance conditions may be a simpler and better method—but who will bell the cat?

Lack of directors' financial acumen: There is a terrible shortage of qualified directors, particularly of those possessing the ability to comprehend crucial financial nuances, identify systemic control weaknesses and understand business intricacies. Many countries have restricted the number of boards the directors can sit on, and there are not enough trained directors to repose confidence on.

Inadequate independence of independent directors: Independence of independent directors has often been the subject matter of investor debates. Legislations have made it compulsory in many countries for corporates to have a minimum number of independent directors. But just because the directors are not related to the majority shareholders or do not hold enough shareholding interest in the company, does not mean they would exercise their judgements independently. This matter came into intense public scrutiny in late 2016 when Cyrus Mistry, **Tata Sons** chief, was shown the door, seemingly without any cogent reason disclosed. He was then asked to resign from the Tata Group companies. Some directors voted in favour of the ousting motion. Some did not (incidentally the directors who did not vote in favour of Mistry's sacking were also eased out shortly thereafter from the Tata Sons board). Should the independent directors have voted in favour of ousting Cyrus as the chairman when little reasons were disclosed for his ouster? This will remain a case study for long regarding the independence of independent directors.

Tailpiece

Ultimately, it is the shareholders who will need to keep a keen eye on the company performance with the aid of information provided by the government and the auditors. To help the government, market regulators and accounting bodies or boards need to play an active role in ensuring good behaviour from company managements. The auditors need to be truly independent and ethical in their work. These should augur well for ensuring better corporate conduct.

In Closing

Good corporate governance ensures production and supply of quality goods and services consistently at a fair price. It ensures the creation of satisfactory stakeholder value through transparency and accountability. If the systems and processes ensure these basic deliverables, governance can be claimed to be adequate. It is not about ticking the boxes under any corporate law, though meeting the regulatory requirements help in the quest to enhance better governance. There is enough evidence to show that continuous poor governance ultimately takes businesses into oblivion.

Enough evidence exists that the investment funds observing environmental, social and governance (ESG) standards in their strategies have outperformed those that did not. Hence, investors are getting convinced that if they are good to the planet and people, they are benefiting themselves. To cite an example, during 2007–2017 while the MSCI EM (measures equity-market performance through large and mid-caps across 24 emerging markets) index remained static, the MSCI EM ESG index was up over 50 per cent, depicting ESG stocks outperforming the emerging markets benchmark.

For good corporate governance, there is no one-size-fits-all solution. There is no one guideline which will ensure compliance.

Unless the quality of people managing a corporation is worthy and ethical, unless greed is not forsaken by the board and the management, unless long-term goals get precedence over short-term gains, nothing will work, not even the toughest regulatory fixes and frameworks.

References

1. Hindustan Times. Mallya offers 3kg gold at Tirupati: Report. Hindustan Times [Internet]. 2012 Dec 19. Available from: https://www.hindustan times.com/india/mallya-offers-3kg-gold-at-tirupati-report/story-aIvIu JRHzWHglCStc9umqI.html

2. Gilblom K. BP, Shell to face new shareholder challenge over climate in 2019. Bloomberg [Internet]. 2018 Dec 10. Available from: https:// www.bloomberg.com/news/articles/2018-12-10/bp-shell-to-face-new-shareholder-challenge-over-climate-in-2019

3. Financial Times. Activism in banking is tougher than on the fringes of finance. Financial Times [Internet]. 2018 Jul 23. Available from: https://www.ft.com/content/b1fdd91a-8c36-11e8-b18d-0181731 a0340

4. Makortoff K. SIG appoints EY as Deloitte faces probe over audit of company's results. Independent [Internet]. 2019 May 4. Available from: https://www.independent.ie/world-news/sig-appoints-ey-as-deloitte-faces-probe-over-audit-of-companys-results-37079416.html

5. Morrison C. Deutsche Bank sacks chief executive John Cryan after three years of losses. Independent [Internet]. 2018 Apr 9. Available from: https://www.independent.co.uk/news/business/news/deutsche-bank-john-cryan-sacked-fired-christian-sewing-share-price-london-jobs-a8295476.html

6. The Guardian. Myer chief Richard Umbers quits after third profit warning. The Guardian [Internet]. 2018 Feb 13. Available from: https://www.theguardian.com/business/2018/feb/14/myer-chief-richard-umbers-quits-after-third-profit-warning

7. Financial Times. The Novo Banco debacle and the rule of law in Europe. Financial Times [Internet]. 2018 Jan 19. Available from: https:// ftalphaville.ft.com/2018/01/19/2197893/the-novo-banco-debacle-and-the-rule-of-law-in-europe/

8. Financial Times. Banco Espírito Santo secretly lent funds to controlling shareholder. Financial Times [Internet]. 2014 Sep 11. Available from:

https://www.ft.com/content/8e00b1d6-399c-11e4-93da-00144 feabdc0

9. EY. 14th Global Fraud Survey 2016: Corporate misconduct—individual consequences. EY Report [Internet]. 2016. Available from: https:// www.ey.com/Publication/vwLUAssets/ey-global-fraud-survey-2016/$FILE/ey-global-fraud-survey-final.pdf

10. BBC News. Rolls-Royce apologises after £671m bribery settlement. BBC News [Internet]. 2017 Jan 18. Available from: https://www.bbc.com/news/business-38644114

11. Thomas K. Valeant, distancing itself from its past, will change its name to Bausch Health. The New York Times [Internet]. 2018 May 8. Available from: https://www.nytimes.com/2018/05/08/health/valeant-name-bausch-drugs.html

12. Financial Times. Sunny outcome in solar bankruptcy. Financial Times [Internet]. 2017 Dec 12. Available from: https://www.ft.com/content/799e7b6a-ca35-11e7-8536-d321d0d897a3

13. BBC. Theranos: Scandal hit blood-testing firm to shut. BBC News [Internet]. 2018 Sep 5. Available from: https://www.bbc.com/news/business-45418615

14. Leggett T. How VW tried to cover up the emissions scandal. BBC News [Internet]. 2018 May 5. Available from: https://www.bbc.com/news/business-44005844

15. Financial Times. Car emissions scandal: Loopholes in the lab tests. Financial Times [Internet]. 2018 Aug 6. Available from: https://www.ft.com/content/2a123e88-9582-11e8-b747-fb1e803ee64e

16. RTE. Mazda, Suzuki and Yamaha improperly tested vehicles for fuel economy and emission. RTE [Internet]. 2018 Aug 10. Available from: 84229-three-more-japanese-car-companies-caught-up-in-emissions-scandal/

17. Financial Times. Bosch reaches $328m settlement in VW emissions scandal. Financial Times [Internet]. 2017 Feb 1. Available from: https://www.ft.com/content/964a2f72-e898-11e6-967b-c88452263daf

18. Bremner B, Joshi A, Sanjai PR. How credit rating agencies missed the IL&FS crisis. Livemint [Internet]. 2018 Sep 28. Available from: https://www.livemint.com/Companies/kDBrz7DB4Ti4Pz2TdxG85N/How-credit-rating-agencies-missed-the-ILFS-crisis.html

19. LiveMint: Sebi moves against 3 rating agencies over IL&FS crisis: Dec 13, 2018: https://www.livemint.com/Money/2COset9mxPdob9zsre S1mO/Sebi-moves-against-3-rating-agencies-over-ILFS-crisis.html

20. The Financial Express. Ranbaxy sale: Setback for Singh brothers; Singapore court slaps ₹3,500 crore damages. The Financial Express [Internet]. 2018 Dec 22. Available from: https://www.financialexpress.com/industry/daiichi-case-setback-for-singh-brothers-singapore-court-asks-them-to-pay-rs-3500-crore-as-damages/1421727/

21. The Economic Times. Ranbaxy to ruins: How the Singh brothers turned from business whizkids to fraud accused. The Economic Times [Internet]. 2018 Dec 20. Available from: https://economictimes.indiatimes.com/industry/healthcare/biotech/pharmaceuticals/ranbaxy-to-ruins-how-the-singh-brothers-turned-from-business-whizkids-to-fraud-accused/articleshow/67176061.cms

22. Raymond N. Mylan, U.S. finalize $465 million EpiPen settlement. Reuters [Internet]. 2017 Aug 17. Available from: https://www.reuters.com/article/us-mylan-epipen-idUSKCN1AX1RW

23. Vincent M. Audit fines show self-interest is bigger than a big four problem. Financial Times [Internet]. 2018 Aug 30. Available from: https://www.ft.com/content/5ec5718a-ab90-11e8-94bd-cba20d67390c

SKIDDING ON INNOVATION

Life or business cannot progress without innovation. Look around and think about the things you use: whether it is the book or the e-reader you are holding, the pen you write with, the mobile phone you use or even the clothes you are wearing, each one of them is the outcome of innovations.

Innovation is the calling card to the future; if you do not try, you do not connect. In a 2010 EY survey of 263 of the world's most successful entrepreneurs (winners of EY Entrepreneur of the Year awards), 90 per cent in the United States and 85 per cent in the Asia-Pacific region said that the ability to innovate is critical to the growth of their organization. They felt that it is the one genuine advantage they had over their rivals.

In a PWC report, *Unleashing the Power of Innovation*—discussing the role of innovation within businesses and the ways companies innovate are being transformed—three very important shifts were noticed. First, in a survey of 2013 involving 246 CEOs around the world, three-quarters of CEOs regarded innovation and operational effectiveness as equally important. Second, the CEOs are seeing innovation as their own agenda rather than delegating down the line, showing innovation rising significantly in importance. Last and the most fundamental shift, businesses are now looking at innovation to provide whole new sources of revenue rather than just improved products and services. To make all this happen, creating an organizational culture and mindset to encourage innovation will be the key.

Organizations which innovate will also have faltered. We normally will not get to know the failures faced within the hallowed walls of any corporate. However, when the result of innovation is launched in the market, we do get to see the result. Unfortunately, some innovations fail to fire the imagination of potential customers. Legendary **Harley-Davidson** launched perfumes and colognes—flopped in the market as the heavyweight motorcycle fans could not correlate their love for fast rides to the innovated 'hot-road' branded eau-de-toilette fragrance.[1] **Colgate** thought its toothpaste brand can naturally be extended to frozen dinners like beef lasagne, only to find that the two just did not go together.[2] Innovations linked to diversification have often bombed.

The innovation-related failures revealed to these companies the way forward—how to look at the customers' perception of their brands. If they did not attempt, these companies would not have been where they are today. As babies falter when they try their first steps, so are failures while you innovate, the first stepping stones to progress. If you do not fail, you are not trying enough.

Usually, companies that last long preserve their core values while making progress stimulated through innovation. Look at McDonald's. Innovation has changed the way we eat. The ultimate fast-food experience was launched in the 1950s, with utmost innovation in finding the so-called bliss-point of the ultimate combination of salt, sugar and fat, to create our cravings. Look at Marico, the 'Parachute' brand coconut hair and edible oil Indian company. It stuck to the core since the early 1990s but kept innovating, converting tin containers into consumer friendly round plastic packaging with significant brand extensions. Look at Tesla Motors. It manufactured its first electric vehicle Tesla Roadster in 2008, and ever since remained focused on its core of developing electric vehicles and components.

But a classical example of a company which lost out on accepting innovation as a tool to succeed is Xerox. The company failed to conquer the personal computing market despite developing revolutionary technology in the 1980s. The lack of organizational alignment and commitment in the pursuit of innovation led to the fiasco.

It's a grave mistake if innovation is given a short shrift—be it with existing businesses or through a diversified foray.

Innovation is imagining the impending: the power that enables businesses to develop new, feasible offerings to meet consumer demand, respond to market trends and find new ways to accomplish onerous tasks. Innovation drives the development of new products, processes and services every day. Hiccups will appear on its way, but do not dither on innovation as failures, if any, will teach lessons for success.

It Is All about Timing!

Innovation is like a fickle-minded mistress! Reasons for innovation-linked fiascos could be many. It need not be the poor product innovated. One of the biggest risks of an avant-gardist is that the market may not be ready for the creation when invented—thereby allowing someone else to reap the benefits several years later.

Let us take an instance where an innovation was continuously overlooked. The inventor of photocopying device Chester Carlson ferried his innovation to over 20 companies, including **GE** and **IBM**, between 1939 and 1944, but none showed any interest. Even the National Inventors Council dismissed his work. Many companies thus made the cardinal mistake of not being able to foresee the future of a huge commercial success. They believed there was no market for this technology. Finally, in 1944, the Battelle Memorial Institute, a research organization, became interested and began to develop the process together with Carlson. And in 1947, Battelle entered into an agreement with a small photo-paper company called *Haloid* (later to be known as *Xerox*), giving them the right to develop a xerographic machine. It was not until 1959, 21 years after Carlson invented xerography, that the first convenient office copier using xerography was unveiled. It was a phenomenal success.[3]

In another instance, the implementation timing of an innovation went haywire when Godfrey Hounsfield, the corporate scientist of

EMI, named in 1979 as a Nobel Prize winner in physiology, had loads of lamentations to do. EMI was a music company best known for promoting the Beatles, and then it diversified into the medical industry. When Hounsfield was asked why the company was plagued by medical scanner losses, he bemoaned saying, 'The only problem is that we're a little bit late in getting the machines manufactured.' He developed the first CAT scanner (for computed axial tomography) in 1967, showing a detailed picture of a slice of the body by rotating the X-ray tube completely around the patient. Unfortunately, EMI was too late in getting the machines made, with the first production despatched only in September 1979, a decade after its invention![4] Very strangely, one of the finest-ever medical inventions brought grief to the company responsible for its development—primarily due to delayed implementation.

The British company's early success was threatened by a dozen competitors, some large and experienced. Later entrants such as GE, J&J, Philips and Siemens had already commenced capturing CT scanner market share. Early mover advantage slipped out of the hands of EMI, which was also plagued by internal organizational problems and government regulations.

It is not enough to just innovate. It also needs timely upgrades. Nick Woodman, a young man, went for surfing in Australia. Wanting to take close-in action pictures of the brilliant sun, sea and human interactions, he observed there were no reasonably priced alternative to shoot. Stirred by this desire, **GoPro** was floated to make wearable cameras for use in filming—skiing, surfing and racing, including underwater scenes. In spite of a great idea, GoPro is struggling. Lot of competition and too little innovation enhancement is affecting it. The Silicon Valley-based company has been slow to improve its editing software and the launch of new-generation cameras, both of which have long been in development. Lack of improvement in early innovations provides competition space to exploit opportunities.

Think of BMW, Audi and Mercedes-Benz, a byword for quality and high performance, accounting for 80 per cent of the global luxury car market, and their risk for the future where forces of digitization could sweep away the auto sector's pre-eminence, especially when companies like Google have forayed into cars, energy and robotics. Will the Germans still lead when the world shifts to self-driving, electric cars and software takes over engines as a vehicle's most important constituent? Time lag in innovation may leave them behind in a not-too-distant future—the fear is spreading.

Tailpiece

Delay kills. It is more so in business. Time to market is the king. In innovation, procrastination is the worst malady. Financial constraints are an impediment though, but intent will help to fix the problem as you go along. Not recognizing that speed is important in business will be a big gaffe.

Unable to Capitalize

One of the best examples of businesses unable to capitalize on a lifetime opportunity was when **Tatas** launched, marketed and bungled on Nano, the ₹1 lakh ($2,000) car that the then Tata chairman Ratan Tata dreamt of.

How can anyone produce a car at the targeted price when even three-wheelers were costlier? But the Tatas did it, perhaps the best innovation by an Indian auto maker—but by cutting all corners. No one, and surely not the youth, the target customers, wanted to see themselves driving the cheapest car—it was not cool at all to drive Nano to college! When the first models hit the roads in 2009, customers got put-off by noticing the base model had no air conditioning, no stereo and just a single windshield wiper. Then, in 2010, a Nano car caught fire, leading to terrible publicity. Imagining Nano was Beetle or Mini was a big mistake.[5] This is a case study for brilliant innovation not being able to capitalize due to serious mismatch of customer perception, pricing and product offering.

Another classical business tragedy is the story of **Xerox**—a company which was incidentally borne out of someone else failing to capitalize on innovation—failed to exploit its own in-house inventions. Many of the innovations were developed in its very own PARC research centre, a Xerox subsidiary created to build the office of the future, in the 1980s and 1990s. PARC had developed many technologies that defined the personal computer business, such as the graphical user interface. It was Steve Jobs, the Apple co-founder, who on a visit in 1979 picked up the ideas what was to eventually become the Macintosh. Jobs could not believe his eyes what he was seeing at PARC. He commented, 'You are sitting on a goldmine; I cannot believe Xerox is not taking advantage of this.' The Xerox managers rejected the inventions in personal computing space, saying they need to focus on its 'core' and not something else. How mistaken was the company, only posterity depicts![6] It remains one of the best examples of missed opportunities of playing an active role in the evolving digital age.

The biggest name in mobile phones, **Nokia**, floundered similarly. It is a typical case study for failing to capitalize on its head start. A clear leader in cell phones in the 1990s, it developed the first smartphone. Even I used one for years. But Apple and Android phones just crushed Nokia. Being hardware and marketing focused, Nokia failed to realize the importance of software in smartphones. The rest is history. Unable to bear the ever-falling market share, Nokia sold its mobile handsets business to Microsoft in April 2014. But 18 months later, Microsoft sold the brand again and got out of the Nokia mess.[7] Numerous instances exist of even big names missing on innovation, change and adaption.

Ideas are precious. Fresh ideas do not appear from the heaven as often as we would like to have. Try various permutations and combinations, and attempt several options, perhaps to find something which could be worth at least an attempt to commercialize. Often new theories, suggestions and solutions are ignored by the management, either due to lack of understanding or assuming ineffectiveness in the marketplace or under the ostensible belief of preserving cash.

Sadly, many companies have been innovators but slow to commercialize their breakthroughs, unable to bring to fruition their notions. Hovercraft, radar, jet engine and telephones are examples of companies quick to innovate but late to cash in.

Tailpiece

Innovation is about anticipating future, responding to changing customer needs or creating a new need for customers to consume. Organizations need to rekindle the innovative magic of entrepreneurship. Businesses cannot afford failure to capitalize on opportunities to change. In fact, most innovating firms do not survive to milk their revolutionary ideas. Countless examples exist where early movers and innovators could not take advantage of their brilliance and creativity. In fact, they move into oblivion within five to ten years and leave the market leadership to someone else.

Unable to See Change

Failure to adjust in response to the advent of any low-cost competitor or changing customer choice is the most significant reason why businesses stall. The answer primarily lies in extracting value out of investments in new products and services.

Most of us would have used a **BlackBerry** to send official e-mails. Each one of us would have albums of old family pictures taken through **Kodak** films. Typewriters typically from **Remington** or **IBM** were the only way to type letters and reports from our homes and offices. Today none of them exist.

There are companies who are able to reinvent themselves from time to time. They are able to see and read what competitors are doing. They can smell the threats. However, there are organizations which tend to rest on their laurels for far too long, only to be despatched into oblivion through competitive activities.

The ability to see what the customer wants is the prime moving force for growing any business. Staying ahead of times provides an edge.

Let us look at the mobile phone industry, the one device without which most of us cannot live. This device has perhaps undergone the widest and biggest metamorphosis since its invention. This industry is an apt illustration depicting the necessity to imbibe the changing times and the compulsion to stay ahead of the competitive curve.

In 1997, I got my first mobile phone—Nokia 6110. And the best it had three inbuilt games to keep me busy during empty hours. Then I shifted to the coolest device those days in 2004—Motorola Razr V3. It would make a satiating 'clap' sound when shut.

My company in 2009 picked up a Motorola Iridium satellite-based phone, so that we could connect with our sales teams in far-off locations. It was too heavy and worked only when outside.

Come 2010, BlackBerry's iconic keyboard function made an over-whelming case to shift for sending e-mails quickly. The BlackBerry Messenger (BBM) was such a hit that it became the only mode of communications among my friends and contacts.

Blackberry's highly obsessive nature, which led to the 'CrackBerry' nickname, meant some of us rarely putting the handset down when we came back home from work. A friend of mine had his BlackBerry addiction cited in his divorce papers as one of the reasons on his ex-wife's list of 'irrational conduct'. I was distinctly unhappy to learn BlackBerry abandoning its smartphone manu-facture in September 2016.

The story behind BlackBerry's demise is an interesting read. Its co-chief executives, Mike Lazardis and James Balsillie, refused to take the iPhone seriously. They countered saying the iPhone, which was launched way back in 1997, was too unwieldy to type long and serious work-related e-mails. They surmised the iPhone to be a toy, and assumed that organizations will never allow its employees to handle such a device for official work.

To top it all, the BlackBerry top management refused to upset the existing apple carts. They believed that BlackBerry's huge existing clientele cannot be disturbed with any technological changes.[8] This is a problem with many organizations when innovation needs to be thought of to make things move to the next gear.

Even when competition seems to be breathing down the neck, many organizations get stranded in their prevailing play areas. Protecting their existing turf becomes more important. The future is sacrificed at the altar of the present—a problem that plagues many.

While iPhone was difficult to use for sending longer e-mails, BlackBerry management missed the point that iPhones could do a lot many things much better. It was a more secure device, had ease in synchronization with Apple PCs and could do many more technology-related stuffs—and ultimately the iPhone toy became a tool.

Around 2014, my BlackBerry handset started misbehaving. Samsung smartphone based on android technology made a strong case for me to change, which combined the features of a cell phone, camera, pocket computer and multimedia player. Many of my friends had moved to Apple's iPhone.

Technology kept shifting. Companies became irrelevant. Iconic brands mentioned before and which were dear to many of us, such as Motorola, Nokia and BlackBerry, moved into obscurity. Companies such as Samsung and Apple, and a host of relatively new Asian players, such as Huawei, Vivo, Oppo, Xiaomi, Lenovo and LG, that could keep pace with changing consumer choice flourished, and the old order faded. The mobile phone sector, thus, went through a metamorphosis, with many iconic companies succumbing to competitive innovation lunge.

Another interesting but may be unheard of story of failing to see change was that of a brilliant Chinese immigrant to the United States, An Wang. For all those of you who would have been used to typing on computers in the late 1970s and early 1980s, you may recollect that the main computing device used in most parts of the corporate world was a word processor made by **Wang Laboratories**, founded by Wang. He was very successful, and his dream was to overtake IBM in his mini-computer business. He used to maintain a chart on his table comparing his sales with that of IBM and visualizing to beat them somewhere in the mid-1990s.[9]

But IBM created its first personal computer, which could not only do word processing but a lot more things. Unfortunately, Wang clung to his belief that people would only need to do typing and use word processing, trusting there is no space for a holistic computing device. And that was the beginning of Wang's end. Wang Computers declared bankruptcy in 1992 unable to keep pace with technological changes with shifting times, unable to upgrade the so-called gloried typewriters to the next level.

Perhaps the most widely discussed failure to see change coming in pertains to **Eastman Kodak**, the photography company founded in 1888. The company developed the combination of roll films and camera in the early days of its existence. Kodak continued to hitchhike on its success for the next 100 years.

Kodak was aware that the digital technology was getting developed but ignored the change thinking analogue system will never die. They argued how can anyone not print pictures and store for posterity? An employee even developed a digital camera in 1975, but the management team ignored the development.

For Kodak, the age-old analog film business was a money-spinner even until 1999. By that time the digital technology had already spread its wings, and it was too late for Kodak to adapt it.

Kodak was overtaken by nimbler competitors who could foresee how people would want to capture and share pictures in the wired world. Kodak's business collapsed and the company filed for Chapter 11 bankruptcy protection in 2012.[10] It emerged in 2013 as a much smaller and leaner company selling imaging equipment and services. But it was never the same Kodak with which we have all grown up, capturing our history in pictorial formats.

A good example where change will need to be forecasted is our minimalistic mechanical device—the pencil. Will it survive?

Most of us have used the world's best-known pencil—**Faber-Castell**. Set up in 1761, it is the world's largest maker of wood-encased pencils, pens and crayons. This German company's focus has been on design and engineering, developing an aptitude for turning everyday products into luxury goods. With the advent of digital technology and the world of iPads, is there any certainty of the future for coloured pencils, crayons and ink markets?

Until now, for over 250 years, Faber-Castell has overcome various technological shifts. For example, it shifted from slide-rulers to electronic calculators in the 1970s. Over centuries, the basic design of pencil remains similar. In the late 1990s, Faber-Castell developed triangular shaped pencils with raised dots, for ease of grip. It became an instant hit.

'I think it (the pencil) will always be a part of mankind's experience to draw and write,' says Daniel Rogger, who was appointed the CEO in June 2017, after the death in 2016 of the eighth-generation Count Anton Wolfgang von Faber-Castell. Rogger also notes that even the current fad of doodling is an uptick in the popularity of some form of pencil use of late.[11]

Time will tell whether Faber-Castell leadership is right in assuming pencil business is immortal in this age of computers and smartphones, and the ever-waning habits of writing by hand.

What should you not do to trip by circumventing change? How to prevent your business from becoming sick as you either could not stay ahead of the curve or could not catch up with the developments?

The top management must have the ethos to change: a holistic tactic to management rather than taking a silo approach—like manufacturing ignoring what R&D is developing, ability to mould business to changing conditions, and having an all-round interactive approach to connect the innovation dots into an organization to make change effective.

Tailpiece

'The pessimist complains about the wind; the optimist expects it to change; the realist adjusts the sails,' said the inspirational American writer William Arthur Ward—perhaps summarizing unknowingly his take on business necessity to see change and adapt it to suit new buying habits—but many miss to notice the apparent.

Honey, Innovation Needs Money!

There is always a degree of luck involved in case of novelty and new projects. Efforts may or may not yield in commercial success. But to embark on development efforts without adequate capital backing is a recipe for adversity.

To innovate, there need to be a number of trials. Trial and error is the fulcrum of newness. Thomas Edison, the inventor of the electric light bulb, is understood to have tested over 6,000 possible materials to find the right filament that will fit the bill—carbonized bamboo. It is clear that some ideas and efforts need to necessarily fail to germinate the seeds of a successful outcome. What is the threshold of failure for an entrepreneur? After how many attempts will an innovator give up? What price is an innovating entrepreneur willing to pay for success?

The threshold will vary among organizations, depending upon their varying risk appetite. More important, working on innovation needs money and some may not have adequate economic muscle power, making financial constraint as one of the most important barrier to innovation. The quantum of money available could limit the innovation threshold.

Canada's **Bombardier**, a business jet maker, had a development budget of $3.5 billion but it overshot to $5.5 billion. To fight competition, it got preoccupied by the expensive and time-consuming route of trying to break into the narrow-body commercial jet market. The company ran out of cash. The project to launch new variants got delayed. (The company has since ramped up a large long-term debt load of $9 billion.)[12] Unless the company improves its cash flow, the future looks challenging.

Hawker Beechcraft, operating in the similar, yet very competitive business jet field, failed to differentiate itself from the crowd and invested heavily in developing aircraft with lighter but costlier material. The market refused to pay a premium for the newly developed lighter version. The company, a manufacturer of smaller corporate jets, ran out of cash and entered bankruptcy in 2012 due to mismanagement and poor capital allocation[13] (the company emerged from bankruptcy protection in 2013 after jettisoning its unprofitable business jet operations).

Similar experiences have also been inflicted upon the automotive sector. This industry has continuous development projects, but on a smaller scale compared with the aerospace industry but equally critical. It was the comparable issue of allocating too little capital to product development by the United States' big three—**GM, Ford** and **Chrysler**—which failed them in the recent past to compete effectively with foreign competition.

Innovation and development activities may or may not work. But if you do not try, you do not get to know what works! A degree of risk and element of providence is inevitable.

Tailpiece

Before embarking upon research and development actions, it is good to assess likely 'capital' cost (one-time expense with long-term advantage) and 'revenue' cost (benefit unlikely to last more than one year). Fund availability should be estimated. It is good to have about next 12 months' development-related fund requirement budgeted and ideally set aside. Financial constraint is the greatest killer of the innovative spirit of a business.

Pitfalls to Avoid

Salesforce.com, Tesla, Amazon, Netflix and Hindustan Unilever are among the best innovating companies in the world, according to Forbes Listing 2018. What do the innovative businesses do so very right which makes them the world-beaters? Alternatively, what is it that the companies need to avoid to be winner-innovators? An EY survey of 2010 found certain answers to how companies push growth by igniting the fuel of innovation from within.

1. *Be flexible:* Disruptive forces sometime sweep customer needs. Organizations need to be able to adapt to business

tectonic shifts. Take a look at the tech world. The market moved through mainframe computers to the internet and smartphones. These waves of change have created havoc to many of the old giants. IBM and HP keep struggling. And some like Compaq, HCL and Honeywell, unable to keep pace with time either got acquired or dumped the computer business for good.

2. *Inspire creativity:* Give people enough time away from their normal jobs to work on creative ideas. But set up formal processes to make sure the ideas generated are not wasted. At *3M,* considered one of the most innovative companies in the world, employees are allowed 15 per cent of their time to think of new ideas. If an idea looks promising, the company officially funds it.

3. *Encourage employees:* Employees have lots of ideas. Tap them. Encourage all to participate in the innovation dialogue. Did you know that it was Google engineers and not the auto industry that started the work to produce self-driving cars? How was it done? Google expects every employee to spend 20 per cent of their time to create something new—and just see the result: Google map, Google earth, Street View, all to help us to hit the roads, hands-off in the near future.

4. *Diversity helps in innovation:* Assemble and unleash a diverse workforce. *Google's* employees in India come from various cultural and religious backgrounds, speaking different languages. This diversity helped in creating 'Google Finance'.

5. *Provide career for thinkers:* Innovators are non-conformists. Design a career path for your innovators. Traditional ways of advancing their careers may not work. At Microsoft, Robbie Bach and J. Allard (both of whom worked many years and retired from the company ultimately), creating the software giant's Xbox game console, would not have been possible had Microsoft not provided them with encouragement and career moves.

6. *Explore government support:* Most countries have subsidies for R&D efforts including tax breaks. Do not ignore them. For example, in India, innovations through an approved R&D cell of a corporate can obtain tax breaks.

7. *Be prepared for failures:* Failed projects should not be a hurdle for innovation. Failures are harbingers of success. Take into stride failures, intellectual property squabbles, financial risks and internal conflicts. HP, the IT giant, tried to grow big through acquisitions, but realizing its hazard, it has reversed its course.

8. *Institutionalize innovation:* Make innovation-related activities inseparable from organization's operations. It is the ability to harness the collective power of ideas efficiently and transparently, encouraging employees to generate more and more new ideas. This will enable continuous innovation—the best way to become a market leader. Infosys, the Indian IT major, has successfully used the concept in its enterprise application services, generating patentable innovations and business solutions for clients.

Tailpiece

Innovation is about disagreeing with the past. Innovators are thinkers. But only if their brilliance is enmeshed with business sense, logic and sustaining efforts, can the wise men convert their hearts and minds to a wallet full of money.

In Closing

The seismic shift that reverberates through the business world disrupts all but a small handful of organizations that are either flexible or simply lucky to adapt. In the technology world, for instance, the shift from mainframe computing, to minicomputers and then to PCs and now smartphones, has brought successive waves of old companies dropping off and bringing new companies to the fore. Food and beverages business is another disrupter where healthier fare is snubbing processed foods and carbonated drinks.

The true value of a business is not that it has been around for a long while, the real worth is that it should be missed if it is not around. For achieving this, businesses need to continue innovating by constantly challenging themselves and setting dauntingly haughty targets to withstand the sands of time and not sink in them.

Success in business and innovation are inseparable. Without innovation it is difficult to keep the consumers interested, or else profits will remain elusive. Look at Apple—from near bankruptcy to the most valuable company—inventions like MacBook and iPhone convinced shoppers its products are indispensable. But innovation need not always be the answer in every occasion if it gets somehow detached from consumers' desire. Look at the genetically modified food, a brilliant innovation but its removal further from the 'natural' state is stretching adversely the business concept including the sector's mentor, Monsanto, since acquired by Bayer.

Relevant innovation is the key—or else, the durability and financial success of a business will elude. New businesses will always emerge to replace the failing ones. Make no mistake of not reinventing and not adapting quickly to changing circumstances.

References

1. Rafferty T. The rise and fall of Harley-Davidson perfume. Rideapart [Internet]. 2017 Jun 6. Available from: https://www.rideapart.com/articles/253742/the-rise-and-fall-of-harley-davidson-perfume/

2. Schanen N. Colgate's beef lasagna, coffee flavoured Coca-Cola and Donald Trump's board game among biggest flops at Museum of Failure. Mirror [Internet]. 2017 Apr 21. Available from: https://www.mirror.co.uk/news/world-news/colgates-beef-lasagna-coffee-flavoured-10262672

3. Lahman S. Chester Carlson's long journey. Democrat & Chronicle [Internet]. Available from: https://www.democratandchronicle.com/story/money/business/2013/10/17/sean-lahman-chester-carlsons-long-journey/2993265/

4. Independent. Obituary: Sir Godfrey Hounsfield. Independent [Internet]. 2004 Aug 20. Available from: https://www.independent.co.uk/news/obituaries/sir-godfrey-hounsfield-550312.html

5. AutoWeek. The Tata Nano failed because nobody aspires to own a cheap car. AutoWeek [Internet]. 2018 Jul 11. Available from: https://autoweek.com/article/car-news/tata-nano-failed-because-nobody-aspires-own-cheap-car

6. Mui C. The lesson that market leaders are failing to learn from Xerox PARC. Forbes [Internet]. 2012 Aug 1. Available from: https://www.forbes.com/sites/chunkamui/2012/08/01/the-lesson-that-market-leaders-are-failing-to-learn-from-xerox-parc/#6ed9643f6829

7. Surowiecki W. Where Nokia went wrong. The New Yorker [Internet]. 2013 Sep 3. Available from: https://www.newyorker.com/business/currency/where-nokia-went-wrong

8. Gustin S. The fatal mistake that doomed BlackBerry. Time [Internet]. 2013 Sep 24. Available from: http://business.time.com/2013/09/24/the-fatal-mistake-that-doomed-blackberry/

9. Smith E. The great failure of Wang Laboratories, the David to IBM's Goliath. Motherboard [Internet]. 2017 Feb 21. Available from: https://motherboard.vice.com/en_us/article/vvxby3/the-great-failure-of-wang-laboratories-the-david-to-ibms-goliath

10. Mui C. How Kodak failed. Forbes [Internet]. 2012 Jan 18. Available from: https://www.forbes.com/sites/chunkamui/2012/01/18/how-kodak-failed/#450ad7106f27

11. Olson N. Faber-Castell makes the pencil popular. Forbes [Internet]. 2018 May 14. Available from: https://www.forbes.com/sites/nancyolson/2018/05/14/faber-castell-makes-the-pencil-popular/#316433732ab9

12. Bogaisky J. Bombardier fights to regain altitude. Forbes [Internet]. 2018 Nov 6. Available from: https://www.forbes.com/sites/jeremybogaisky/2018/11/06/bombardier-fights-to-regain-altitude/#165505ec490d

13. Voorhis D. Hawker Beechcraft's recovery a long process. The Wichita Eagle [Internet].2012 May 5. Available from: https://www.kansas.com/news/business/aviation/article1091647.html

THE DEBT TRAP

Debt is a double-edged sword—it helps to do business; it can also ruin one.

Do you know what caused the biggest recession in the recent times? Believe it or not, the reason was 'debt'. Taken to build homes—a just cause indeed—housing loans given by some of the largest US banks to the not-too-deserved borrowers turned out to be the biggest blunder. It made the debt-providing banks sick, not being able to recover loans made against 'subprime mortgages', meaning loans given with little hope of recovery. With housing loans given easily, more houses were in demand, leading to price surge. But when it loomed that the borrowers were incapable to repay, mortgaged properties got sold to settle the overdue loans. A housing bubble emanated, originally created by the credit boom. Fears about the inability of borrowers to repay or refinance the debts caused the 2008 crisis the worst economic downturn since the 1930s, hitting the world's underbelly, creating waves of global slowdown.

Debt levels grew enormously in the rich world from 1980 to 2007. Post the financial crisis of 2008, private-sector borrowers scrambled to reduce their debts. The problems became more intense with subprime mortgages, as the owners of such assets committed the error to leverage themselves, meaning they had bought their assets with borrowed money. They were forced to sell the homes to repay their debts. And when some could not meet their debt obligations, confidence in the system went for a toss.

In turn, it affected the lenders too. They started attempting to shrink their lending to cut further losses on their bleeding balance sheets. The resultant credit contraction led to the global financial calamity.

The financial crisis of 2008 was all debt led—mistake on one part of over-leveraging, and a fraud on the other when some banks bundled subprime mortgages with normal loans to create collateralized debt obligations (CDOs) for onward sales to investors. These substandard loans were thereafter hived off by banks to investors across the world.

Banks made investors believe that they were buying risk-free investments as they were rated AAA by rating agencies. Whereas these were poor-quality debts backed by borrowers with little ability to repay the loans they had taken. With borrowers failing to repay the loans when they were called upon to do so sometime in 2006–2007, the investors of CDOs lost millions of dollars and the financial crisis set in. The players to the game were banks such as **J.P.Morgan**, **Bank of America**, **Wells Fargo** and **Citigroup**.

'Debt' thus resulted in the implosion of the world's financial system—such is the nuisance value of the deadly instrument of debt—when failure to service emanates.

Though Shakespeare in 'Hamlet' said, 'neither a borrower nor a lender be', in reality, the availability of debt and the willingness to take it are critical components of economic progress as these allow individuals, businesses and governments to make investments which they otherwise would not have been able to make. It involves the movement of money from creditors with an excess of funds, to debtors who are short of it.

Archaeologists have unearthed Babylonian tables of sun-dried clay demonstrating incurrence of obligations pertaining to the period of the third millennium before Christ.

Despite debt being in existence since ancient times, misgivings always surrounded it. Debt is an unforgiving instrument—it must be paid on time when due, whatever happens. It strongly distinguishes from equity-like instruments, which are more merciful and flexible. Even the German word for debt—'schuld'—means guilt, blame or fault. Such has been the reservation for the venerable instrument where indiscretions formed fault frontiers.

Mistake not—borrowings do have merits. It lets businesses do things which otherwise may not have been possible—start an operation, buy an asset, repay an old loan, acquire an enterprise, pay for working capital involving buying raw material, labour, rent and energy.

Debt also has other upsides. Interest on debt is tax deductible, while dividend on equity is not. In addition, debt does not dilute equity ownership.

Higher debt automatically is not a problem—debt is a beneficial way for creditors and borrowers to spread their cash flow requirement over time. Rising debt levels may be a sign that the lenders are looking at the borrowing corporate more positively. No lender would lend unless there is reasonable chance of recovery—but, of course, mistakes do take place.

The positives of debt often drive corporates to drop their guards only to get exposed to its vagaries.

Loans have a cost and could turn out to be a huge downside. Not only the borrower has to pay interest, the debt also needs to be repaid on time, usually in instalments. Money is lent usually against security of some assets such as land, building, machineries, receivables and inventories. If the borrowing is not serviced through timely payment of interest and instalment obligations, the lenders would have the right to acquire the borrower's assets securing the loan—a big risk if things go wrong.

A typical soft spot for debt is mounting business losses. The adverse situation enhances hunger for money to fill up the emptying coffers. To satisfy the appetite for growth and meet continuing operating cost, debt is easy money to hanker for. Credit binge becomes an addiction. The bait of debt trap gets laid.

There is no definite threshold at which debt levels become 'too high', although debts at the covenant guidelines are usually taken as the 'debt limit'. Theoretically, stacking up more debt benefits shareholders as debt interest is tax deductible—but only up to a point. That level, generally speaking, is reached when lenders start worrying about the enterprise defaulting in their obligations to pay interest or instalments. This is the 'tipping point'. To continue debt flow beyond that threshold may even lead to insolvency of the borrower enterprise.

The mistake of overreliance on debt is what plays havoc. This may take place when a call is made to take on someone else's money to create value. A judicious amount of debt is considered beneficial as financial leverage maximizes return. But debt is also associated with fragility and risk. Debt could mean having less room to manoeuvre if setback occurs. Choice is—giving too much power to the lenders or retaining it within the business!

Call of Covenant

God has an agreement with you and me to look after with unlimited love and to protect us. The Lord is committed to provide unconditional affection, attention and care to all His creations. This is the Biblical alliance between the Almighty and we the human race. In form, a 'covenant' is an agreement between two and involves promise of each towards the other. The notion of covenant between God and His people is one of the central themes of the Bible.

The concept of fulfilling obligations also extends to contracts of loan. No one lends unless the borrower agrees to fulfil certain commitments—to meet some threshold guidelines the lender expects. The mutually agreed deliverables, which could be financial and operational, are known in the commercial world as 'covenants'.

'Financial covenants' are usually ratios that the borrower is required to maintain. Say, maintaining a maximum level of borrowing to enable timely servicing through indebtedness-to-profit (usually EBITDA) ratio of 4:1. There could also be a financial cap on the debt levels. The covenants could also limit the entrepreneur to spend money on, say, acquisition of new assets, change in ownership control, giving of loans, related-party transactions and payment of dividends. The basic purpose is to ensure that shareholders do not suck out money from the company for unrelated business purpose or for extravagant usage, and maintain financial discipline so as to ensure timely servicing of the debts.

'Operational covenants' could include maintaining certain standards of business assets, preparing management information on timely manner and periodical internal control audit by approved auditing firms. These covenants dictate how to run the business.

Breaching of covenants leads to negative outcomes—usually lenders place additional restrictions. It could mean hastening of loan repayments, levying of penal interest, enforcing sale of security, restricting on further fund raising, declaring the borrower a defaulter or needing additional guarantees. It also could have loads of rub-off adverse effects—plummeting credit rating, negative employee morale, plunging customer confidence and reduced market valuation of the enterprise.

Covenant breach essentially leads to lenders taking more control over the enterprise and placing additional restrictions on operational flexibility. While lenders usually feel that such controls and restrictions will improve their chance of recovering their dues, but more often than not, it hastens business sickness if not its ultimate demise. It is thus best to avoid the mistake of committing covenant breach.

Blunders could be many in the arena of covenants.

For example, lenders advance with a sense of optimistic judgement but borrowers fail to deliver; market conditions turn adverse and loan servicing gets challenging; borrowers miscalculate business projections and cash flows do not match expectations; and borrowers misrepresent business plans which lenders fail to decode. Causes could be many—the result remains the same—covenant threshold breach and business sustenance getting difficult.

If the business grows beyond capabilities to handle, covenant breach cannot be ruled out. **CAN Capital Inc**, one of the oldest, most successful online lenders to small businesses in the United States, was forced to stop making new loans in late 2016 when problems were discovered as to how the company reported borrower delinquencies. The firm had covenants on limits of delinquent customers. It is reported that the employees of CAN Capital granted loan extensions when the borrowers failed to pay. The 'grace days' led to non-declaration of delinquent loans and hence under-reporting of repayment failures to investors and creditors. The errors were significant enough to cause covenant breaches with its banks like Wells Fargo. To help a turnaround, the company commenced negotiating with creditors to seek covenant relaxations.

What transpired in companies such as CAN Capital is like getting into new markets rapidly without putting in place proper internal processes and controls. Non-adherence to covenants, a process failure, put brakes in one of the best names in the financial technology space.

High debt was almost leading to a serious debt covenant default for India's resource giant and London-listed **Vedanta Resources**, which was enmeshed with a lot of debt. The mining company looked at all sorts of cash flows to boost its coffers. In early 2016, cash-rich subsidiary Hindustan Zinc declared a special dividend to push up $1.8 billion of cash to India-listed Vedanta Limited, so that a part of the cash can get passed on to the parent, Vedanta Resources, via an intercompany loan. To provide Vedanta some breathing space, the creditors granted a covenant waiver for a certain period allowing the company to breach debt levels of 2.75 times of EBITDA.

Companies in debt look for any cash they can lay their hands on and all possible waivers to keep their noses above water, somehow.

In India, large corporates who had taken massive debts are being declared by the country's central bank (RBI) as loan defaulters since June 2017, dissolving company board power and referring to probable insolvency actions. These companies would have long back breached the loan covenants. The list includes companies such as **Jyoti Structures**, **Bhushan Power & Steel** and **ABG Shipyard**. Many of them are in limbo for multiple years, unable or unwilling to bite the bullet of resolving the covenant rupture clauses.

Many a time the covenant requirements are buried in the myriad of words written on loan documents. More often than not, the loan papers are either not referred to regularly or covenant terms are not taken cognizance of seriously. The consequences of such omissions could be damaging.

Many causes could have led to breaching the covenants, including operational challenges, market downturn, skill shortages or simply poor governance. Hence, businesses need to keep a keen eye on such eventualities.

Tailpiece

Businesses must continuously work out shadow-covenant levels at future dates plotting probable numbers. It is a grave error when organizations do not take all possible steps to prevent tripping on loan stipulations.

Horror of Debt

Borrowing by businesses, households and governments take place on the assumption that their debt liabilities will be met either by paying the principal and interest or by rolling over the debts with new conditions. But this works only if the business performs better to make the debts bearable or to justify new loans. When those ingredients go missing, defaults follow.

Debt is a claim on future affluence: lenders expect to be paid back from wealth created by the business. The level of debt tends to expand at moments when the business is on upswing. Borrowers hope that their income is set to rise, or that the assets bought with borrowed money will enhance in price; lenders too would share that optimism.

But if the business scenario does not improve suitably to justify the enthusiasm, lenders' disenchantment is inevitable. Borrowers may default, leading lenders to cut back further lending, creating a liquidity whirlpool even for borrowers genuinely in need of funding. When challenging clouds threaten business, the debt umbrella is often withdrawn by the lenders. This unfortunately is the stark reality—debt has several ugly faces.

Global debt numbers are rather scary, reaching a new high of $247 trillion or three times of the world GDP in mid-2018.[1] Such enormous debt addiction cannot be without its downsides and goof-ups. This is mainly driven by emerging markets, raising doubts about another possibility of a global debt-related financial crisis. The debt burden is not distributed evenly, with some countries showing deleveraging while others have accumulated very high levels. For regions with rising debt may create headwinds for long-term growth and eventually pose danger for financial stability, as debt cannot keep growing faster than an economy forever.

The debt burden has made many corporations live on oxygen. Once one of the America's largest and most storied retailers, **Sears**—which also owns **Kmart**—has been on its death bed for the last several years. While the buying habits of consumers post the e-commerce era have changed, one cause which created immense pain to Sears is its debt. Its possible bankruptcy is not long away.

Many of us love our breakfast cereals for a seemingly healthy intake in a hasty morning. **Kellogg's** sells its cereals and convenience foods in over 180 countries. And yet it is struggling with high debts. Continuing volume decline in its core cereal business, especially in developed markets including North America, Europe and Asia, has created great challenge. To top it all, the company committed grave errors in the past by returning cash to its shareholders through enhanced share repurchase and dividends, only to add more debt. With about four times debt to equity (i.e., leverage position), it was rated by mid-2018,[2] to almost a junk grade investment company (BBB minus by Fitch Ratings[3])—a not too happy financial position for a company with great recognizable brands.

India is going through debt dismay. Many businesses launched aggressive debt-fuelled growth strategies over recent years, especially during 2003 and 2007, only to come unstuck as growth slowed or investment projects were delayed by India's red tapism. Most Indian banks lent ardently and often adventurously to corporates building large-scale projects in steel, power and infrastructure, only to find many borrowers unable to service their debts, often due to project delays, poor management or simply, poor governance.

The corporate indebtedness scenario in India is bad. Credit Suisse has produced an infamous list[4] of most indebted companies in India, the 'house of debts'. Ten business groups feature in the list. It includes big names like **Jaypee**, **GVK**, **GMR** and **Anil Ambani**-led **Reliance** Group. It shows that their debt levels kept climbing and despite attempts at deleveraging, the financial stress at these groups intensified. The business canvas of India is splashed with indebted moguls, ranging from big conglomerates such as **Essar**, **Adani** and **Vedanta**, to a long tail of enterprises in sectors such as mining, steel, power and infrastructure. No wonder such development on the part of the heavyweights has resulted in Indian banks crumbling under the weight of bad loans and borrowing companies are being throttled of their growth ambitions.

Many of you, who are in India, must have used consumer durables bearing the names like Allwyn, Kelvinator and Electrolux. The Indian group which owns these well-known brands is **Videocon**, another famous name. Growth ambitions festered by its chairman Venugopal Dhoot by getting into unrelated areas like telecom and multiple acquisitions, mainly through debt funding, has taken its market valuation falling off the cliff—due to its default to repay its debt obligations. It is a sad fall from grace of the well-known consumer electronics brands. Over ambition, expansion into unrelated areas, and high debt are a heady concoction often hard to swallow and digest.

When debts spike and credit rating drops, enterprises agonize. Their ability to source new money gets challenged. Debt enables businesses to do things which they otherwise would not have been able to do. A sinking rating makes debts risky and expensive.

Moreover, lenders get jittery. Big names in businesses have skidded time and again.

Do not commit the error to borrow to the hilt—keep headroom to raise further debts when bad times hit.

Tailpiece

The late Walter Schloss, one of the best-known American value investors, once said—'I don't like debt. A lot of companies get in trouble because of debt. So I tend to avoid companies with too much debt'—mark these words of an all-time great investor!

Debt–laden Acquisition Trap

Optimism is good; over-optimism is bad. Entrepreneurs with high ambition, tall confidence or over-sized ego have dreamt of taking the leap to super growth with acquisitions—both local and foreign. Many of these acquisitions sit on the back of debt. When forecasted business cash flows do not materialize or get stretched, all hell breaks loose.

Tulsibhai Tanti, the Indian promoter-chairman of **Suzlon Energy**, harboured the ambition to become a world player in the wind energy sector and rub shoulders with the globe's high and mighty. To promote his dreams, he acquired in 2007 REpower, a German company, for $1.6 billion, outbidding France's Areva.[5] This was one of the many high-profile overseas acquisitions by Indian businesses—the deal earned Tulsibhai a reputation for careless expansion. No doubt this acquisition propped Suzlon as the world's fifth-largest wind turbine company—but only to be submerged with costly debts on its balance sheet.

The German business had to be sold in 2015 at a loss to a US private equity group—for €1 billion ($1.2 billion) to repay the debts. Tulsibhai said on the completion of the sale—the proceeds will be used 'for debt repayment thereby reducing interest cost'.[6] In fact, the German business REpower (renamed Senvion) was the most profitable piece of Tulsibhai's business empire. The German arm had to be sold as part of wider plans to save his Indian business that had come close to bankruptcy. The golden goose had to be sacrificed to save the geese.

The enigmatic Indian steel conglomerate, **Tata Steel**, gave years of growth to its shareholders, till Ratan Tata, its former chairman, decided to go global and challenge the hegemony of ArcelorMittal, the world's largest company headed by another Indian, Lakshmi Mittal. Ratan Tata bought the British-Dutch steel maker, Corus, in 2007. It had outbid CSN of Brazil for the British steel operations for $12 billion,[7] seeking to gain access to European markets. Not only was the takeover ill-timed, being just before the 2008 global financial crisis, but the price paid was excessive through an overheated bidding process. And to top it all, the huge acquisition was debt funded—with half raised on Corus's books and the balance funded by using foreign currency debt raised in its Indian books. Tata Steel, of course, became the fifth-largest steel company in the world in terms of output, from its earlier position of 56th, but this debt-laden acquisition sunk the ever-blooming Tata Steel into a thorny plant. Since the takeover, the Tata Steel share price by and large has lagged behind the metal share price index—only to prove how the transaction of debt-filled acquisition was an awful self-goal. The company's obsession with adding capacity mainly through debt keeps its liabilities tantalizingly bloated, keeping anxious investors worried.

Tailpiece

Pumping up egos of entrepreneurs by acquiring assets holding bankers' lending hands has fallen foul in many cases. Unless the cash flows are sustainably adequate to pay for the incremental loan instalments and interest, taking debt for M&A is a poor strategy to follow. Historical evidence shows that it does not pay to borrow to buy someone else.

Slip-up in Lenders' Lending

Debt—a double-edged knife—involves a giver and a taker. The borrower often makes mistakes while borrowing, and the stories around it are many. But what about the lender? If a debt goes bad, is the lender not to be blamed too.

A glaring example of bankers making cardinal errors of giving loans to the undeserving is **Kingfisher Airlines**. Millions of dollars of debt remained outstanding when Mallya flew away in early 2016 from India to the United Kingdom, not to return to face the bankers who have filed dozens of cases to recover the debts.

The airlines had a slew of instances where bankers kept giving loans at a time when there were reasonable reasons to believe that the loans may end up bad.

The Indian investigating body, CBI, is investigating five high-level officers of **IDBI Bank** for a ₹950 crore ($150 million) loan sanctioned in 2009, which the airline has failed to repay. At that time, Kingfisher was already in a full-blown financial crisis, with losses reported in March 2009 of ₹1,600 crore ($250 million). The CBI is questioning why the loan was given at all. Believe it or not, the bank referred the loan proposal for credit rating (a loan sanction prerequisite), almost a week after the disbursement of the entire loan amount. In addition, the CBI has reasons to believe that the airlines did not use the money for the purpose it was given.[8]

Sadly, Kingfisher was not the only beneficiary of the lackadaisical loan process of IDBI. According to CBI, there were many other corporates with poor credit rating which were sanctioned loans by the bank. It is learnt that several Indian corporates such as **Strides Arcolabs** (renamed **Strides Shasun**), **Sun Direct TV, Kolte Patil Developers, S Kumar's, Aircel** and **Marathon Realty** have been benefitted by IDBI Bank's largesse.

Let us take another example how bad lending leads to loss for lenders. **S Kumars Nationwide**, an Indian textile company, is a glaring example. With great apparel brands such as Reid & Taylor, S Kumars and Belmonte, the company went into oblivion by 2015, leaving the banks to rue losses of over ₹4,500 crore ($690 million) of outstanding loans.[9] Not only did the banks give loans when they should not have according to the CBI charge sheet, the banks did very little when they found the balance sheets untenable. Between 2008–2009 and 2012–2013, the company showed receivables in excess of 40 per cent of sales, with the figure jumping to 55 per cent in 2012–2013. Very clearly, either the debtors were bogus or were propped up to show higher revenue with little or no possibility of recovery.

With a lack of oversight from the bankers, the borrower company went belly up under their very nose. The lenders committed the mistake of letting the company drift into extinction without repaying the borrowed funds.

Tailpiece

If lenders are not careful, who should be? It is our money which the bankers lend. They are trustees of our money. But when they play foul or depict sheer carelessness, the outcome is calamitous.

Less Debt, More Charm

'Leverage' implies exertion of force by means of a 'lever'. Lever means a rigid bar resting on a pivot, used to move a load with one end when pressure is applied to the other. Debt is exactly like a lever. It has the ability to thump business returns upward, or it can swing an enterprise into distress when the fixed interest cost becomes too high to bear or cash flows are insufficient to repay loan instalments. It always remains a double-edged blade!

Funding for any business is a mix of equity and debt. A higher proportion of debt intrudes on the credit rating of a firm. Good credit rating helps to reduce the long-term cost of capital as it helps in sourcing debt at cheaper rates. Keeping debt low necessarily helps.

More debt means more risk. If the profits of the corporation are not good enough to even pay off its interest, obviously the company's growth will suffer. With profits being inadequate—which is usually depicted as EBITDA—lower than the interest liability, there is but no option for the company but to throttle operations to arrest cost and try enhancing its surplus. In addition, the cash flow needs to be adequate to pay for the debt instalments.

A major incentive for managers to seek debt funding is when their remuneration has dollops of stock options—a great way to line up the pockets of senior executives. Debt is a quick way to show short-term returns—cost of debt is corporate tax deductible while dividend on equity is not.

Debt funding also helps to enhance earnings per share (EPS). EPS, a popular methodology for markets to value companies, can also be enhanced by buying back shares. The method reduces the number of outstanding equity shares, thereby buoying up the earnings in terms of a single share.

Creating a leveraged balance sheet may not be value accretive but some managements choose to chase quarterly earnings and push up EPS. In the long run, the actions could be treated as grave errors, but who cares! Quite a few top executives are more concerned about their personal bottom line, and if that gets propped up, little else do they bother.

Tailpiece

Entrepreneurship stands on medication of debt and equity; but improper dosage of debt may aggravate sickness with grave side effects.

Lenders Forcing Correction

A weak credit culture in India has led to cycles of borrower defaults, hurting the economy and taxpayers. The origin of the current Indian banking stress lies in the credit bubble inflated during the boom years before the global financial crisis, and the short burst of recovery thereafter. Banks were either goaded to lend due to political connections or under corrupt undertones.

A relatively new law in India, the Insolvency and Banking Code 2016 lays down a time-bound and transparent framework for resolving cases of debt defaults. The regulation seeks to break the bad equilibrium among the borrowers, lenders, bureaucracy and politicians, by shifting power from borrowers to creditors. The code bolsters the sanctity of the debt contract and aims in correcting the numerous blundered lending by the banking sector.

Egged by India's central bank and bolstered by the insolvency regulations, banks are forcing borrowers to put sale tags on their wares such as mines, plants, refineries, roads, ports, guesthouses, private jets and status symbol corporate offices. Indian banks are cracking the whip on the defaulting bigwigs—to sell their assets and pay off the debts due. Or else, the companies are being put up for insolvency resolution, which would result in change of ownership of the assets. The top 10 business house debtors alone owe over ₹450,000 crore ($64 billion) to the banks.[10]

The outcome of the mistaken strategy of overloading with debts has seen several corporate ownerships flipping—recalcitrant ex-entrepreneurs losing control over their assets. The steel major **Bhushan Steel**, with an outstanding debt of ₹56,000 crore ($8 billion), one of the biggest loan defaulters in India, has become Tata Steel in September 2018.[11] Banks took a one-third haircut. The erstwhile promoters, the Singhal family, committed the grave mistake of fraud. The Serious Fraud Investigation Office has accused the entrepreneurs of fraudulent manoeuvres to siphon-off loans.[12] **Monnet Ispat**, one of India's foremost steel makers, with an outstanding loan of ₹11,000 crore ($1.6 billion) bleeding with huge losses, has changed hands—AION–JSW Steel consortium has taken over the troubled borrower. Their blunders were high debt, inappropriately acquired coal mines cancelled by the Supreme Court and product mix not good enough to compete with cheaper Chinese imports.[13] The outcome was bankruptcy. The new Indian bankruptcy laws compelled these recalcitrant owners to hand over the ownership of their stressed companies.

Tailpiece

Many businesses commit the error of growing at a breakneck speed. This heady desire of growth is often fulfilled through the mistaken step of lenders adding debt to the borrower's coffers without considering the fallouts of their poor possible future cash flows and the risk of non-repayment. Optimism is good, but over-optimism on the borrower risk profile is a very bad business.

Un-jumbling Junk

While countries and governments may be keen to latch on to superior credit ratings, but enterprises are perhaps thinking otherwise. The *Economist* stated that the median rating of the companies assessed by the rating agency Standard & Poor's has fallen from 'A' in 1981 to 'BBB minus' by 2010 (and continued to remain downgraded even till 2018).[14] This rating is the lowest possible 'investment grade' or, to put it simply, is just one notch above the 'junk' bond status.

This definitely suggests that creditors as well as borrowers have had a change of heart over time. Customarily, the investment funds that held the bulk of corporate bonds were only allowed to procure investment-grade securities. (Credit ratings 'BBB' and above are known as investment grades.) But nowadays, many issuers are double-B and triple-C rated companies, meaning they are below investment-grade category. Many of the bonds have become 'junk' because of deterioration in the issuing enterprise's balance sheet quality, but it was not that way when it started earlier.

Investors, however, like 'junk bonds'—a non-investment-grade fixed-income debt instrument providing higher yields. They are also politely called 'high-yield bonds'—instruments with inherent nature of higher risk of defaults where borrowers are financially stretched.

The world's love affair with junk bonds has resulted in its share rising now to almost half of the global bond market against one-quarter in the 1990s. The prevalent market low rates of interest and the desire to make higher returns at any cost have made high-yield debts quite popular.

To chase higher yields in a world of sinking interest rates, investors are willing to take riskier investments to make some extra percentages of gain. The additional yields paid by companies reflect the possible risk of default. Investment-grade bonds usually trade four to five percentage points higher than the near risk-free government bonds. Junk bonds obviously are priced much higher based on their risk profile.

With interest rates falling, the companies have used junk bond proceeds to refinance high-cost debt, a step that saves interest expense. This is a good move. But the lousy news is that some corporates are using the proceeds to pay dividends to private equity owners, a move that can weaken a company by increasing its debt load without strengthening its underlying business. While this move enriches the private equity holders, it results in business sickness, job losses and potential bankruptcy.

From an investor's point of view, junk bonds have all the trappings of a risky venture—lowering yield or non-payment is part of the spectacle. Global uncertainties and swinging oil and commodity prices may make the yields sway. Make no mistake of putting all the investment eggs in one basket—junks can turn sour.

Junk bonds are a more expensive way of raising money. The availability of funding under this mode should not be mistaken to be easy money. These bonds come with quite a few covenants and missives (standard high-yield bond covenant involves a 'two times coverage ratio', meaning a company cannot take more debt unless its EBIT or 'earnings before interest and tax' is large enough to cover its interest costs twice over). This puts limitations on future borrowings.

Tailpiece

Junk bond is a $1.5 trillion rough and tumble business arena. As befits a junkyard, it is full of ups and downs—many trash but with a few traces of goodies. Do not mistake that low market rates, high yield and tall risks are a delightful brew for an intoxicating experience for the not so faint-hearted in the world of finance.

How to Solve the Debt Riddle?

As we all know, to conquer addiction, the first thing to resolve is to acknowledge there is a problem. Debt is like liquor or pot—the more you take the more you want. Businesses often get hooked on to a debt obsession. Easy money flowing in gives a huge kick—only to realize later that the past indiscretions were costly compulsions.

Debt-related problems would never arise if both the lender and the borrower were working with perfect information and act with complete rationality. Usually, there is information asymmetry between the lenders and their borrowers. Lenders may not analyse all data, and borrowers may not provide all information to which they are privy.

The problem with debt is that it is not like any cooking oven, where the parties to the debt cookery can instantly see if something is wrong. It may take years for the mistakes to become evident. By that time, the harm could have already happened.

Nations such as China, Argentina, Greece and Italy have relied for long on credit-fuelled growth, so have many businesses followed this mantra to their own peril.

Lanco Infratech, once listed among fastest growing in the world, and **Alok Industries**, once a darling of the Indian stock markets, burnt their fingers through debt reliance, getting them into the defaulter's list of bankers, failing to pay their dues. On the other hand, there are companies such as *Lupin Laboratories* and *Wockhardt Limited*, which were almost crushed under debt in the mid-1990s, but could come out of it through debt restructuring. While most succumbed under debt, some could climb out of the debt dungeon.

What should a business do to avoid the debt trap? How does a business deleverage itself should it fall into the debt pit?

- *Recognize there is a problem:* Awareness that there is a problem is the first step to emancipate oneself from any debt muddle.

The optimism of the entrepreneur, the board or the senior management that the situation will improve in the near future to service the debt is the biggest impediment to save any business from debt potholes. Numerous enterprises have suffered from this ever-presence sense of hopefulness.

I know of a very large business house headquartered in Mumbai whose debts were getting so large that every month it would be a struggle to pay the banks' instalments. Lenders would be called to provide grace days. Finance team would run helter-skelter to find new methods of funding to repay the old debts—an improper practice commercially known as 'ever greening'. But business plans for expansions were neither curtailed nor arrested. All signs showed of an impending debt trap. After several years of optimism and non-recognition of the debt crisis, the group is now declared as a defaulter by the lenders—a mistake which could have been avoided by timely recognition of the debt problem.

- *Equity, and not debt:* You have heard that equity is more expensive than debt. Loans get tax shelter, while dividend on equity gets none. Another upside for debt is getting money without ownership dilution. But the downside is debt obligations need to be met whether the business is doing well or not, while dividends are declared only out of profits. Thus, a struggling business will not have any dividend cash outflows, but lenders' dues cannot be ignored. Hence, to look for equity funding or debts with long payment holidays are best ways to avoid the debt noose, even though equity looks pricier on books. Programmes to look at swapping debt for equity should not be ignored.

Think of the relatively new e-commerce companies such as Uber, Ola and Flipkart. They are incurring millions of dollars of loss. But they are still growing with high valuations. The success of their business stories is investment through equity and not falling into the booby trap of the lenders.

- *No loans for cash-strapped businesses:* You must get more bang from debt. That, in theory means, choking off credit to underperforming businesses or restructuring those to get better repayment terms. Loans should flow to better cash flow-generating businesses, isolating struggling businesses from regular cash outflow requirements to meet lenders' compulsions.

- *Forex debt, only when forex earnings:* Borrowings are sometimes done in foreign currencies, including issuing of bonds. This makes debt servicing risky in terms of local currency of the debt issuer, if the borrowing currency strengthens. The debt-issuing company should ensure that either they have adequate export earnings or their future foreign exchange-related cash outflow obligations are hedged. Essentially, firms with sizeable foreign revenues such as multinationals or export-based businesses will be able to cope better with shifts in exchange rates.

  An instance is the rising external commercial borrowings, including the foreign currency bonds of Indian corporates. Things do not look kosher. Concerns exist against the claims made by many borrowers that they have a 'natural hedge', which suggests that foreign exchange assets or earnings adequately cover their foreign exchange liabilities. But doubts exist whether the assets and liabilities are well matched, especially in the case of real-estate, metals, oil and utility firms—another error in the funding strategy which is avoidable.

- *Avoid covenant breach:* Breaching covenants could lead to serious adverse consequences. Listing down the covenants is a good practice. Not all covenants are critical. Hence, to keep a tab on the important ones is imperative. Maintaining a good relationship with the bankers is a must. Continuous dialogue and sharing of business performance with the lenders make them retain confidence in the enterprise. In hours of crisis, bankers are said to look after their engaged clients better.

Some of the key covenant-related areas which should be focused upon while entering into a loan agreement could be as follows:

- Obtain as much covenant latitude as is possible. It is better to gain maximum leeway in covenants than bargain hard for interest reductions.

- Build covenants considering the seasonal pattern of the business. If monsoon season results in lower sales, then the relevant quarter should have higher covenant headroom.

- Get a remedy period before the lender can pull the rug from under the feet if breach happens. The grace days help the borrower to work on cures if default happens.

- Make sure that the board and senior management understand the key covenants and fallouts of breaches. Any potential covenant fissure can then be resolved with concerted collective wisdom and corrective measures.

Tailpiece

There can never be an exhaustive things-to-do list for borrowings. Awareness of its pitfalls will provide great solace to businesses in the hours of crisis. Prevention is better than cure—the popular phrase—applies very well to this entrepreneurial craving called debt.

In Closing

Debts are like electric currents: wrong connection will give you shocks over a long period, but the right ones will light up your business. There will perhaps never be the right answer for a debt quagmire. The need is to watch out and plan carefully for this elixir of business.

References

1. Turak N. Global debt hits a new record at $247 trillion. CNBC [Internet]. 2018 Jul 11. Available from: https://www.cnbc.com/2018/07/11/global-debt-hits-a-new-record-at-247-trillion.html

2. MarketWatch. Kellogg Co. MarketWatch [Internet]. 2019 Jan. Available from: https://www.marketwatch.com/investing/stock/k/profile

3. CBonds. Fitch Ratings downgrades. CBonds Financial Information [Internet]. 2018 Oct 12. Available from: http://cbonds.com/news/item/1048009

4. Livemint: Debt continues to weigh down India's top conglomerates: Oct 22, 2015: Available from: https://www.livemint.com/Companies/ny8WpQMe9LES9vpdFciVKI/Debt-continues-to-weigh-down-Indias-top-conglomerates.html

5. Reuters. India's Suzlon Energy completes REpower acquisition. Reuters [Internet]. 2007 Jul 13. Available from: https://in.reuters.com/article/repower-suzlon/indias-suzlon-energy-completes-repower-acquisition-idINBOM474320070602

6. Livemint. Suzlon sells German arm Senvion for €1 billion in all-cash deal. Livemint [Internet]. 2015 Jan 22. Available from: https://www.livemint.com/Companies/RPeXiOxA5jx6WzuJOx7wsL/Suzlon-sells-Senvion-for-1-billion-crore-in-allcash-deal.html

7. Tata Steel. Tata Steel completes £6.2bn acquisition of Corus Group plc. Tata Steel press release [Internet]. 2017 Apr 2. Available from: https://www.tatasteel.com/media/newsroom/press-releases/india/2007/tata-steel-completes-62bn-acquisition-of-corus-group-plc/

8. Livemint. Vijay Mallya case: CBI suspects IDBI Bank loan to Kingfisher Airlines was diverted to seven nations. Livemint [Internet]. 2017 Jan 31. Available from: https://www.livemint.com/

9. The Hindu Business Line. Bombay HC orders folding up S Kumars. The Hindu Business Line [Internet]. 2018 Jan 17. Available from: https://www.thehindubusinessline.com/companies/bombay-hc-orders-folding-up-s-kumars/article8820063.ece

10. Money Control. Top 100 debt/liability figures. MoneyControl [Internet]. Available from: https://www.moneycontrol.com/stocks/marketinfo/debt/bse/index.html

11. Mehta S. Tata Steel completes ₹35,200 crore purchase of bankrupt Bhushan Steel. The Economic Times [Internet]. 2018 May 19. Available

from: https://economictimes.indiatimes.com/industry/indl-goods/svs/ steel/tata-steel-completes-5-2-billion-purchase-of-bankrupt-bhushan-steel/articleshow/64224367.cms; Mazumdar R. Bhushan Steel renamed as Tata Steel BSL. The Economic Times [Internet]. 2018 Oct 1. Available from: https://economictimes.indiatimes.com/markets/stocks/news/ bhushan-steel-renamed-as-tata-steel-bsl/articleshow/66030595.cms

12. Thomas T. Tata Steel buys Bhushan Steel, to settle dues of ₹35,200 crore. Livemint [Internet]. 2018 May 18. Available from: https:// www.livemint.com/Companies/zQJ1nAquZndCvPo0baMCeO/Tata-Steel-unit-completes-acquisition-of-Bhushan-Steel.html

13. The Economic Times. JSW Steel, promoters acquire around 88% stake in Monnet Ispat. The Economic Times [Internet]. 2018 Sep 4. Available from: https://economictimes.indiatimes.com/industry/indl-goods/svs/steel/jsw-steel-promoters-acquire-around-88-stake-in-monnet-ispat/articleshow/65676876.cms

14. Where will the next crisis occur? The Economist [Internet]. 2018 May 3. Available from: https://www.economist.com/finance-and-economics/2018/05/03/where-will-the-next-crisis-occur

MORTAL MISTAKES

There is no end to the fumbles in our quest to survive. No one can ever say, 'I do not commit any faux pas.' No mortal can claim, 'I am flawless and faultless.' Perfection is not human.

Visualize the heart-rate monitor equipment—it goes up and down intermittently when we are alive and kicking but would smoothen itself on our last breath. Businesses are no exception—always oscillating between correctness and calamities, success and failures, good and the bad, depicting their existence and potency.

It should, however, be in our interest to make businesses as stable as we possibly can—to ensure consistent quality, smooth performance, steady deliveries and predictable financial performance. And this is where difficulties arise, challenges occur and inexactitudes ensue.

Have you noticed how many restaurants open in your town and how many of them close down in not too distant time? This phenomenon arises when businesses are either started without carrying out market demand estimate, or they lack competency, or they have inadequate capital, or they are just following someone who is seemingly doing well. It is rather common to see businesses starting with fanfare and only to find, sooner than later, an unscalable wall.

There are many unsound decisions and rickety steps we take which could be avoided to make our businesses steadier and sturdier. Let us look at some of the common mortal mistakes some of us commit—avoiding them will make immense sense barring unforeseen circumstances.

Long and Short of a Strategy

Short termism seems to have become a disease. Investors are not only holding investments in shares for much lesser period than they used to do earlier, but they are also expecting faster gratifications like share buybacks and higher dividends. US Senator Mark Warner, quoted in Politifact Virginia, said in 2016 that the average holding period of stocks, back in the 1960s was eight years; now it's an average of four months. One reason, however, could be computerized trading. Short-term in many cases is prevailing over long-term view.

Together with the investor attitude to hold the investments for shorter period, managers are feeling the heat, being hounded to provide for cost cuts, jack-up quarterly profits and buy back shares—short termism all the way.

Too much attention on short term affects business decisions adversely. *Harvard Business Review* in February 2017 reported a study observing companies deliver superior results when executives manage for long-term value creation and resist pressure to target excessively on meeting quarterly earning expectations. Research by McKinsey's and FCLT Global found organizations that operate with a true long-term mindset have consistently outperformed their industry peers between 2001 and 2014 across almost every financial measure that matters.

I have had years of investor quarterly calls—explaining sometimes not so encouraging company performance parameters under trying business conditions. Almost all questions from the analysts were focused on the ensuing 'quarter'—note, the singularity of the term, quarter. Their primary focus was: What is the guidance for the next quarter—'Can a 14 per cent' (believe me, the figures were so accurately asked) 'sales growth be expected'? How on earth, I wonder, can any CFO ever predict such precise growth numbers—unless he has 'cookie-jar' reserves created which can be dipped into; or unless the numbers are suitably 'played' with to suit market expectations!

It was sheer short termism in the analyst questions as opposed to attempting to understand what the company's tactics could be for the not too distant future. Attempting to extrapolate business performance uncertainties to predict likely share price movements have been the ultimate motive of the stock market experts.

I cannot blame the analysts. Economic newspapers and business-TV analysis necessarily need to predict the share price graph. 'Buy' or 'sell' recommendations are expected to be made. 'Breaking news' or the first-off-the-block broadcast syndrome are required to be met. These can happen only when the next quarter can somehow be a crystal ball gazed into! This approach is a sheer mistake of 'long-term' sacrificial lamb being offered at the altar of 'short termism'.

The culture of fear of not meeting guidance takes away a lot from the management bandwidth. They may attempt value-destructing immediate actions of dumping products on distributors, pushing credit sales, sacking people, curtailing advertisement and curbing R&D costs—the list could be long.

Over the past several years, many a company has discontinued hazarding guesses on the next quarter's financial performance. Ford, UPS, Coca-Cola, AT&T, Berkshire Hathaway and Google have dumped the practice of regularly posting quarterly forecasts.

Contrary to popular belief, McKinsey's, in its 2006 study, observed that frequent guidance does not result in superior valuations in the marketplace; indeed, guidance and valuations do not appear to be providing any significant relationship—regardless of the year, the industry or the size of the company in question. Why should management incur cost, time and stress on this exercise?

Management would do better to provide an understanding of the market, business environment and challenges, the underlying value drivers, possible capital expenditure plans, R&D, M&A, probable sources of funding and their business strategy—in short, to convey their understanding of business's long-term health and provide glimpse of their short-term performance. Analysts and investors would then be much better equipped to make business performance prognosis and to draw their own conclusions about business values.

It will be a healthier practice to discontinue quarterly guidance and substituting thoughtful discussions about company's long-term business fundamentals. Businesses could then signal better their commitment to creating a long-term sustainable value. It will be a blunder not to encourage investors to adopt a similar outlook.

Working on 'medium' and 'long term' does not mean bypassing the 'short term'. Only when the bumblebee sits on the first flowers can other flowers for future be pollinated. Think of big names like **AT&T**, **Digital Equipment**, **Kodak**, **Polaroid**, **Xerox**, **Silicon Graphics** and **Sun Microsystems**. All had significant R&D agendas, playing on long-term arenas. The trouble was none could bring their long-term investments to think of short-term fruition. They remained stuck in the future.

An example where short termism killed the biggest name in the toy industry is **AC Gilbert**. This American company, founded in 1909, had an unparalleled reputation of meeting the science and engineering learning needs of youngsters. Their bestseller was Meccano-like Erector engineering sets that had captivated the minds of millions of young learners. In a desperate move to meet the changing market conditions of the 1960s, the company opted for the disastrous strategy of making low-cost, low-quality toys. The plan backfired, and the company went out of business in 1967.[1] Short termism resulted in throwing out of the window 50 years of hard-earned reputation.

In business, a time-horizon perspective is crucial in trying to ensure enterprises to endure. Like farmers, managements need to simultaneously harvest the current crop, prepare the ground for the next season, and sow the seeds of the future. Long term (over five years) exists only when short term (current year) is treaded, and medium term (two to three years) is tackled. When enterprises find themselves caught off guard by the changing business environment, management is often found wanting in failing to invest sufficiently in the medium- and long-term horizons. The reverse is also true. Too much focus on long term will sweep businesses off their feet by short-term competitive tornados. Short termism does not always destroy value, nor does long termism promise success. A decent balance is most desirable.

The fact that some investors still value long-term strategic intent necessarily implies long-term investments are still given importance by a lot of stockholders. Capital will, hence, continue to pour into organizations like *Tesla, Flipkart* and *Paytm*—highly valued firms where breaking even is still years away. It would be a mistake to pick short termism as a quick fix investment strategy in every case.

Tailpiece

A long-term view will continue to sway its influence for times to come, even when short-term financial result forecasts will keep investors hedging their bets.

Why Many Launches Fail?

Many of us have a herd mentality—joining the bandwagon of buying shares or booking a home. Often this is a mistake. Just because others are doing something does not mean you should do the same. Why not evaluate your own option and action?

Similar stories exist in the business world. Is there a market for the product or service you are getting into? This is a key question to be asked before mistakes are committed.

Look at the retail mall-market scenario in India. With GDP on an upswing during recent years, several cities had a surfeit of new shopping malls. Many started only to be closed or to languish after heavy investments. Dozens changed their use to offices, educational institutes and banquet halls. Why is this industry in such a mess? It is sheer poor market-demand estimate. Many rushed to the already crowded space with me-too-malls—and the result is quite stark. Some market research would have reflected that there is already excess capacity. Hence, investments in new malls are unlikely to show results, unless the fresh offerings are different from what is already available in the market, like areas over 300,000 sq ft, presence of big brands and a good mix of food, beverages and entertainment.

Market research into consumers' buying habits is often overlooked by businesses. Sadly, entrepreneurial self-hunches habitually overshadow logical and professional inputs. Over one-half of new retail and consumer-packaged products fail to make any dent in the marketplace. One obvious cause is the inflexibility of consumer shopping behaviour. Even P&G, which regularly rolls out fresh products, faces unsuccessful launches in most cases, especially in the initial years. The main reason for failures could be no consumer demand, product not working, capacity inadequate or improper promise of performance.

Products could fail during test marketing due to a myriad of reasons: the recipe could be deficient, concepts may have shortcomings, insufficient value for money and packaging not attractive enough. Essentially, it usually flops when the product does not demonstrate perceptible benefit to consumers as compared to competing products. Market research is meant to replicate the *bazaar* situation, and not taking cognisance of the study findings would be a mistake.

Another big issue for market launch failure is the lack of preparation. Businesses often commit the error of getting too focused on crafting and making the new products, missing out on the hard work to understand consumers and getting ready for the market until it is too late.

Tailpiece

Gut feel is good but is not enough in every sphere of business. Marketing without information is like driving with eyes closed. An American author, W. Edwards Deming, had rightly commented: 'Without data you're just another person with an opinion.' Don't commit the mistake of going up the unfamiliar pathway of business without a data compass.

Missed Opportunities

History is replete with examples of companies which have passed up golden opportunities which, if taken, would have changed the way the world of business functioned or how the fortune of the companies would have turned up.

Just think of the stories of companies initially rejecting hovercraft, the hybrid vessel, not being able to distinguish whether it was a boat or an aircraft; makers of board-games rejecting Scrabble on the ground that it was too boring and dull; the management of Westinghouse, United States, which rejected Formica thinking it will be a commercial failure; and William Orton, the president of the Western Union, deciding in 1876 not to pay $100,000 for Alexander Graham Bell's telephone patent, asserting the apparatus little more than a toy, agreeing to offer $25 million only two years later.

The music and publishing industries overflow with stories of missed opportunities by companies. The illustrious JK Rowling was in the boat of rejections when 15 publishers rejected *Harry Potter and the Philosopher's Stone*.[2] But the Oscar for missed opportunities goes to British music company Decca Records' Dick Rowe, the man who turned down the Beatles, almost 50 years ago.[3] Dick Rowe made himself inadvertently but perpetually synonymous with disastrous commercial oversights.

The misjudgement club have many members. Some put their mistakes behind and move forward, and some get stuck in the muck of missed opportunities.

Tailpiece

How many times would you have miscalculated and bought shares of companies only to find it to be duds? Errors in thinking are part and parcel of our existence. No one misjudges deliberately. Hindsight lets people know that past decisions could be incorrect. It would be a mistake to brood over mistaken judgements. Be that as it may, it is best to recognize that these things happen; and if it does take place, forget them to forge forward.

Why Need a Barometer?

You cannot drive a car unless you know whether there is adequate fuel, you are exceeding the speed limit or not and have sufficient coolant. The car dashboard lets you know the basics.

Similarly, businesses cannot be run without having a control panel telling you how you are performing. Every business carries on numerous transactions of buying and selling. When these are recorded in a scientific manner, it helps to tell you whether you are making profits or losses, how much assets and liabilities does the business have and how are you doing in your fund management. But this is not enough. You would need to know much more information in a simplistic manner regularly, may be monthly or a shorter frequency. This is produced through the management information system—MIS, as it is popularly known.

I know of a company in Delhi which was making flexible solar panels, a recent development with multiple usages. The management was very happy that their manufacturing capacity was fully booked and sales were taking place at a brisk pace. But within a year, they ran out of cash. This is preposterous! How can this happen? A close look at the affairs of the business let the company know that it was not maintaining proper and regular MIS. They did not know whom did they sell, how much amount to be collected, when the amount will become receivable and how old are the existing outstanding customer dues?

In short, the organization did manufacture their products well, which led to good market demand, but they did not have proper MIS to capture the crucial information on credit sales made to customers and to follow up on collections. Simple issue, but the mistake led to severe cash crisis, which took them a long time to resolve.

Tailpiece

Making money is the barometer of business reality. But you cannot generate surplus unless you have a regular snapshot of key business performance parameters. MIS helps to focus your eyes and ears on the big stuff, ignoring the trivial.

At What Cost?

Businesses are meant for selling above cost, so as to generate some profit. But a key issue is: What is the 'cost'?

For a trader, determining cost is easier—the purchase price of the product which is traded-in plus incidentals such as interest, advertisement and selling expenses will normally be the cost.

The problem, however, arises when it comes to products manufactured or services rendered. It is often not easy to find the proper cost. Costs are of various types—'variable cost' such as raw material and energy; 'fixed cost' such as staff salaries, travelling, office rent, advertisement and many more. Organizations with debt will have interest as a cost, and manufacturers will have depreciation expense to be set aside. All this is fine, but someone needs to calculate it. Cost helps to provide guidance for arriving at the selling price. Even where products are based on market-driven pricing like steel, information on cost incurred helps to take action to chop-off portions of it to survive in the cut-throat competitive world. Not knowing the cost is a poor management practice.

A company making laboratory furniture in Mumbai once asked me to look into why it was financially stretched when its factory was working to capacity. It all boiled down to its incorrect product pricing, which was based on its owner's own hunches of cost incurred. It had no formal system to calculate the cost of every custom-built furniture item made to fit into specific customers' R&D laboratories. I observed that it was under-recovering its factory running cost, leading to making losses on most of their orders. Not calculating costs led to its bleeding financially.

Tailpiece

Profit is the monarch, and cost decides who will be the tsar. If you do not know what is the cost, then how will anyone know how much to sell at, to make profit?—Simple thing, but often ignored by many.

Why Have Cash?

Which businessman does not like to see revenue growing? But there is no point in enhancing sales if customers do not pay on time. A large receivables (customers owing money) balance means very little if the outstanding amount is not recovered on time. Similarly, procure your input items maximizing credit period from suppliers. A great business mantra is to buy on credit (pay later) and sell in cash (receive cash quickly) if you can, like restaurants and e-commerce groceries do.

Many FMCG companies in India, such as Hindustan Unilever, follow this model, and see how profitable they are and how healthy is their business balance sheet.

In times of financial difficulties, which arise more often than expected, it would be a mistake not to focus on one thing: relentless emphasis on unearthing cash and holding onto it. Neither growth nor profits are as important. When crisis happens in our personal lives, we may survive on credit cards, though paying obscene interest. But corporates do not have such privileges, barring undrawn bank facilities.

Even if there are good times, it would be a mistake to think that slip-ups will not take place. It would be a serious goof-up not to follow some golden guidelines: maintain emergency funds normally created when business has been performing well; do not utilize full borrowing limits and keep some undrawn balance from working capital debt facilities; keep an action plan ready to cut costs fast and precisely if there be a need; and prepare a weekly cash forecast to depict potential fund gaps for comparing with actual performance as you go along.

The popular saying 'Revenue is vanity, profit is sanity, but cash is king' is true for every business.

Tailpiece

It is all about money, honey! If money runs out, the pot of honey remains a distant dream. It is a grave mistake not to capitalize your business adequately or having sources of fresh funding if required. Hoping for divine intervention will be a big bungle.

Can You Manage It All?

Dreams we all have—to make it big. Some of us have entrepreneurial streaks within ourselves. But do we have the all-round education, expertise and experience to fulfil our vision to make it big in business?

If we cannot do it ourselves, we would need professional help. But many among us, especially the small-scale industrialists, may not have the intent or the financial muscle to appoint specialists. This is where many entrepreneurs blunder—thinking he has the aptitude and skill but the reality could be different. Another reason why professional help may not be taken could be lack of financial power. Try and seek some help even on part-time basis. Fully relying on one's own ability may be a mistake.

I know of a person who is an excellent plastic manufacturing engineer. He has worked in a plastic plant for over 20 years. He was bitten by the entrepreneurial bug. Being a product specialist himself, he commenced his journey to start on his own. He failed miserably when it came to raising funds—his ability and knowledge of the financial market was limited, and he started the business with inadequate funding. The new venture collapsed within three years. You will perhaps know of many other similar instances.

Business involves producing, planning, procuring, logistics, financing, selling, marketing, human resources, IT, taxation and a lot more. Most of us do not have the managerial ability to handle each of these areas. Evaluate what skills you possess, which ones you can get help from your known circle of contacts and where you would need outside professional intervention.

Tailpiece

No human can be a jack of all trades. An entrepreneur not planning to seek the 360-degree capability for business support will be hara-kiri. Money may be a constraint to employ professionals but awareness of areas of weakness will help business persons to seek support whenever feasible.

Don't Defer Delegation

You cannot do everything yourself—no one can. However, many managers are notoriously reluctant to delegate and give up control. How can a busy manager get more productive when there is only so much time in the day?

One simple answer: Delegate more of what you do not have to do yourself. This frees up your time to enable you to do what is really important. It is no wonder that the management schools teach to 'manage by exceptions'.

Do you prefer to be copied in every e-mail? Do you ask for frequent updates about things? Do you laser in on every detail and take pride or suffer pain in making corrections? There are innumerable instances of entrepreneurs and managers trying to hold on to everything. This necessarily delays decision-making, demotivates managers and organizational progress becomes tardy.

The attitude of micromanagement leads to the streaks of do-it-yourself syndrome. No one likes to be micromanaged. It is discouraging and demoralizing. Yet some controlling bosses cannot seem to stop themselves from paying attention to every minute detail.

Tailpiece

While managing through nit-picking may provide short-term results, it is a poor managerial trait. Just as no one wants to be micromanaged, similarly no one wants to be the much-despised micromanager. Do not commit the error either to adopt or to adapt this crummy behavioural trait.

Why Biased Hiring?

In China, **J.P.Morgan** hired the children of the well connected. 'He was the worst candidate they had ever seen, and we still had to extend him an offer,' shrieked an internal e-mail. Jobs were offered to the offspring of potential clients, including those in the government or at Chinese government companies. J.P.Morgan earned about $100 million revenue from the 200 junior employees hired as favours in the Asia Pacific region between 2006 and 2013. 'Client referral programme' was practised to work around the internal hiring guidelines. The bank paid in 2016 a penalty of $264 million to settle a US probe for hiring the 'princelings' to win Chinese business.

Many businesses across geographies flourish through the business–politician–government nexus. These linkages often lead to bribery being given to the politician and government connections. These hirings often misfire, leading to bad-will to the businesses when the hiring gets known.

Some business groups in India are known for their tireless cultivation of political contacts. In 2015, **Essar** was forced to defend its drill of hiring friends of politicians at their request[4]—a practice which does not augur well for any business and is best avoided.

Businesses cannot be run by bricks and mortar. You need people to run it. Your business is as good as your people. Wrong hiring is a blatant blunder, more so when these recruits are people with 'connections'. Neither will you be able to provide them with negative feedback nor can you throw them out if their performance is suboptimal.

Tailpiece

Bad hires are like having a tasty fish for dinner but with the fishbone getting stuck in your throat which you are neither able to swallow nor take it out.

What to Do, to Evade Errors?

Normally mistakes are not committed knowingly. It is typically an unintended outcome of some action or inaction. It is good to take steps to avoid the gaffes. Some precautions, certain steps, a few do's and don'ts should help to minimize bloomers and blunders:

- *Be realistic, and do not be over ambitious nor be excessively hopeful:* Over-optimism is like speculation—you feel that you may win whenever and whatever you attempt; but business is not so simple. Optimism is good but over-optimism is a mistake.

- *Implement a sound management system and control:* Or else, your efforts could be systematically drained. Have 'four-eyes' principle for every cost item—someone's work should be checked at least by another. Don't believe that the world consists of only sages; in fact, there are too many cheaters prowling around.

- *Make a business plan, and do not keep everything in your head:* Do not keep hoping things will work out the way you want them to be. Draw your monthly plan—likely costs, estimated sales and fund requirement. Update the business plan regularly but definitely once a quarter. The best plans will go awry, and adjusting these to ground conditions will make your business plans definitive and action oriented. Compare plans with actuals, and study why there were variances, especially the negative ones.

- *Maintain simple and good MIS:* This should match broadly with financial accounting numbers on a quarterly basis. It will help to provide early warning signals of impending blips. Potential business crisis can be unearthed for quick action.

- *Estimate the right amount of capital required, without over borrowing:* Negotiate a loan repayment moratorium for new businesses or projects, and a two-year repayment holiday would be good. Loan comes with responsibilities to repay the sum borrowed over instalments and the interest component. Non-payment makes further raising of new money well-nigh impossible and lenders start hounding on you, taking much of your time to fend them off.

- *Understand the supply–demand scenario first:* When you start a new business or a fresh line or any diversification, try to understand what the customer wants, and debate whether you will be able to meet their expectations. Do not underestimate your competition—remember they are probably thinking the same way as you are.

- *Select the suitable and relevant technology*: Vendors may be making a sales pitch or you may have liked what you have read or seen recently. Examine whether the technology, including any second-hand equipment, is appropriate for the present and the future? Is there a good after-sales service facility available? Is maintenance cost reasonable? Is the yield, wastage and energy consumption in line with industry standards?

- *Evaluate the critical business skills available:* Can your team handle all the critical matters either internally or you have someone to fall back upon? No one can know all; hence, you may need someone knowledgeable in certain disciplines and functions.

- *The best asset a business can have is cash:* Remember, profit is not cash. Cash is often stuck in inventory and debtors. Keep monitoring the two key items, and anything dated should be liquidated before it erodes value. Globally, good companies maintain piles of cash reserves as a cushion against eventualities. For instance, Apple's cash hoard was over \$230 billion by mid-2018.[5] So does Infosys, the Indian IT multinational, and many more, having large cash reserves stashed up. Keep focusing on your cash pile, and you will never regret it.

- *Practise the 'what', not the 'how':* Tell what to do, but not how to do. Do not be a control freak. Delegate authority but seek responsibility to deliver from those delegated. When you find that you are being swamped with work and unable to decide on new tasks, it is time to delegate. An organization's outcome is a joint effort of many, and no single mortal can build any business empire. So let it go!

- *All of us are mortals:* Every manager, every employee, will need to ultimately secede office. But experience shows that most companies are ill prepared for succession planning. Lack of preparedness when a key manager or employee leaves, retires or dies is half the story. Executive development programme dovetailed with senior management succession planning ensures organizational endurance. Just remember, each one of us has a finite lifespan, but an organization carries on in perpetuity—it is immortal after all. Forgetting this inevitable truth is a serious blunder!

In Closing

When any organization is accustomed to almost continuous success, it becomes difficult to contemplate failures. It is very difficult to own up a mistake—especially a costly one. The fact remains, each one of us blunders, regularly. From some slip-ups we learn, while on other goof-ups we rationalize. It is good to take responsibility, decide a plan for remedy and fix what is wrong. This will enable anyone to gracefully handle aberrations. Though it sounds simple, repercussions of a mistake once committed are difficult to handle in real life.

To err is human—and no one is above this innate human attribute. It is also not possible to lay down every mistake one can make. The illustrations in this chapter (and, of course, in this book) should help one know how some have agonized. These should provide ideas to conjure up to cope with any of the rather common eventualities.

Mortals we are, mistakes we shall make and mending is a must, though a mammoth mission.

References

1. Eli Whitney Museum and Workshop. AC Gilbert: The demise of AC Gilbert and Company. Eli Whitney Museum and Workshop [Internet]. Available from: https://www.eliwhitney.org/7/museum/-gilbert-project/-man/a-c-gilbert-scientific-toymaker-essays-arts-and-sciences-october-6

2. Dawn R. J.K. Rowling's original 'Harry Potter' pitch was rejected 12 times. Today [Internet]. 2017 Oct 20. Available from: https://www.

today.com/popculture/j-k-rowling-s-original-harry-potter-pitch-was-rejected-t117763

3. Viner B. The man who rejected the Beatles. Independent [Internet]. 2012 Feb 12. Available from: https://www.independent.co.uk/arts-entertainment/music/news/the-man-who-rejected-the-beatles-6782008.html

4. Sharma B. Essar emails suggest pressure from Pranab Mukherjee to hire family and friends. Huffpost [Internet]. 2015 Jun 12. Available from: https://www.huffingtonpost.in/2015/06/12/pranab-mukherjee-_n_7559714.html

5. Feiner L. Apple now has $237.1 billion in cash on hand. CNBC.com [Internet]. 2018 Nov 1. Available from: https://www.cnbc.com/2018/11/01/apple-now-has-237point1-billion-in-cash-on-hand.html

MANGLED BUSINESS MODELS

Two of the most recognizable brands in India nowadays are the e-commerce giants **Flipkart** and **Snapdeal**. Tiger Global Management, an investor in Flipkart, got dissatisfied with the way the business model was getting structured, allowing space to its competition. It flipped Flipkart's co-founder Binny Bansal in 2017 for its own employee Kalyan Krishnamurthy. In May 2018, Walmart bought over 77 per cent of Flipkart's stake for $16 billion, forcing Binny Bansal to sell his 5 per cent stake, though he did not wish to do so from a company which he co-founded a decade back. Kunal Bahl and Rohit Bansal, the co-founders of Snapdeal, admitted in April 2017 that their company's fate was out of their hands. In both these cases, the investors took control, rejigging and redesigning the business models, control mechanisms, pricing techniques, product portfolio and funding requirements.

Let us take another example where business models have created havoc. **Bitcoin** and many other cryptocurrencies, not monitored by any government agency, have been structured as an alternative to regular monetary system. Bitcoin price-swings have been wild—from $1,000 in the start of 2017 to $19,000 during Christmas the same year, and then doing summersaults. Some have made millions, while others have lost their life-savings by mortgaging homes to take positions on Bitcoins. Only time will tell whether this recent block-chain-based business concept of pseudo-currencies is flawed or not.

Business models are never cast in stone. Even if these have stood the test of time, these need to be revisited over and over again—to pick holes, repair them and build new ones trying to make these as much watertight as is feasible.

When you look at the list of long-lived companies, the one lesson which stands out clearly is flexibility. It could involve change of business, product lines, technology or the leader.

Changing Consumer Custom

Consumer habits have changed rapidly over time. Dresses, bags, books, phones, groceries and so on are now disproportionately being bought online, compared with consumer preferences earlier. The touch–feel–trial requirement while buying shirts or frocks seems to have been given a go-by. A wide choice, attractive price and home-delivery ease are all taking precedence over the physical shopping experience. The list of changing consumer habit is unending. When businesses do not adapt to these changing tastes quickly enough, grave error is the outcome.

Tesco, the supermarket chain, has been hit hard by continuing shifts in shopping habits and the rise of discounters like Aldi and Lidl. Crushed by debt and crippled by online competition, a 60-year-old brand, **Toys 'R' Us**, filed for bankruptcy in September 2017. The retail giants **Kohl's**, **Dillard's** and **Nordstrom** are all struggling to keep pace with changing times.

Some businesses have adapted e-commerce gainfully, while many are still trying to figure out how to make the best use of it. For instance, the Indian pioneer of organized retailing, Kishore Biyani of **Future Group**, was too late to get onto the e-commerce bus, and it seems to be rather costly for the group, though they refuse to acknowledge it.

E-commerce not only provides consumers with wider shopping options sitting home, through giants such as Amazon, Alibaba and Flipkart, but it also offers manufacturers, especially the smaller ones, a new way to reach consumers. The archaic ways of dealing with retail and department stores with poor payment terms are now a passé for many vendors. However, many manufacturers detest e-tailing as enhanced competition, and cut-throat pricing sometime affects the bigger ones.

Thousands of businesses fail to recognize consumer habit shift. They keep basking in past glory—only to topple miserably sooner than later. **HMV** and **HMT** are classic examples of generic brands failing to keep pace with changing times.

HMV, the name synonymous with music, is a typical story of not discerning the shifting tunes in the melody-business game. It failed to recognize the threats coming from online retailers and downloadable music. The biggest mistake HMV made was its failure to invest in its online offering throughout the 1990s. The global music company was overtaken by changing technology, and when it began reinventing itself, it was just too late.[1]

The epochal HMT, India's timekeeper, stopped ticking since 2016. The enviable brand failed to keep pace with quartz-analog technology, attractive designs and competition from the home-grown brand, Titan.[2]

Some businesses are adapting while many are struggling. For instance, tobacco companies have somehow coped with the stigmatization of its unhealthy heritage products, by investing in e-cigarettes and enhancing the cost of consumer packs. Coca-Cola, once a single-product company selling the dark and sweet soda since 1886, is now besieged with health concerns of the discerning consumer.

Tailpiece

It is important to remodel business in line with the shift in consumer behaviour. While every business may not be able to anticipate and identify the change, it can play along with the consumers' changing consumption habits. It will be foolhardy to assume that consumers are stupid, and their transforming behaviour is just a flash in the pan. Businesses must play the game with consumers, keep adapting and reinventing along with shifting consumption habits. Or else, disaster will be knocking at the door.

Culture: A Cause for Collapse

Why do some businesses get maimed and mangled, while others prosper? The ethos of achievement and effectiveness against the habit of sloppiness could be a reason. Many entrepreneurships fail when philosophy of benevolent leadership is amiss. Most M&As fail when the cultures of two organizations do not congregate.

A lack of proper business culture can be calamitous. **HP**, an office-equipment conglomerate, failed over the last two decades under successive CEOs where the focus was on top-line while under investing in R&D, leading to tech deficit. Successive CEOs drove their own agendas. Carly Fiorina controversially purchased PC maker, Compaq, Mark Hurd acquired the IT services company, EDS and Léo Apotheker disastrously overpaid in the $11-billion deal for a software company, Autonomy. The company in all spent around $70 billion, more than the combined market value of the main two surviving HP enterprises. By 2017, the outcome was dreadful: 100,000 lost jobs, $19 billion in write-offs, $10 billion of restructuring charges and a series of spin-offs, resulting in the maiming of the world's most incongruent tech giant. (Meg Whitman, during her six-year CEO stint ending in 2017, ultimately had to undo the mistakes her predecessors did. Break up the company, as it was too unwieldy to handle.)

Not learning from mistakes is a matter of poor corporate culture and is unpardonable.

Pfizer, the largest pharmaceutical company on the planet, has over the years repeatedly paid fines for its drug-marketing misdemeanours. Over several decades, Pfizer has been at the centre of controversies for overpricing its products, inappropriate advertising and marketing, bribery, environmental issues, human rights and tax practices. A senior manager at Pfizer, Kopchinski, once said, 'The whole culture of Pfizer is driven by sales, and if you don't sell drugs illegally, you are not seen as a team player.'[3]

A bank of great stature, **Goldman Sachs**, has flunked time and again, making mistakes as it strode the path of a money-making machine. It has paid billions of dollars as penalties, its chief executives assured of good conduct every time, only to slip again into the toxic culture of poor corporate behaviour. Behind its closed doors, Goldman straddles the line between conflict of interest and legitimate deal-making, and upholds a culture of power struggle and toxic paranoia—states William Cohan in his book, *Money and Power*.

In 2013, **Ryanair**, the Irish budget airline, for the first time accepted that it was suffering from a reputation of treating its passengers shabbily. It had a culture of being macho and abrupt, complained many. Action replay in 2017. The culture of working at Ryanair 'has gone very miserable … even in our head office', moaned chief operations officer, Peter Bellew.[4] These are typical examples where the psyche of providing poor customer service and not listening to staff members were pulling the company down, though it had done a lot in cost-cutting and competitiveness.

No wonder that Ryanair has been rated in 2018 as the worst airline for the sixth consecutive year by '*Which?*' with the consumer group claiming that the Dublin-based carrier serves bad food and provides uncomfortable seats. As expected, Ryanair dismissed the survey as 'unrepresentative and worthless'.[5] Continued hara-kiri on the airline's side in not accepting the reality.

Cultural contours can vary. One of the most successful start-ups of recent times—**Uber,** the ride-hailing app company—depicted a horrible culture through its 40-year-old boss Travis Kalanick, who was ultimately sacked. A 2017 independent review of its workplace practices revealed a sickening free-for-all corporate attitude, including bullying drivers, grabbing intellectual property (Google's accusations) and sexual harassments (200 odd complaints). Uber followed aggressive and unrestrained work culture, tainting its hard-earned brand name.[6]

Culture in an organization can take various shapes and forms. Some corporates could encourage employees staying late at their desks, while others could be a paragon of informality.

Tailpiece

Culture is difficult to define. It takes a mystical form, often eroding a company's way of working and serving its customers. Shame, peer pressure and negative public opinion often prevent managements not to fall short of poor culture of execution threshold. A cocky culture could be a silent killer, negating years of effort in putting together a business venture.

Global Structural Shift

Oscillating global trade is generating debates whether the recent longish slowdown since 2008 is a permanent shift or is cyclical, as global growth is again showing some upturn since 2017. Challenging times make organizations look to shift business models.

The recent global stagnation can be attributed majorly to economic slowdown in China. This resulted in impacting its declining appetite for commodities on several emerging markets where growth is dependent upon feeding the Chinese hunger for metals and minerals. In addition, a continued lack of traction from emerging economies, such as Latin America and Africa, adds to the anaemic growth in global commerce.

However, these are not the sole reasons for the insipid display of global trade. There are other reasons in play, which businessmen need to be aware of, to avoid mistakes in their strategies.

The foremost reason is China's emphasis to rebalance itself from a manufacturing and export-led economy to one focused on domestic consumption.

Almost half of the post-2008 crisis slowdown could be attributed to 'structural', rather than to 'cyclical', reasons. China is moving towards swallowing up major portions of supply chain. This means Chinese manufacturers are increasingly producing many of the intermediates which it used to import.

Many countries have commenced bringing production closer home as it has happened in the United States, India, Africa and elsewhere. Auto and pharmaceutical makers, and intermediate manufacturers like fabric and electrical parts, have commenced producing closer to the place of consumption, resulting in shrinking volumes of global trade.

Increased automation and new manufacturing technologies such as robotics and 3D additive manufacturing are likely to accelerate the change. These do not bode well for global trade.

The images that we have of shiploads carrying tonnes of goods to far-flung locations may slowly dwindle.

In fact, instead of global trade and commerce increasing, it is the digital world which is bringing sweeping global changes. While the flow of goods and services has fallen from a peak of 53 per cent of global output in 2007 to 40 per cent in 2014, the cross-border data interchange, however, has increased. A McKinsey report has indicated that the flow of digital information around the world has grown 45 times in 10 years, from 5 terabits per second (Tbps) in 2005, to 210 Tbps in 2014.[7]

The exchange of huge data and information, internet of things (network connectivity helping data collection and exchange), next-generation genomics (ability to manipulate genes to improve health and agriculture), and developments in renewal energy storage are making companies avoid shipping boatloads of goods and equipment. Global innovations and digital data interchange are in fact helping companies to manufacture on their own.

For instance, the McLaren Honda F1 Team has made a new trackside addition—a 3D printer—to allow its aerodynamic engineers to make tweaked parts overnight, slashing production time and shaving fractions of a second off race times. GE using 3D printers is making fuel nozzles for jet engines. It expects to manufacture over 100,000 parts using this technology by 2020.

Stalled corporate investments in manufacturing machineries have added fuel to global slowdown. In addition, falling consumer confidence is not helping. While transition away from China can be fired by the demands from Africa, Latin America and India, it is in the realms of the next round of developments for which businessmen need to perhaps wait a while.

Disruptive technologies are likely to change business dynamics, creating entirely new products and services and varying supply chain solutions. Businesses will need to keep their strategies updated in the face of the ever-changing technological changes, so that they can use technologies to stay ahead of the game.

Established business models may need to be challenged, rejigged and recalibrated, updating employee skills and mindset continuously. Not being cognizant of probable changes around you will be a big blunder.

I shudder to think that some companies may be facing massive dilemmas that may go to the core of their business model. There is a growing risk that automakers may discontinue bulk-transporting vehicles to individual buyers, as ride-hailing app companies with their soon to feature self-driving vehicles may displace our individual car ownerships. The new vehicle buyers may instead be fleet services, purchasing in bulk at reduced prices and at locations close to probable use, shrinking global shipping traffic further.

Tailpiece

Risk-mitigating mantras help avoiding missteps which businesses may otherwise commit by sticking to their hitherto old ways of doing business. Mistake not—the vicissitudes in the world of trade and commerce after all are more structural than cyclical!

Fiddled and Flawed Product

Sometimes the difference between success and failure depends upon whether the products meet customer needs. Foolish moves and gargantuan mistakes often lead to crash landings of even the high and mighty.

A glaring example of tinkering with a product and making a mess of it was New Coke. It is such a case study that when a new product backfires in the market, it is called the 'New Coke'. The problem emerged in April 1985, when the **Coca-Cola** Company broadcast a change to its nearly century-old secret formula. The New Coke would have a smoother, sweeter taste—similar to Diet

Coke, but sweetened with corn syrup.[8] Market researchers predicted that it was a product of the millennium.

During the 1980s, Pepsi was breathing down the neck of Coca-Cola, though Coke was number one in the market. The New Coke was launched to take Pepsi head on and make Coke the undisputed market leader. But it bombed. 'I find the Coke too sweet. The old coke was much better', was what a majority of customers harped back. It was a disaster of epic proportions. Pepsi took full advantage by launching a commercial featuring a girl quipping: 'Somebody out there tell me why Coke did it? Why did Coke change?'

Consumer groups got together and petitioned to get the old Coke back. Virtually one and all were rejecting the sweetened new Coke.

In July 1985, the old Coke was brought back, dumping the new Coke. Coco Cola admitted it was a mistake to launch the new Coke. A 77-day fiasco taught Coca-Cola a lesson of a lifetime. Even after 30 years, the company remembers not to interfere with the taste that works.

It is very important not to play with a product which is working with customers for a long time.

A similar experience took place in **JCPenney**, the US retailer. During a thankfully short stint of its chief executive, Ron Johnson, the retailer underwent a makeover, which the customers just did not buy. In 2012, the stores stopped promoting sales and offering coupons and instead made a big deal about its 'everyday' low prices. The regulars stopped shopping there. It wasn't that the prices were bad. The customers just felt that there wasn't much fun anymore in shopping at JCPenney—not to see products being marked down heavily.[9]

What Ron Johnson did was to reduce the prices of certain products on a daily basis. The customers did not get the feel of earning a huge discount by comparing the 'old' price and the new discounted price. A $5 product may be great, but unless the customer sees that it is after a 50 per cent discount on a $10 product, she will not get a good feel. Ron missed this basic psychology—providing an illusion to customers of obtaining a great discount. JCPenney's sales nosedived. Ron was fired in 2013, but the company lost vital time to fight competition especially from the web-world.

A mistaken strategy of pricing—JCPenney might say it's a fair price, but why should consumers trust the retailer? Believe it or not, people do not want a fair price. They want great deals. Consumers infer that they get a bargain based on the reference point provided by the higher pre-sale or anchor price. Without the old price being displayed, consumers have difficulties in determining whether it is a great buy.

JCPenney backtracked on its pricing strategy, offering coupons and running weekly sales again. And it started marking up items to immediately mark them down for the feel of a discount. But damage was done through a strategic pricing blunder.

Look at Colgate. The same old taste for generations. I can still remember the toothpaste which I used as a child. I enjoy the same flavour and taste even now every morning. Colgate, of course, has launched other variants, but it has retained its original toothpaste without much fiddling, though changing a few aspects of the formulation. A similar example applies to Unilever's Close Up gel toothpaste. Over the decades, I continue to like the same tingling sensation while brushing my teeth.

My two all-time favourite oral cares continue to be the grand old Colgate and mouth-freshening Close Up. It is perhaps true with many of you. These are classic cases of the manufacturers not making the mistake of fiddling with the products which are working in the marketplace.

Tailpiece

Consumers are normally resistant to changes. Try they may, but a whole hog shift in their purchasing habits takes time. **Kellogg's** came to India way back in 1994, spent millions of dollars to change habits of Indians by offering them alternatives in breakfast, lost loads of money over decades and yet could not make much dent.

Attempt not to mess around with consumer preferences. Launch new variants or options after market research into local tastes and habits. Not spending time enough to understand what customers would like is a massive mistake.

To Brand or Not to Brand

There are numerous entrepreneurs selling their many wares—some with a brand name, others anonymous. Is branding better? Does it not cost a bomb to build a brand name?

Research has shown that non-branded businesses typically earn gross margins anywhere between 3 and 5 per cent. But they are constantly at risk of being undercut by cheaper rivals. Branded companies usually earn chubbier margins (hopefully in double digits) and would have more loyal customers. These firms will have more resilience against competitive activities.

It is a mistake to possess visions of becoming big without building a brand. Most of the time when we think of branding, the B to C (business-to-consumer) business model conjures in our mind. Of course, there could be great brands but lousy businesses. There are several instances of poor business practice leading to decimation of superb brands like **Pan Am** airlines, **Polaroid** camera, **HMV** music stores or **Borders** bookshops. While these businesses would have lost their way due to various reasons like not keeping up with changing competitive scenario or high debt and the like, it does not take away the premise that branding helps after all.

Brands could also be in the B–to-B (business-to-business) domain, like *Bilcare* and *Caprihans*—makers of PVC films used for blister packaging of medicines (Disclosure: I have run both these companies some time or the other.) These brands promise price, quality and functionality. Having a brand name behind the ostensibly innocuous primary packaging material has helped these B-to-B companies to make a name.

Tailpiece

Though businesses try endlessly to delight customers, ultimately most consumers make their buying decisions automatically. They look for what is familiar and easy to buy—the presence of a brand name provides the consumers this purchasing comfort and ability to recall the stuff they wish to procure. If we as humans can have a name, why should products or services not have brand names? If it helps to identify a particular characteristic or emotion, why should it not be practised? It takes time to build a brand—it does not happen overnight. But not working towards it will be a value destroyer.

Stop Loss

Every investor in stocks and commodities expects transactions to end in a profit. A buyer of stocks would like to see the stock price going higher than the purchase price. The investor could either hold on to the stocks or sell at a profit. But what if the market price goes below the purchase price? Should one wait for good times to come? Many investors do not wait for stocks to collapse endlessly but exit when the market price of the investment reaches or falls below their pre-decided threshold. 'Stop loss' is a common term used by investors to limit their loss.

Should the same strategy exist in business models?

If a particular business is not meeting expectations of the entrepreneur and efforts to turn it around are not yielding results, should one exit? When should a 'stop-loss' decision be taken?

Entrepreneurs owning only one business, say, a restaurant, will make best efforts to turn it around. But should the person own several eateries, it would be rational to churn the business portfolio around and possibly to close the outlets which are either incurring loss or not meeting expected return on investments. Stop-loss syndrome plays in to escape mistakes made.

The current Tata Chairman, Chandrasekaran, declared that 'we will exit if we aren't getting returns today and we don't think we'll get them tomorrow'.[10] He again reiterated in October 2017: 'We would like to see ourselves as 5, 6, 7 groups as opposed to 110 companies; the more we see ourselves as 110–120 companies, nothing will be done.' Obviously, the 'stop-loss' theory is at work. But walking out of businesses for the group is not normal. Persistence sometimes pays, and of course it may back fire. Tata's jewellery brand, Tanishq, and its IT arm, Tata Consultancy, are examples where perseverance and long-term perspective paid off. These are more of exceptions than the rule.

As the Tatas have openly declared that they are evaluating their long list of nonperforming businesses acquired or started over a long period, so should all managements carry out their spring-cleaning exercise. This is commonly known as 'portfolio analysis'.

Every business, be it a multiproduct multi-business or single-product organization, is known to add trash over time. This happens in our homes too—look at your drawers and see the quantum of junk accumulated!

A relatively simple portfolio analysis tool which is fairly popular is the 'Boston Consulting Group growth-share matrix'. It is a framework to evaluate strategic positioning and evaluate potential of businesses and brands.[11] The general objective of the analysis is to help understand which businesses or brands the firm should invest in and which ones should be divested—a potential sanitization exercise for your businesses so that duds are not carried and muck is not accumulated.

The matrix contains four quadrants into which a firm's businesses can be classified:

1. *Dogs:* These businesses hold low market share compared with competitors and operate in a slowly growing market. It is better not to invest in these businesses as they generate low or negative cash flows. A potential stop-loss candidate. Strategic options: divestment, liquidation.

2. *Cash cows:* The most profitable segment should be 'milked' to extract as much cash as is possible. The cash gained from

'cows' should be ideally invested into 'stars' to support their further growth. Strategic options: product development, innovation.

3. *Stars:* Usually operate in high-growth areas and maintain high market share. 'Starry' businesses are both cash generators and cash users. We need to invest in stars so that they can become cash cows of tomorrow and generate positive cash flows. Strategic options: vertical and horizontal integration, market penetration and development.

4. *Question marks:* Businesses and brands that require much closer evaluation. They hold low market share, consuming funds and probably bleeding. These businesses may not succeed and, even after pumping in investments, could continue to struggle and eventually become dogs. A potential stop-loss case and exit could be a good option. Strategic option: divestment.

In life, the 80/20 principle mostly works. Look around, and you will find this principle working all over—80 per cent effects coming from 20 per cent of the causes. Twenty per cent of employees do most of the work; we generate 80 per cent of output during one-fifth productive daily time. Business is no exception. Twenty per cent of brands or products will normally provide 80 per cent of enterprise's profit.

Many companies keep weeding out 'stop-loss' brands. Unilever, the Anglo-Dutch FMCG major, in the late 1990s slashed its brand numbers from 1,600 to 400. The majority were occupying crucial retail shelf-space without generating the desired revenue. Signal toothpaste (rechristened as Pepsodent) and Erasmic Shaving creams, my two favourites, got the axe—the general consumers obviously did not perceive these brands as favourably as I did!

Tailpiece

It is but natural to get rid of duds in your portfolio—be it stocks, commodities, or any brand or business. Lugging deadwood never pays. Hope keeps us alive, but hoping against hope is bad business judgement. Not keeping in mind the concept of 80/20 would be sheer mismanagement. Keep cleaning your stable of flops—it helps to manage things better.

Starting Start-ups

The evolutionary world will always give birth to new, with the old succumbing or fading away. Every day, across the globe, thousands of new entrants are commencing to wet their feet and swim in the deep waters of business.

Just think of all those apps on your mobile phone. They were nowhere to be seen even a few years back. These are the creations of new-generation entrepreneurs, the so-called start-ups. Sitting in your home, you can order almost everything that you need in your daily lives, from shoes to clothes, from plants to books. A whole new world of business model is under launch, hoping to change the world and bring a new way to deliver benefits to consumers. Uber, the tech's most valuable company, Paytm, India's new way of making payments instantaneously through your mobile, are just a few unicorns making their presence felt.

Needless to mention, today's mature businesses were once a start-up too.

The questions are: Do all start-ups work? Do they do the right stuff most of the time? The quick answers are: No, most don't succeed: Three in four fail. Several vanish into oblivion. Many bleed financially.

Some of the common business-failure causes, mentioned all over this book, are inadequate capital, inability to have a 360-degree view of business, stuck in technology temperament, absence of marketing focus, bickering co-founders, lack of professional inputs, too much optimism, inappropriate area of business, demand–supply mismatch, intense competition, business model ahead of time, and the list is rather large.

News of start-ups shutting down is aplenty. Some are inevitable, whereas others come as a bombshell. It came as a surprise when

America's **Sprig** and India's **TinyOwl** downed its shutters, in the beleaguered food-delivery service space—with both having marque investors and launched with much fanfare.

The most startling shutdown in 2017 has been the seven-year-old hotel aggregator, **Stayzilla**, which had raised $34 million funding and was billed as India's largest homestay network. The budget accommodation space and the Indian version of Airbnb looked attractive due to the potential size of the Indian tourism market. But monetization became difficult. Stayzilla ran up losses of ₹95 crore ($14 million) against the paltry revenue of ₹14 crore ($2 million) in 2016.[12] Investors became more cautious, and cash-burn funding dried up, making business continuity unsustainable.

Most start-ups fail not being able to keep pace with 'logistics' requirement, being inept in 'operation' details and unable to raise funds. High cost of running operations and inability to find top-up funding take a heavy toll on many start-ups.

The Mint newspaper analysed 43 Indian consumer internet companies having a revenue of ₹26,000 crore ($3.9 billion), which showed a loss of ₹19,000 crore ($2.8 billion) for the year ended March 2017.[13] A pathetic reading indeed for India's start-ups.

Cash-burning start-ups are in plenty. Would you believe that the most-valued start-up **Uber**, the tech taxi-hailing company, incurred a loss of $4.5 billion on a turnover of $7.5 billion in 2017?[14] Can you also believe that one of India's largest start-ups, **Quikr**, a classified ad-platform, with a turnover just under ₹64 crore ($10 million), incurred a loss of over ₹300 crore ($46 million) in 2016–2017?[15] This is simply unsustainable and cannot continue forever!

Most of the times, it is a question of being able to keep up with a leaking finance pipe owing to losses while starting a business, and whether one can tap inlet money pipelines to keep funding the losses.

Rising competition, inability to keep pace with operational jigsaw puzzles and lack of funds to meet continuous cash burns are the chief causes for the start-up cessations and closures.

Although many big names have survived in the market till now, but with fund crunch and investor desire to exhibit returns in invested businesses, it will now be the show time for the players, big or small, to carry on with their expedition innovatively.

Continuous cash use and leaning heavily on investors cannot be the survival strategy for long. Much of the expansion in online shopping and grocer-owned delivery models has been funded by investors who had very modest immediate return expectations. But the funny money cannot flow into start-ups endlessly. No investment can run on losses over infinite time.

A pioneering product and service strategy with a sustainable business model will be the order of the day. It will be a blunder to assume that cash-burn marketing gimmicks of high discounts with little customer loyalty and squeezing deep pockets of investors will continue forever.

Tailpiece

Thomas Edison once said, 'I have learned 50,000 ways it cannot be done and therefore I am 50,000 times nearer the final successful experiment.' The new-age entrepreneurs should learn from the past and move into the future with renewed zeal of not repeating the mistakes made earlier. Every inexperience is an experience.

Speculative Quick Bucks

When a purchase manager decides to buy an input item, should he procure for replacement needs or stocking for speculative gains? Should a business hold inventory of finished goods and hope to sell dear at a future date?

Many of these decisions have speculative undertones. Procuring now, locking up scarce working capital and hoping that the price would go up later is a dirty game. Entrepreneurs often cannot resist the temptation of blocking capital, take a position on stocks and hoping that the call taken for a future price movement will turn out the way predicted. It is obvious that any reverse price movement entails loss.

My personal view with over decades of experience have proven that you cannot make money through speculation over long term. Short-term favourable swings are possible. But one wrong call may wash out several positive calls. Profits made on some occasions would in all probability be offset by losses at other times with gains and losses evenly poised. In the long term, business is a great leveller.

Let me cite an example. You would have heard of *Nutrela* soya chunks. The brand owner **Ruchi Soya**, India's largest maker of edible oil, crashed into great financial mess when castor seeds procured to make castor oil turned out to be its nemesis. While soybean and palm oil are its major inputs for edible oils, the company's penchant for trading in castor seeds in commodity exchange resulted in its downfall.

Dinesh Shahra, the company chief, took positions on castor seed price. The castor price crashed globally in early 2016. The company got stuck with higher priced castor seeds. The debt ballooned, resulting in bankers and creditors hounding the company management. To top it all, the company was charged with fraudulent behaviour in manipulating the Indian commodity exchange NCDEX price of castor.

The prime cause of the muddle was the speculative view on castor seed prices. It must have worked well in the past, but one bad instance made the company suffer no ends.

Tailpiece

There is no shortcut to making money. Speculation and gambling could be someone's trade, but for the many, it is a mistaken trait, which is avoidable.

Technology Threats

Hailing a public taxi has become rare with the advent of Uber and Ola cabs. Airbnb has made most of us reluctant to move into a hotel, pay through our nose and miss out on the cosiness of a home. Buying music compact discs is a passé with mobile phones letting us access millions of songs through Wynk and Google Play Music-like apps. Technology has made life so different—simple, easy and cost effective.

Is further automation and digitization going to affect many more industries? Are some business models under serious threat?

Brick-and-mortar banks may give way to online banking; financial intermediaries such as banks, financial brokers, insurance companies and pension funds may be replaced by 'shadow-banks' like pawnshops, peer-to-peer lending websites, hedge funds and bond-trading platforms set up by technology firms; Bitcoin-like cryptocurrencies may replace banking notes; automated robo-advisors may replace financial planners; travel shops may become extinct with online booking gaining popularity; 3D printing may adversely affect components and the prototype industry; driverless cars under careful control of computers and cameras may eliminate risk of accidents, thus acutely hitting the motor-insurance industry; electric cars with hardly any moving parts may not need repair garages anymore; and artificial intelligence and robotics may replace many of us eventually.

There are boundless options of technology changing the way we will eat, live, work and enjoy our lives in the not too distant future. Sometimes it looks rather comforting, but quite crazy and scary at other moments! Will delivery drones being developed by Amazon, UPS, Walmart and Google replace distribution vans? Will augmented and virtual reality, voice-activated assistants and physical gestures replace our omnipresent smartphones? Will credit card payment for a cool drink on a beach be replaced by VISA sunglasses, having a small contactless chip inside? And there is that 'internet of things'—which may remotely control every object on earth, especially our homes, like refrigerators that order milk when supplies run low.

A stocktaking of the ongoing developments reveals quite a few potential threats. It will be a mistake on the part of the threatened industries not to take cognizance of the likely risks of obsolescence due to technology-related threats.

Tailpiece

Since the beginning of civilization, human race has always evolved. Old has given way to new; business models changed; discoveries and inventions led mankind to find novel and better ways to live; advanced skills developed, leading to fresh ways to work; living became less challenging as days passed by.

Changes of late are more defining and led by technology. The invention of computer and internet has significantly changed the way we read, write, live, work and enjoy. Mankind and governments are struggling to ensure that developments touch one and all and not only a few—it is now the task to deliver shared prosperity instead of benefiting a handful.

Every one of us needs to be conscious of the ever-changing world around us, adopt and adapt to the changes in the business models. If not, it will be a serious mistake, which will be hard to erase in the future.

Golden Rules of Successful Business Models

Businesses possessing good ideas, having a differentiating business model, commanding robust domain knowledge, ability to hire and motivate a great team are recipes for success. Certain types of business models, organization structures or methods of governance are more likely to achieve lasting success than others.

Let us take a peek into some success formulae.

1. *Ability to change:* One of the best books I have ever read is *Who Moved My Cheese?*, a slim book by Dr Spenser Johnson. Speaking through rodents and tiny humans, the book beautifully explains that change is always for the better, that smart people will be brave enough to move ahead quickly and find a new niche, and that the inflexible will perish. Not following this simple dictum is a grave gaffe.

   Founded in 1288, Stora, a Finnish mining and forest products company, is often cited as the world's oldest business corporation. Over centuries, it shifted not only its political alignments but also its business, moving from copper to forest exploitation, iron smelting, hydro power, wood pulp, chemicals, and eventually to biomaterials and green construction products—a classic instance of foresight, to change by reacting early.[16,17]

Shalimar Paints, the 1902 Indian enterprise having over 55,000 colour options for its clients, kept changing over time, moving from ubiquitous distempers to emulsion paints, water-based colours, weatherproof paints and new-age decorative colours. Incidentally, in Rashtrapati Bhavan, where the President of India lives, fresh coats of Shalimar Paints are applied.

The ability to change is helping both Stora and Shalimar Paints in their quest for market success.

2. *Ability to adapt:* Too many technological developments are taking place around the globe. In the face of changing times, the winner will be the one who can adapt and adopt new knowledge and skill.

One industry where significant technical breakthroughs have taken place is the vertical transport industry. Companies such as Kone, Schindler and ThyssenKrupp are operating with great vigour and energy in the elevator sector. But a local Indian company is giving these international giants a run for their money—*Otis Elevators*. This company installed its first elevator in Kolkata's Raj Bhavan way back in 1892. Otis's elevators operate today in Burj Khalifa, the world's tallest skyscraper, hurtling from the 124th floor to the ground level in less than a minute. Otis developed and adapted newer technologies as time went by.

Another example of adapting to technological changes is **Alembic Pharmaceuticals**, an over 100-year-old company. Alembic's factory, in the mid-1930s, was so technologically advanced that it manufactured its own internal combustion engine running on 'power alcohol'—a product that mixed alcohol with petrol in the ratio of 4:1 to enhance engine performance while reducing pollution. Later, in the 1940s, when public sentiment turned against alcohol in Gujarat, Alembic moved on to making cough syrups, vitamins, tonics and antibiotic drugs. And now the company has shifted its focus from commodity-active pharmaceutical ingredients or APIs in short, to higher potential formulations, through enhanced R&D effort.

The stories of Otis and Alembic teach us a lot. The ability to adapt new technology, enter fresh segments, attract unique customers and source from different vendors kept them going in the face of severe competition.

3. *Ability to re-engineer:* The average lifespan of companies is shrinking. It means that companies are becoming irrelevant rather soon. Hence, organizations have to constantly re-generate themselves.

Many companies have a single product, possess old systems, lack enthusiasm and fail to re-engineer themselves. 'Good companies' show dynamism and the ability to reinvent based on environmental developments. 'Very good companies' are constantly reviewing their performance, evaluating on a continuous basis, perhaps quarterly, their relevance and altering their strategies.

Taking an example, *Netflix* re-engineered from a DVD sales and rentals company to becoming the most popular streaming media service company, turning its irrelevance to utter relevance.

4. *Ability to bounce back:* Companies which can go through episodes of great difficulty and yet can come back has a sure recipe for long-term success.

An apt example is IBM. This technology player, almost died in 1990, after the rise of personal computing threatened

IBM's mainframe-centric business model. Of late, cloud computing is threatening to change the game. Customers are turning their back on procuring their own technology to run on their own servers and datacentres. They are instead looking at outsourcing their IT needs to companies like Google Compute Engine or Amazon Web Services. While IBM is trying to join the bandwagon, it is still way down in the stacking order—once again the company will need to depict its skills to get back.

You are aware that jute as a medium of packaging and textiles is almost dead. With changing times, hundreds of jute companies have gone extinct due to the emergence of plastics and synthetic fibres. The Kamarhatty Company Ltd, a Kolkata-based outfit commencing its operations way back in 1887, still remains an exception. It is using technology to reduce labour and increase production efficiency, manufacturing close to 30,000 tonnes of jute every year using almost three-fourths of its installed capacity—a credible example of getting back into the game in the midst of a dying industry.

Tailpiece

One thing which becomes loud and clear—business endurance is directly proportional to its ability to adjust quickly. Businesses need to navigate risk—market, financial and political. It will also involve anticipating risks, having resilience and adapting itself to altering conditions.

An important factor which is often believed to influence triumph is lady-luck. It will be a mistake to underestimate the power of Dame Fortune!

In Closing

Faulty business models take toll on business durability. How long will a corporation last? Richard Foster, the Yale University professor referred to in the *Financial Times*, calculates that in the 1920s, US companies on the S&P index would last for about 65 years. Today, that is down to 18 years, and he thinks it could eventually fall to 10. It is a dog-eat-dog world. Hence, whoever has a sound business model, makes best use of available capital and adapts to change will last the longest. No business wants to die; but achieving corporate immortality looks more difficult now than ever before.

The setbacks that challenge business models and bring businesses to an end can be many, including financial reversals, changing markets, poor management, unethical practices as well as accidents. To survive and prosper, companies have to be able to cope during the down phases of business cycles, adjust to shifting political landscapes and manage changing business conditions.

A successful business model theory is complex and hazy. Mistakes are bound to take place. Learning from them is the key; but being beaten by these is abject surrender.

References

1. Beeching P. Why did HMV fail? The Guardian [Internet]. 2013 Jan 15. Available from: https://www.theguardian.com/commentisfree/2013/jan/15/why-did-hmv-fail

2. Vadukut K. Why did HMT fail? Livemint [Internet]. 2014 Sep 12. Available from: https://www.livemint.com/Opinion/BxhKMMvIA7tPjzoyQRLMHP/Dj-View--Why-did-HMT-fail.html

3. Harris G. Pfizer Pays $2.3 Billion to Settle Marketing Case. The New York Times [Internet]. 2009 Sep 2. Available from: https://www.nytimes.com/2009/09/03/business/03health.html

4. The Irish Times. Ryanair culture 'gone very miserable', says airline executive. The Irish Times [Internet]. 2017 Dec 19. Available from: https://www.irishtimes.com/news/ireland/irish-news/ryanair-culture-gone-very-miserable-says-airline-executive-1.3332320

5. Topham G. Ryanair ranked 'worst airline' for sixth year in a row. The Guardian [Internet]. 2019 Jan 5. Available from: https://www.theguardian.com/business/2019/jan/05/strike-hit-ryanair-ranked-worst-airline-for-sixth-year-in-a-row

6. Newcomer E, Stone B. The fall of Travis Kalanick was a lot weirder and darker than you thought. Business Bloomberg [Internet]. 2018 Jan 18. Available from: https://www.bloomberg.com/news/features/2018-01-18/the-fall-of-travis-kalanick-was-a-lot-weirder-and-darker-than-you-thought

7. McKinsey & Co. Digital Globalization Report: The new era of global flows. McKinsey & Co [Internet]. 2016 Mar. Available from: https://www.mckinsey.com/~/media/mckinsey/business%20functions/mckinsey%20digital/our%20insights/digital%20globalization%20the%20new%20era%20of%20global%20flows/mgi-digital-globalization-full-report.ashx

8. Nocera J. The inside history of the 'New Coke' debacle. Bloomberg Opinion [Internet]. 2017 Nov 3. Available from: https://www.bloomberg.com/opinion/articles/2017-11-03/the-inside-history-of-the-new-coke-debacle

9. Mourdoukoutas P. A strategic mistake that still haunts JC Penney. Forbes [Internet]. 2017 Feb 24. Available from: https://www.forbes.com/sites/panosmourdoukoutas/2017/02/24/a-strategic-mistake-that-still-haunts-jc-penney/#65b876be1bcf

10. Chandler C. How Tata's new chairman plans to fix India's biggest company. Fortune [Internet]. 2017 Jul 21. Available from: http://fortune.com/2017/07/21/tata-sons-india-biggest-company/

11. Jurevicius O. BCG growth-share matrix. The Strategic Management [Internet]. 2013 May 1. Available from: https://www.strategicmanagementinsight.com/tools/bcg-matrix-growth-share.html

12. Pani P. Stayzilla shuts operations. The Hindu Business Line [Internet]. 2017 Feb 24. Available from: https://www.thehindubusinessline.com/info-tech/stayzilla-shuts-operations/article9557756.ece

13. Dalal M. Despite cutting costs, consumer internet start-ups struggle to turn profitable. Livemint [Internet]. 2018 Feb 7. Available from: https://www.livemint.com/Companies/DKoREWzoPQ8LV8pQIqt83O/Despite-cutting-costs-consumer-internet-startups-struggle.html

14. Lashinsky A. This is Uber's biggest problem. Fortune [Internet]. 2018 Feb 14. Available from: http://fortune.com/2018/02/14/uber-2017-financial-results/

15. Srinivasan S. Quikr FY17 revenues grow 55% to ₹64 crore, losses dip 42%. ETTech [Internet]. 2018 May 18. Available from: https://tech.economictimes.indiatimes.com/news/internet/quikr-fy17-revenues-grow-55-to-rs-64-crore-losses-dip-42/64224790

16. Sullivan A. Stora's Story: A Company as old as the millennium puts on a new face. The New York Times [Internet]. 1999 Nov 27. Available from:https://www.nytimes.com/1999/11/27/your-money/IHT-storas-storya-company-as-old-as-the-millennium-puts-on-a-new.html

17. Financial Times. Founders' vision keeps engine running. Financial Times [Internet]. 2015 Nov 10. Available from: https://www.ft.com/content/9e3b2740-7ec2-11e5-a1fe-567b37f80b64

EPILOGUE

Life is never without blemish. Unexpected events—whether in business or in personal lives—often affect us. The worst is that with the benefit of hindsight, it is easy to expose the follies and criticize the faux pas.

Setbacks need to be tackled. If hiccups and hold-ups derail your vision, then fulfilling ideas and desires will remain a pipe dream.

As you live, you will falter. But if you learn from your mistakes, you will become a better person. It is how you handle adversity not how it affects you that matters.

Remember the profound statement: 'Tough times do not last; tough people do.'

Errors Escort Excellence

Think of doctors. They train extensively, but even then it is not enough to make perfect judgements all the time. When doctors commit mistakes in diagnosis or surgery, it is an invaluable opportunity to learn. But often a doctor would rationalize it by saying—'It is the patient who could not adapt to treatments; everything that we could do was done.' This is a deadly blunder. The doctor then misses a chance to learn from the errors and the reasons remain unidentified.

Preventable mistakes are a big killer in the medical world. It is estimated that, worldwide, over 40 million people are affected every year due to medical errors, and in India the number stands at about 5 million. Hence, unless doctors learn from mistakes, the situation will never improve.

Business scenarios are no different. Previous success is also no guarantee for its continuity. A faux pas, a few mis-steps, some judgement errors or certain wrong calls could wipe out many a good deed. Inexperience provides us with experience. Blunders teach us a better way to build. Errors committed teach us many a lesson.

Take the instance of James Dyson, the British inventor for the dual-cyclone vacuum cleaner. He worked through over 5,000 prototypes, learning each time from the mistake of the previous one. Finally, he cracked the modern way of household cleaning. Failures led to ultimate success.[1]

Best forecasters are those who learn from mistakes. On receipt of fresh data, a forecaster or an economist should be willing to rework the assumptions and conclusions, instead of just sticking to earlier predictions. Have you noticed the economic or market predictors yapping away on our TVs? Once they make a prediction, many of them carry through it in spite of new data suggesting a different outcome, not admitting mistakes.

Customers are always looking for high quality and good service at a low price. Businesses are ever striving to achieve this conundrum. In the quest to achieve this demanding market desire, businesses take actions which may or may not turn out the desired way. It is painful to admit that we have made a bad decision. It is human to be optimistic and believe things would just turn out the right way. But when ominous signs emerge, recognize that there is a problem and drive quick actions to undo mistakes committed. Shoving problems under the carpet would only add to the misery.

Tailpiece

Open a business newspaper—and most stories are of accomplishments. Journalists and analysts generally do not get access to negative reports. The PR departments will always feed news agencies with positive announcements—and that is their job. Very little information is available in the public domain on the goofs and gaffes businesses make. Learning from whatever bloomers you encounter would be a huge lesson. Ignoring it is a big blunder.

Mistakes and failures will never disappear howsoever hard you may try. But the good news is they are enlightening. You can learn as much from failures, oversights and howlers as you would from your trials and triumphs.

Mistakes Could Be Unforgiving

More and more businesses are nowadays funded by venture funds, hedge funds and private equity investors. They usually retain good stakes in their invested companies, expect continuous good performance and keep asserting themselves. Mistakes and slippages are not often pardoned by these neo-investors.

But there are thousands of companies where minority shareholders cannot influence the controlling groups to perform, often suffering at the hands of the majority.

Shareholder activism has been on the rise across the globe. Investors are working to influence the running of companies in which they invest, primarily through the casting of shareholder voting. The objective is to deter lackadaisical performance and poor governance that might pose a long-term threat to the profitability of the companies invested in. Of course, there could also be the ulterior motive of making a fast buck, by forcing the invested company to take actions as would benefit the shareholder activist.

Some investor activism ends disastrously. William Ackman meddled into the management of JCPenney in 2013 and the result was catastrophic. In another occasion, Ackman, shorting the stock, kept saying *Herbalife,* an American nutritional product company, is a pyramid scheme which is bound to collapse. But it did not. (Ultimately in February 2018, six years after Ackman took the bet that the stock price will tumble to zero, exited his position by letting go his wagering against Herbalife.)[2] However, his negative spiel kept affecting the company adversely.

Shareholder activism has sometimes helped to lift the faltering companies from the trough they have been in. To cite an example, Daniel Loeb bought shares in Yahoo in 2011 and forced a CEO change, and its stocks rose. But it could be a mixed bag for some. Caving under activist investors' pressure, ThyssenKrupp had to decide to split the German diversified industrial goods giant into two (TK Materials and TK Industrials) in September 2018. The shares rose 17 per cent immediately, but since then the price has shown a southward trend.

There could be other intent of the activists, including forcing companies to use cash to pay higher dividends or to buy back shares; their own list of desirables could be long.

By pushing the envelope of activism, some shareholders—sometimes termed as barbarians, corporate raiders or extortionists—use media and board pressures to get their propositions worked upon by companies. It may sometimes be good for the shareholders in general or could just suit a few. It is common knowledge that markets reward companies that govern themselves well. Ideally, activist shareholders or large institutional owners should use their expert judgement to vote bad boards out of office.

Mistakes are generally condoned if these do not result in significant loss or do not get noticeably noticed. Corporate life is no different. If a particular ownership group is in command of a business, then repercussions on faltered actions are minimal. But if some sections of the corporate ownership, including activist shareholders, notice unbecoming corporate outcomes or some extracting opportunities, the outcome could be unforgiving, especially when these shareholders are able to exercise their influence by hook or by crook.

Coming Out of Failure Closet

It is important to get comfortable with failures. If you are an investor, you should be able to cut your losses when your judgement calls do not seem to be going your way. In personal life, if you have committed a mistake, it is best to recognize it and move on. Keeping failures under wraps provides less of an opportunity to rectify them and take cognisance of lessons learnt. Acknowledging lapses and learning from errors is a virtue.

A conference management outfit, FailCon, holds seminars for technology entrepreneurs, investors, developers and designers to study their own and others' failures and prepare for success. The philosophy is to encourage entrepreneurs to hear from each other: that it's okay to fail, it doesn't mean the entrepreneur is worthless. It helps learning from each other's mistakes and building something bigger next time.

It is all about bringing the world of failures out in the open—take it out of your closet and spread it out to see what went wrong. The more people do this, the greater will be the learning. It is a question of finding how to flourish from fiascos.

Easy to say, but very difficult to practise: take responsibility for gaffes, convey plan for remedy and fix what was wrong. Blunders are perceived as a sign of weakness. Hence, no one finds it easy to own slip-ups, especially the serious ones.

I know of a technocrat CEO who procrastinated writing a letter acknowledging the customer complaint and letting know the root cause. He misjudged, mistimed and misunderstood the customer requirement, and procured the wrong stocks. The businessman did not acknowledge his error on time. The customer shifted to an alternative supplier source. What a grave lapse!

'I am sorry' and 'will replace it'—would have been the healing words that could have brought the customer confidence back.

It all starts at the top—developing a culture where people feel comfortable admitting mistakes. Subordinates watch their leaders for clues on acceptable conduct and decorum. The management must encourage the practice to accept imperfections, admit wrongdoings, heed feedbacks and seek corrective steps—even when these could sometime be rather embarrassing.

No one can avoid snags and snare. As businesses become more complicated, it becomes more critical to avoid pitfalls. And when encountered, contrary to perhaps the suggestions of the lawyers, it is good to 'own up'. It helps to cleanse the past and get a fresh start—the long-term benefit will mitigate short-term pain. Not acknowledging blunders is not worth its while.

What Should You Do When Blunder Is Committed?

Learning from blunders and not repeating it is what life is all about. All of us make errors—but almost none will be life-threatening. The ability to tackle obstacles and lapses will set you apart from the rest.

All mistakes are not bad. There could, in fact, be deliberate ones. Look at the entrepreneurs around you. They may have taken risks on ten ideas; four may have worked, balance failing miserably. But when the ideas were thought of, no one knew which ones would come to fruition. And when some work well, willy-nilly the risks taken to confirm assumptions turn out to be good mistakes.

We are humans—fallible and sometimes irrational. We need to recognize that the path of wilful errors is full of burning pebbles and best avoided. But when it happens unintentionally, recognize and resolve. Forgive and forget when others commit errors, more so when abnormal. And when it comes to yourself, accept and acquiesce—you will profit.

A few ideas which have worked for many will help you to tackle mis-steps and bad decisions.

Take Time to React

Irrespective of the impediments and mistakes made, you can control one thing. That is your reaction.

Do not react immediately. Take time to retort or else you may regret it later. Carry on as if nothing has happened. Things will improve. Another side to the story is responding rather than reacting. Responding is more thoughtful. Responses contain reasoning. Reacting is sporadic and emotional. Hence, respond rather than react.

Tomorrow Is a New Day!

Every day is a new day. No two days are the same. So have faith and hope. Things may just recover. Every day provides us an opportunity to get ourselves on track. Successful people always absorb the pain of an error, brush aside the failure, and move on to re-emerge and re-energize the next day.

Monica Johnson, the famous American screenwriter, once said, 'Learning from the past helps to ensure that mistakes are not repeated.' Mistakes provide experience and learning. Take these positively, and you will be a winner.

Failure Is Not Permanent

It is often difficult to swallow failures by the ambitious and successful. Who likes to fail? Nobody.

Think of the child who learns to walk for the first time. How many times the wobbly toddler would have fallen to learn to walk? How many falls does it take to learn riding a bicycle? Unless you get back and try again, neither we would have ever walked, nor would we have learned to ride a two-wheeler.

Every time you were by-passed for a promotion, you needed to get back to try harder for the elevation the next time. Every time an idea did not work, bring back new ways and means to do it—and it may work someday.

Acknowledging fiascos is itself a good step forward. For instance, **Zomato**, one of the most talked about Indian food technology firms, sacked over 300 employees in 2015.[3] Amid backlash from employees, CEO, Deepinder Goyal, wrote to the entire workforce admitting his mistake of adding headcounts without concomitant sales increase and the need to correct. Failures are temporary setbacks, though initially it looks to be everlasting.

Let Bygones Be Bygones

Do not dwell upon the past. Successful people always focus on the task on hand and how to get it done. They learn from mistakes made in the past. What has happened cannot be undone. There is no point crying over spilt milk.

Wasting time, energy and money on beating a dead horse will lead us nowhere. While playing a game of cricket, if you have bowled a bad over, let that not affect your next bowling turn. Clear your mind of the past and focus on the next bowling-over to execute, as if you are beginning all over again.

Expect the Worse

Hope for the best but prepare for the worst. Expecting good to happen keeps all of us going. But if we get prepared to handle tumbles, the outcome would be supremely better.

Once you can smell rot creeping in, handle it in two possible ways. Either solve on your own or study what others have done to resolve similar predicaments.

Take Extraordinary Actions When Required

During tough times, everyone needs to share the pain. Many businesses try unprecedented tactics to get over hard times. From getting rid of people, reshuffling management, off-loading businesses, fiddling product formulations, eliminating costs, pumping equity funding instead of debt to save interest, and the possibilities are endless.

The Japanese electronics maker **Sharp** has been going through a rough patch for some time. First, it cut wages, but then it took a bizarre decision at the end of 2015. For the long suffering employees, the struggling electronics group set them targets to buy company goods such as televisions.[4] The unusual tactics testify the extent of Sharp's troubles and its serious attempts to stay afloat.

Tailpiece

No matter what you do, bloopers and bungles will take place. Talking of blunders is not about poking fun on businesses. Anyone of us can make a bad decision; it could be a wrong move; it could just be a bad day. Maybe an incorrect price paid, or the wrong person hired, or a mistaken investment made. It is quite natural to think that decisions taken will turn out to be correct. But only time would tell that things might not be going your way.

Identify, assess, control and review are the four superstructures on which business 'risk management' stands. So make mistakes and commit blunders—recognize, evaluate, regulate and analyse; and then move on, perhaps to commit the next blunder for further experience.

In Closing

There is no magic wand to wish away the fallout of any blunder. There is no one solution to take care of negative implications. Recognize first that there is a problem and cut your losses; practise tough-mindedness and resilience; think through and identify the remedy; take time to understand where you went wrong; and share the lessons learnt with colleagues. Build a defence mechanism to resolve possible negative outcomes of bloopers.

It is difficult to admit mistakes. But once you do, work on a remedy fast and fairly; it will have a lasting impact on your self-esteem and business. The more you will learn from mistakes if you do not get busy denying them.

While as a child, parents and teachers would have told you to learn from the errors. As we grow up and get involved in the business of life, we start dreading to commit and own up goofs and gaffes. The reality is: forget and forgive slip-ups; get up and move on; it is only human to fumble and flub once in a while.

Make no mistake—perfection is a myth.

References

1. Mochari I. Lessons from James Dyson's invention of the vacuum. Inc: Try, Try Again [Internet]. Available from: https://www.inc.com/ilan-mochari/vacuum-innovation.html

2. Banerjee A. Ackman ends public battle with Herbalife, takes stake in United Technologies. Reuters [Internet]. 2018 Feb 28. Available from: https://www.reuters.com/article/us-pershing-square-utc-stake-idUSKCN1GC2N0

3. Prasad A. Zomato lays off 300 employees as it shifts focus to transaction based business. Inc42 [Internet]. 2015 Oct 17. Available from: https://inc42.com/buzz/zomato-lays-off-300-employees/

4. Financial Times. Sharp tells workers to buy company goods. Financial Times [Internet]. 2015 Nov 18. Available from: https://www.ft.com/content/1ce287ea-8dba-11e5-a549-b89a1dfede9b

INDEX

Index

Scan QR code to access the
Penguin Random House India website